Learn Microsoft® Visual Basic® .NET

In a Weekend®

JAY MILLER
LLOYD WORK

Premier
Press

Premier Press, Inc. is a registered trademark of Premier Press, Inc.

Publisher: Stacy L. Hiquet
Marketing Manager: Heather Buzzingham
Managing Editor: Sandy Doell
Acquisitions Editor: Todd Jensen
Project Editor: Karen A. Gill
Editorial Assistant: Margaret Bauer
Technical Reviewer: Michelle Jones
Copy Editor: Karen A. Gill
Interior Layout: Marian Hartsough
Cover Design: Mike Tanamachi
Indexer: Sherry Massey
Proofreader: Suzannah Walker

Microsoft and Visual Basic are registered trademarks of Microsoft Corporation. Crystal Reports is a registered trademark of Crystal Decisions. Delphi is a registered trademark of Borland Software Corporation. All other trademarks are the property of their respective owners.

Important: Premier Press cannot provide software support. Please contact the appropriate software manufacturer's technical support line or Web site for assistance.

Premier Press and the authors have attempted throughout this book to distinguish proprietary trademarks from descriptive terms by following the capitalization style used by the manufacturer.

Information contained in this book has been obtained by Premier Press from sources believed to be reliable. However, because of the possibility of human or mechanical error by our sources, Premier Press, or others, the Publisher does not guarantee the accuracy, adequacy, or completeness of any information and is not responsible for any errors or omissions or the results obtained from use of such information. Readers should be particularly aware of the fact that the Internet is an ever-changing entity. Some facts may have changed since this book went to press.

ISBN: 1-931841-95-0
Library of Congress Catalog Card Number: 2002104494
Printed in the United States of America

02 03 04 05 RI 10 9 8 7 6 5 4 3 2 1

For my wife and children.
The most precious things I have in this world!

Joshua 24:15b

—Jay

For Amy, Isaac, and David,
who bring joy, peace, laughter,
and happiness to me every day.

Colossians 3:23

—Lloyd

ACKNOWLEDGMENTS

This book is the effort of many people to whom I owe thanks. I especially want to thank Todd Jensen, acquisitions editor, for providing me with the opportunity to write this book. Also, Karen Gill, project and copy editor, for the patience and guidance she provided during development of this book.

—Jay

This book would not have been possible without the key involvement of several people. First of all, thanks to everyone at Premier who supported us on this project, especially Todd Jensen and Karen Gill for all their help and allowing us to be flexible with our schedule and content. Thanks to Michelle Jones for doing the tech edit. Thanks to Brad Jones for giving me the heads up to the project. Thanks to my friends at Astra and my family who put up with LOL (Lack of Lloydage) on a regular basis. Finally, I wish to thank my friends at Grace Community Church: the drama team, whose weekly meetings and goofball get-togethers are the highlight of most of my weeks; Rick Drumm, who provided much encouragement and many a prank call; Joe Schroedle, who helps keep me accountable and goes so far as to laugh at my jokes; and finally, thanks to my community group, for listening to all my techno-jive even though you probably understood less than 1% of it. "A friend is one who knows us, but loves us anyway." (Father Jerome Cummings)

—Lloyd

ABOUT THE AUTHORS

JAY MILLER has worked for the past 13 years in the information technology field. Jay received his computer science degree from Indiana University. Before joining Astra Digital, Inc. recently, Jay worked in a variety of industries encompassing financial services, government contracting, insurance, telecommunications, manufacturing, and education. Although Jay has used a wide range of technologies including C, C++, FoxPro, SQL Server, and MTS, his passion for the past seven years has been Visual Basic. Jay looks forward to seeing what .NET will do to revolutionize software development. Contact Jay via e-mail at JMiller@AstraDigital.com.

LLOYD WORK has been in the information technology field for 15 years. He is the president of Astra Digital, Inc., a software development firm based in Indianapolis, Indiana. Lloyd is a native of Plymouth, Michigan (Go Blue!) and received his college education from Taylor University in Upland, Indiana. Lloyd has published several articles and books and has a wide range of experience in many different technologies including VB.NET, ASP.NET, C#, Delphi, C, C++, Visual Basic, PowerBuilder, Oracle, InterBase, SQL Server, MTS, Midas, ASTA, and many others. Lloyd has written commercial software packages for many clients and has worked in the insurance, health care, banking, merchandising, manufacturing, pharmaceutical, education, and publishing industries. Contact Lloyd via e-mail at LWork@AstraDigital.com.

CONTENTS AT A GLANCE

CONTENTS

SATURDAY AFTERNOON
Exploring the Visual Basic .NET Programming Language 83

INTRODUCTION

If you haven't yet heard about Microsoft's new .NET platform, then let me be the first to personally welcome you back to earth. It seems that everywhere I turn today—newspapers, magazines, TV advertisements, radio spots and, of course, splattered all over the Internet—is propaganda surrounding all things .NET. With an advertising budget only slightly lower than the country's gross national product, Microsoft has ensured that I can't turn a page, channel, or profit without being reminded of how much I need .NET. So far Microsoft has done a good job of convincing technical personnel within corporations and programming enthusiasts that .NET is a giant leap for nerdkind. When the day comes that my mom calls me on the phone to talk about .NET, I'll know that Microsoft has flexed its marketing muscle once again.

The reality for all of us in the modern age is that .NET is a revolutionary step in computing and will inevitably change our lives. Perhaps not everyone will be programming with it, but certainly we all will be affected by it. As this book is being written, thousands of applications from Microsoft and other vendors are being written for the .NET platform. New devices are being programmed to support .NET. Thousands of Web sites are being reconfigured to use the .NET platform's new, powerful ASP.NET technologies. Mobile phones and personal digital assistants are also undergoing a change in preparation for the .NET age. In essence, within a few short years, anyone who owns, touches, or uses a computer will in some way, shape, or form be affected by .NET. In all likelihood, many modern accessories such as household appliances, automobiles, and other devices will be made "smart" by the integration and support of .NET technologies. Of course, every application, Web site, Web service, and device that supports .NET will need one or more brilliant developers behind the scenes making it all happen.

This is where you enter the picture.

Whether you've never programmed before or you consider yourself God's gift to propeller heads, rest assured that diving into .NET headfirst is a big leap in the right direction. Even if your corporation is not yet adopting .NET, you would do well to learn what it is all about now instead of trying to pick it up when you've just been told that tomorrow's your last day and you're left holding nothing but a mostly blank résumé with a few years of ALGOL under your belt. Even if you're not a Microsoft bigot, you should pay close attention to what's happening with .NET: Many vendors who initially were leery or hesitant to support .NET are now jumping on the bandwagon, realizing the impact it will have on the future of computing. Most of my colleagues, even the ones who are traditionally anti-Microsoft, now are realizing that to ignore .NET is like ignoring air: You can only hold your breath so long before you turn blue and start gasping.

Learn Microsoft Visual Basic .NET In a Weekend will help you get an accelerated start on your .NET career and give you ample information to form a solid base of knowledge for future development work. If you want to get up to speed quickly with .NET technologies, then you've come to the right place.

Who Should Read This Book

Regardless of whether you have a background with Visual Basic, you'll find this book helpful in getting you started with Microsoft's new VB.NET language and the .NET platform. Certain portions of this book are geared toward the absolute beginner, assuming nothing but a simple knowledge of computers. Okay, so you should know the basics, including how to navigate around Windows, use the mouse, control the interface, and perform general operations such as store and retrieve files/documents from the computer. If you aren't yet comfortable with your computer and its environment, you might want to skip this book for now and get an introductory book on Windows or computers. Otherwise, you might wind up bruising your head while banging it on your desk numerous times and throwing neighborhood computer book burning parties.

Certain portions of this book are geared toward those of you who have used Visual Basic before. Perhaps you've been using VB since version 1.0. Perhaps you were there even earlier, back in the days when GW-BASIC was a commonly known programming language. Perhaps you were there in the *very* beginning, using BASIC on older platforms, shortly after the earth cooled. Whatever the case, you'll find sections in this book that are dedicated to helping you get the most out of VB.NET. For many of you who are attempting to upgrade from an older version of VB to VB.NET, you'll find some helpful tips on how to make the upgrade process as smooth as possible. So, pay close attention to these sections for valuable timesaving tips. Otherwise, you might wind up bruising your head while banging it on your desk numerous times and throwing neighborhood computer book burning parties.

Although most of this book will be technical in nature, it will be presented in a lightweight and easy-to-read manner. If you're looking for an in-depth look at the inner workings of the effects of Itanium optimization on stack variables versus heap allocations within multi-threaded COM Interop applications in a non-managed CLR-compliant language on a portable solar lunar device, you definitely have the wrong book. However, if you're curious about VB.NET or the .NET platform in general and want to know what it is and how you can use it, you've come to the right place.

This book is presented in everyday English with simple concepts and good examples that will help you grasp the big ideas and know how to put them into practice. Wherever possible, nerdy technobabble is avoided in favor of language and wording that we can all understand. Use of Three Letter Acronyms (TLAs) is allowed only when the TLA is fully explained and the concept has been broadly laid out for you to understand.

What You Can Do in a Weekend

Well, obviously most of us can do a lot in a weekend: go camping, blow our life savings in Vegas, sleep, watch TV, go to church, or catch a ballgame. You, being the brave person that you are, have chosen the higher path to enlightenment by choosing to lock yourself up for the weekend to learn VB.NET. Congratulations—you chose right.

Whereas many of your colleagues will come in Monday morning with stories large and small concerning their weekend activities (recalibrating the clocks in the house, cleaning out the refrigerator, cow tipping, and so on), you will be able to hold your head high and boldly walk in on Monday knowing that you have a grasp on the foundational elements of VB.NET.

You will be the subject of the water cooler scuttlebutt, dominating every conversation and brewing immense curiosity about your technical endeavors.

Your weekend will start at the 50,000-foot level. I'll be presenting concepts and topics at a high level and allowing you to grasp the big ideas before diving deep into the technical subjects. Then, you'll have the chance to get your feet wet with some real-life hands-on application development. You'll learn what .NET and VB.NET are all about. You'll create Windows applications, Web applications, mobile applications, Web services, and more. You'll learn about the VB.NET language. You'll even learn about advanced coding techniques and best practices so that you'll be prepared to enter the corporate world of .NET with more than just book knowledge—you'll have real-life examples, tips, and advice under your wing.

To get you started on the right foot, here are some helpful tips on reading this book:

➤ **Block off a weekend to read the book.** The "In a Weekend" series is not just another cute title—it really is designed to be read in a weekend for continuity reasons and to better concentrate on the tasks ahead. So, go ahead and tell your wife and kids that you need to work. Get a room at Motel 6. Lock yourself up in your office. Do whatever it takes to clear the weekend so that you can get the core concepts of this book down by Monday morning.

➤ **Follow the book's curriculum.** I know it might sound weird, but a lot of people pick up technical books and read some chapters and skip others. Some people start at the middle of the book and read random sections. This book is designed to present the technical material in an ordered fashion—it starts with the high-level concepts and then moves on to the more technical concepts. So, the order of the book is important and should not be ignored. When examples are given, take the time to run them and see for yourself what they mean. When asked to take a break, please do so. Following the book's outline will help you understand all the new concepts and features of VB.NET.

➤ **Focus on learning.** Try to focus on learning the core material of the book—understanding the core concepts and practices that are presented. If you need to, repeat certain exercises or reread sections that are confusing. Don't forget that VB.NET comes with great, dynamic context-sensitive help. In addition, Microsoft and many other third-party sites are available to help you grasp the core material. So, don't be afraid to augment what you're learning in this book with outside resources. Sometimes this is needed to drive home tough topics.

What You Need to Begin

This book revolves around the .NET Framework and associated technologies so, of course, you'll need some basic tools/components/libraries to get through it. Here's a list of what you'll need:

➤ **A Visual Studio .NET-compliant computer.** Yes, it sounds dumb, and you probably already thought of this, but you'll need a computer that can run Visual Studio .NET on it. No, you won't be able to get away with using the family's Windows 95 Packard Bell 100MHz special. First, .NET won't run on it; second, you'll be interrupted 100 times over the weekend for important things like instant messaging someone or checking your e-mail. So, before you embark upon this book's journey, do yourself a favor and find a capable machine that you can dedicate to the task.

➤ **A .NET-compliant operating system.** Even though Windows 98 and Me support the .NET Framework, I don't recommend that you try to develop on those platforms. It is true that you can get away with using a simple text editor to edit, compile, and run some of the samples, but you'll be missing out on a lot by not having a fully featured developer-friendly operating system to back you up. I highly recommend that you get Windows 2000 or XP (or at least NT). In addition, you'll want to make sure you have Internet Information Server (IIS) installed so that you can test all the Web applications and services you'll be writing during the course of this book.

➤ **The .NET Framework SDK.** Visual Studio .NET will not run on a machine without the .NET Framework SDK installed on it. Typically, when you go to install Visual Studio .NET, the Framework and all associated "core" components will be installed on your system first before any other tools.

➤ **Visual Studio .NET.** Although it does not matter which *version* of Visual Studio you have, you'll at least need the tool installed on your machine as a bare minimum.

What This Book Covers

This book teaches you about the new Microsoft .NET Framework and VB.NET in a series of sessions, divided up by morning, afternoon, and evening. Here is a list of the sessions:

➤ **Friday Evening.** In this first session, you'll learn some basic information about Microsoft .NET and its history. You'll also learn some information regarding Visual Basic and its history. Then, you'll dive deeper into the .NET Framework and VB.NET and learn what they're all about. Finally, for those of you who have used VB before, you'll learn what's new in VB.NET.

➤ **Saturday Morning.** In this session, you'll learn how to create "traditional" Windows applications with VB.NET. You'll become familiar with Windows forms, controls, graphics, and printing. You'll even learn how to deploy your first Windows application.

➤ **Saturday Afternoon.** In this session, you'll learn about the core elements of the Visual Basic language: data types, keywords, expressions, operators, and more. You'll learn about objects and classes and how to effectively use them in your applications.

➤ **Saturday Evening.** In this session, you'll learn how to work with files and folders. You'll also learn about manipulating database information using ADO.NET and how to write reports for your applications.

➤ **Sunday Morning.** In this session, you'll learn how to create Web applications with ASP.NET and Visual Basic. You'll also learn how to create mobile applications.

➤ **Sunday Afternoon.** In this session, you'll learn how to create and consume Web services using Visual Studio .NET and Visual Basic .NET.

➤ **Sunday Evening (Bonus Session).** This session will focus on professional tips and guidelines to help you make the transition from this book into the real world and get started on the right foot. Pay close attention to this chapter before embarking on any software projects on your own—some of these tips and guidelines can save you a lot of grief and help you be more successful as you begin your .NET ventures.

Special Features of This Book

This book contains several special features such as Notes, Tips, Cautions, Buzzwords, and Find It on the Web references. Each of these will be highlighted by a special icon appearing to the left of the text in the book. Pay close attention to these sections because they are important and can help you learn key concepts and ideas. Here are some examples of what you'll see:

Notes bring to your attention special information relevant to what you are learning and help you understand the core material better. Notes often point out information that is important to know so you don't get tripped up or confused.

Tips give you professional hints and suggestions on how to apply what you're learning. Pay close attention to these because they can be real time-savers and save you a lot of frustration. Tips help point you in the right direction.

Cautions are warnings of certain issues you might face while you're learning the material. These are like tips, except they attempt to keep you from going in the wrong direction by pointing out possible trip-ups and hazards you might face along the way.

Buzzwords are words known within the industry that are specific to .NET technologies and are important to know.

This icon is found in places where Internet-based content can be found that will help augment the material in this book and enhance your learning experience.

In addition to these special icons, all code listings, keywords, data types, variables, statements, loops, properties, expressions, operators, blocks, functions, constants, and other VB.NET language constructs will appear in monospace typeface. Bold is used to indicate small changes among listings when listings within a chapter are similar.

Visit This Book's Web Site

Be sure to visit the *Learn Microsoft Visual Basic .NET In a Weekend* Web site at http://www.premierpressbooks.com. You'll find all the code from this book at the site as well as any other errata concerning the material in the book.

In addition, you can download an assessment tool containing dozens of helpful test questions based on the content from this book. This tool helps you assess how much information you have learned from this book and how well you have retained the knowledge presented herein. The questions are ordered by chapter, so you can test yourself as you go through the book and then take a practice exam based on the entire question set for the book.

Are You Ready?

I hope that by now, you've read the entire "Introduction" section and are ready to tackle Friday Evening's session. You'll need several hours' time to get through this first session, so I recommend that you get a cup of your favorite beverage ready and get comfortable. The Friday Evening session will focus on an introduction to the .NET Framework and VB.NET, and is more topical and cursory than the other portions of this book. So, you need not sit in front of the computer for this first session. Instead, find a comfortable chair (not too comfortable!), sit back, and turn the page!

Visual Basic .NET and the .NET Framework

➤ Introducing the .NET Framework

➤ Why the .NET Framework is needed

➤ What is Visual Basic .NET

➤ What's new in Visual Basic .NET?

I t's Friday evening, and hopefully you have some leftover energy to get you through the weekend—and what a weekend this will be! By Sunday evening, you will have been introduced to one of the most revolutionary innovations in software development history—the Microsoft .NET platform. You will have learned how to use the Visual Basic .NET programming language in conjunction with Visual Studio .NET tools to create Windows applications, Web applications, Web services, and more. You will have gotten your feet wet with real-world examples and learned expert advice on how to tackle the overwhelming tasks of software development.

The purpose of this first session is to give you an orientation to the world of the .NET platform. Before I go introducing you to all things .NET, you need to have a solid foundation laid so that you will understand the concepts and examples I will be giving later in the book. I will help you understand what .NET is, what it means in the realm of software development, and why it is so important. I will also give a little history on how we got here and what other similar environments exist. Last, for those of you who have programmed in Visual Basic before, I will give a high-level overview of what has changed.

What you will see in this session is a lot of conceptual information regarding the .NET platform. What you won't see are a lot of code samples or hands-on activities. Although some books get started by having you dive into code right away, I feel it is imperative to give you a firm foundation to build your .NET knowledge and experience upon. So hang in there; now let's get started!

Welcome to Visual Basic .NET

Welcome to Visual Basic .NET—a revolutionary step in the realm of modern computing that will help you create the best software applications possible and ease your role as a developer immensely. Whether you're a seasoned VB developer or you're totally new to VB, this book has something to offer you.

At its core, Visual Basic .NET is an object-oriented programming language for writing applications that target Microsoft's .NET platform. Windows applications, Web applications, Web services, mobile applications, and more are possible with Visual Basic .NET. During the course of this weekend, you will learn all about VB.NET and how it fits in with the underlying infra-structure of the .NET platform. You will also learn how it fits in with Microsoft's new development environment—Visual Studio .NET.

Before we get started talking about VB.NET, however, you might be won-dering what .NET is and what all the hype is about. What is it? What can it do for you? Why do you need it? If you, like so many other developers around the world, have lingering questions regarding .NET, read on . . .

What Is the .NET Framework?

Have you ever asked anyone from Indiana what a Hoosier is? Chances are that if you asked 10 different people from Indiana what a Hoosier was, you would get 10 different answers. The same is true for Microsoft's .NET plat-form; ask 10 people who are familiar with .NET what it is, and you're bound to get 10 different answers.

To sum up the .NET platform in one sentence would probably be too con-stricting, but I'll give it a try anyway. .NET is a software platform residing on top of the operating system that provides a structured hierarchical frame-work for building robust, secure, distributed applications in a variety of pro-gramming languages. There—say that 10 times real fast.

There are actually four primary pieces that make up the .NET platform. The first component is the .NET runtime, which is the software necessary to sup-port all the features and services that .NET provides. Think of this piece as a kind of service pack—it is installed on your or your user's machine to sup-port the runtime operation of .NET functionality. The second component is the .NET Framework, which amounts to a massive class library that is well structured and gives nested, hierarchical access to specific .NET services. The third component is the syntactical element—the programming languages that were written (or revised) for targeting the .NET platform. Visual Basic .NET is one of many such languages. The last component is the software tools necessary for designing, developing, debugging, and deploying .NET applications. In this book, we will be discussing Visual Studio .NET, one such tool. Figure 1.1 shows the different layers of the .NET Framework and associated technologies.

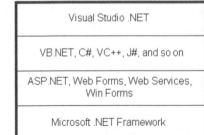

Visual Studio .NET
VB.NET, C#, VC++, J#, and so on
ASP.NET, Web Forms, Web Services, Win Forms
Microsoft .NET Framework

Figure 1.1

Visual Studio .NET and the .NET Framework.

This next section will introduce you to some of the primary concepts of .NET: the Common Language Runtime (CLR as it is often abbreviated), the Common Language Specification, and the Common Type Specification; managed and unmanaged code, intermediate language, assemblies, namespaces, garbage collection, and more. Don't worry if you don't have the foggiest idea what these mean. Rest assured: By the end of this evening, you'll be one step closer to knowing exactly what .NET is and what it means for you. Hang on and get ready to be blown away!

The Common Language Runtime

The CLR is at the core of the new .NET framework. It governs the runtime environment in which all managed .NET code executes and provides numerous services to .NET applications. The CLR is the developer's best friend, assisting in a number of tasks that have traditionally been problematic. It shelters the developer from having to deal with low-level Application Program Interfaces (APIs) that tend to be difficult to use and have disparate implementations between languages. The CLR unifies and helps manage the underlying infrastructure of services on the user's machine, providing the following key high-level benefits:

➤ **Simplified application development.** Because developers are sheltered from having to use complex APIs or come up with their own ways of handling security, versioning, exception handling, and so on, their jobs are made easier because they can now leverage the services that the CLR provides to do such tasks.

➤ **Simplified application deployment.** The CLR provides key mechanisms such as advanced versioning and XCOPY deployment to support a new, powerful, and simplified deployment model that will effectively end what has become known as DLL Hell.

◄◄◄◄◄◄◄◄◄◄◄◄◄◄◄◄◄◄◄◄◄◄◄◄◄◄◄◄◄◄◄◄◄◄◄◄◄◄◄

DLL Hell is the term used to describe aftereffects of having a myriad of DLLs installed on the user's machine and the confusion, mayhem, and quite often technical difficulties that are involved in getting all of them to co-exist peacefully.

◄◄◄◄◄◄◄◄◄◄◄◄◄◄◄◄◄◄◄◄◄◄◄◄◄◄◄◄◄◄◄◄◄◄◄◄◄◄◄

Developers can now safely deploy their applications to users' machines with the assurance of knowing that the CLR will manage the runtime environment.

➤ **Fewer application errors.** Because the CLR manages all execution, the user will have to deal with fewer application errors. With features such as garbage collection, exception handling, and managed code execution, the user will see fewer instances of dangling resources and renegade pointer allocation issues.

◄◄◄◄◄◄◄◄◄◄◄◄◄◄◄◄◄◄◄◄◄◄◄◄◄◄◄◄◄◄◄◄◄◄◄◄◄◄◄

Garbage collection refers to the automatic deallocation of allocated application resources.

◄◄◄◄◄◄◄◄◄◄◄◄◄◄◄◄◄◄◄◄◄◄◄◄◄◄◄◄◄◄◄◄◄◄◄◄◄◄◄

➤ **Better security.** The CLR provides the necessary infrastructure to implement code access security and role-based security. Code access security allows developers to build applications and components with certain trust levels, predesignating what the code can and cannot do. The role-based security model allows for a more robust implementation than the traditional MTS/COM+ models.

➤ **Language interoperability.** Although COM was language independent and a run-time binary standard, it had a lot of undesirable attributes. With the advent of .NET, applications and components now can be created to run under the CLR and interact as if they were all the same language. Thus, .NET is truly language independent and compatible at design time and runtime. The CLR handles debugging, exception handling, inheritance, and disparate calling conventions automatically no matter what language you are creating applications with.

Whether you are new to Visual Basic or you are a seasoned VB developer, many of the terms and concepts that are prevalent within .NET might be new to you, so I will take some time now to introduce you to many of these new concepts. These concepts will help formulate the base of knowledge necessary to grasp the concepts of what's going on in the "big picture" of all that is the .NET Framework and platform.

Managed Code

Any code or resource that runs under the control of the CLR is said to be managed code.

◄◄
Managed code refers to code that is directly managed by the Common Language Runtime. That is, all execution of the code must pass through the CLR before it is executed at the machine-code level.
◄◄

By default, Visual Basic .NET creates managed code for you. This means that any code you create with Visual Basic .NET will be able to take advantage of all that the CLR provides. Other CLR-compliant languages such as C# and J# also create managed code by default.

Unmanaged Code

Any code or resource that does not run under the control of the CLR is said to be unmanaged code.

◄◄
Unmanaged code refers to code that the Common Language Runtime does *not* directly manage. That is, the machine performs the execution and the CLR doesn't oversee it.
◄◄

By default, Visual C++ .NET creates unmanaged code. Visual Basic .NET is unable to create unmanaged code.

Metadata

Many of you who are experienced with COM or COM+ are familiar with type libraries, IDL, and the registry. This is because COM/COM+ required these external mechanisms to describe individual components and services. Collectively, the data used to describe this is referred to as metadata.

◄◄
Metadata is data that describes other data. It is, in essence, data that forms a blueprint (or specification) for the format of other data that is contained within the same document or module.
◄◄

CREATING MANAGED VERSUS UNMANAGED CODE

As an application or component developer, you should always strive to create managed code instead of unmanaged code. Creating managed code allows you to take advantage of all the benefits of the CLR. If you create applications—especially business applications—for a living, your life will be made easier if you strive always to create CLR-compliant code.

For developers who have unusually high performance, flexibility, and execution demands (such as those who create core-level operating system processes or low-level drivers), unmanaged code might be necessary.

However, you should keep in mind that many of the core benefits of the .NET Framework and platform come from the CLR and managed code; therefore, to take advantage of this, you should create unmanaged code only when absolutely necessary. As a Visual Basic .NET developer, you have no choice— VB.NET only creates managed code. However, should you find yourself working with C# or C++ (two languages that support unmanaged code) at some point in the future, keep these guidelines in mind.

With Microsoft .NET, metadata is stored internally within each executable module. This metadata includes declarations of types, members, and references that are used or are referenced by the executable module or assembly. (Assemblies are discussed in the "Assemblies" section later in this chapter.) Additional information on the name, version, and security is also included.

Because the metadata is compiled into the resultant .NET executable module, the components you create with .NET languages are said to be self describing. This is important because you no longer need external files to describe the underlying component you are using or inheriting from. Instead, all this information can be garnished from the component without external dependencies. Therefore, with .NET, individual components do not need to be registered.

NOTE Although individual components or assemblies do not need to be registered, any component or assembly that is to be deployed in the Global Assembly Cache (GAC) must be registered. The GAC is discussed later in this chapter in the section titled "The GAC."

Microsoft Intermediate Language (MSIL)

When you compile your code for the .NET platform, a native executable is not created. Instead, your code is compiled into Microsoft Intermediate Language (often referred to as MSIL or simply IL). The MSIL instructions are then stored in a Portable Executable (PE) file along with any associated metadata. Each compiled code module creates an executable with an extension of either .DLL or .EXE.

Those of you who have programmed with Visual Basic before might be familiar with the concepts of interpreted code and associated runtime. Well, rest assured that the MSIL and the CLR, although similar in some ways to the VB of old, are different in many other very important ways and represent a much better implementation. First, the MSIL that the compilation process creates is a lower-level set of instructions than the VB compilation process created previously. Second, the runtime used in the .NET platform is immensely more powerful than the old VB runtime, providing a plethora of added features and services that weren't available in the old runtime.

CAUTION   Some of you technical types might be freaking out right now, thinking that your code that is compiled in MSIL can be reverse engineered. You need to do two things right now: First, sit down, take a deep breath, and have a paper bag ready. Second, read this: Your code can easily be reverse engineered. Visual Studio .NET even includes an MSIL disassembler called ILDASM, making it easy to do so. While some third-party vendors are busy working on solutions for this, rest assured that the benefits you gain by using the power of the CLR and managed code far outweigh the risks of some hackhead who is locked away in a hotel in North Uruguay trying to sneak a peek at your code.

Because of the prospect of reverse engineering, you should keep in mind that any code or data that you reference statically in your applications and components might be subject to third parties; therefore, never store sensitive information such as passwords in static data. Instead, use runtime authentication techniques and cryptography to keep sensitive information intact and secure.

Just-In-Time Compilation (a.k.a. JITing)

Before you start lamenting a return to the idea of interpreted code, read on. The code you create in .NET is initially compiled in MSIL. When the MSIL is loaded for execution, each procedure or function is compiled into native machine code that can then be executed on the host machine, just as if it were created with a native code compiler. This process is referred to as JITing.

◀ ◀

JITing is the process of compiling the Microsoft Intermediate Language (MSIL) just in time for execution.

◀ ◀

After the MSIL is JITed, it is stored either in memory or in a disk-based cache; this pre-JITed binary is reused the next time it is referenced. Therefore, the MSIL is JITed only once; from then on, the CLR uses the pre-JITed version. This implies a slight performance hit the first time a function or procedure is JITed; every time it is referenced after that, it executes at native machine code speed. Figure 1.2 shows the JITing process at development time and at runtime.

Note that the entire component or assembly is not compiled at once; instead, each individual method is compiled as needed. Therefore, code that is never called will never be compiled. Code that is called time and time again will be compiled once and then run natively from that point on.

• •

Because of Microsoft's design, it is theoretically possible for your .NET applications to run on multiple platforms. This is made possible because all your code is compiled into MSIL and not native machine language. All an operating system vendor would need to do is to provide his own JITing compiler to take the MSIL and convert it into machine-level instructions. Of course, this can't be done overnight and is quite a daunting under-taking, but I believe we will see other operating systems (such as Linux) adopt the .NET architecture because it makes so much sense to do so.

Therefore, some day we might see our .NET applications running on a Linux or a Macintosh machine. You don't think it's possible? Stranger things have happened. Twenty years ago, Bill Gates said that he couldn't imagine anyone needing more than 640K of memory for a computer. Twenty years before that, no one on earth would have imag-ined that we would someday see people land on the moon. History has a way of bring-ing to fruition things that previously would have been thought of as impossible.

• •

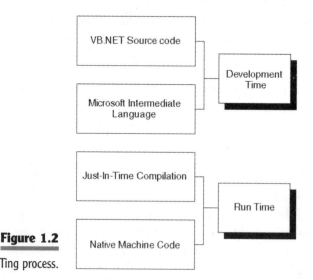

Figure 1.2

The JITing process.

Assemblies

Assemblies are the building blocks of the .NET Framework and any associated applications that are created to run on the .NET platform. Quite simply, an assembly (in the .NET sense) is a collection of one or more files treated as a logical unit. These files can be binary executables, images, resource files, or any other files that are associated with your code. Each assembly carries with it its own metadata (called a manifest, explained in the next section) that contains other important information such as its name, version, locale, and dependencies on other resources.

If you are a VB6 developer, an assembly can best be explained by relating it loosely to a COM DLL. Just as with a COM DLL, you can add many classes to the assembly and assign the assembly specific versions. You can also reuse the assembly in many applications and deploy it similarly. The assembly manifest is similar to COM DLL's type library. The manifest contains all the necessary metadata to describe it to external consumers of the assembly.

Assemblies come with a complex four-part versioning structure called the compatibility version number. The CLR uses this at runtime to determine which version to load and to identify versions of assemblies to other dependent components. Because of the included versioning mechanisms of the CLR, the old days of binary incompatibilities and DLL Hell are gone; with the services of the CLR at your side, you can rest assured that when you deploy an application that depends on a certain version of an assembly, it will be deployed and kept intact on the host machine.

Assemblies are compiled with descriptive names as well as their associated version information. All assemblies must have a name assigned to them, and optionally, they can have a strong name assigned to them.

◄ ◄

A *strong name* is a fully qualified name that is used for assemblies that must be shared. A *shared assembly* is an assembly that is shared with other .NET enabled software on the computer.

The *Global Assembly Cache* is where shared assemblies are stored.

A *private assembly* is not shared with other .NET applications; it is stored in the application's directory or a subdirectory below the application's directory.

◄ ◄

The GAC

If you have multiple applications that use the same component, you should put that component in the GAC. The GAC is a special area designated on the host machine to store assemblies that must be shared at runtime.

When an assembly is referenced, the CLR first checks the local directory for the assembly. If the CLR doesn't find the assembly in the local directory, it checks the GAC. Assemblies that are not found in the local directory or the GAC can be located using codebase hints within a configuration file. Assemblies such as this can be downloaded dynamically via the Internet and stored in what is called the application download cache.

◄ ◄

The *application download cache* is a special area reserved for assemblies that are dynamically downloaded to the application's computer.

◄ ◄

The Common Language Specification

The Common Language Specification (CLS) provides a specification for compiler creators to target the .NET platform and the CLR. Any compiler vendor who wants to fully support the .NET initiative must abide by strict rules that the CLS imposes with regard to types, exception handling, and interfaces, to name a few.

The rules that the CLS imposes are only applicable to those portions of the code and classes that are publicly accessible; that is, only the external classes and methods need to abide by the rules of the CLS. Internally, compiler vendors optionally can choose to support non–CLS-compliant code constructs and mechanisms. This allows for legacy languages to make the jump into .NET and retain some of their original language constructs.

At press time, more than 25 compiler vendors had committed themselves to support the CLS and the .NET platform. This means that you don't necessarily have to code in a Microsoft language (such as Visual Basic .NET or C#) to take advantage of .NET and the CLR. Other languages such as Delphi, Perl, Lisp, Eiffel, Smalltalk, and even COBOL can be used to create .NET components and applications.

In yesterday's world, a developer who chose one language over another inevitably had differing levels of power and capabilities at his fingertips, totally dependent on the language he had chosen to develop with. Now, with the common language support in .NET and the many varied supported languages, a developer can choose which language to use without giving up power or capabilities. Because each language supports the .NET platform, choosing a language is simply a matter of syntactical preference.

The Common Type System

The Common Type System (CTS) provides a specification for the implementation of all types that the CLR supports. In addition, the CTS describes how each type should be defined, referenced, and used. The CTS is a superset of the CLS; as such, not all languages support all types.

At the highest level, all types (including intrinsic types such as integers) inherit from a class called `Object`. The `Object` class provides many core-level methods to implement many important features to support the .NET platform such as type information, garbage collection support, string name, and hash values for the object and comparison operations.

Value Types

Value types are commonly built into most modern programming languages. Value types are usually passed by value within an application and are stack based (not heap based), making them performance friendly.

Value types that .NET supports include `Boolean`, `Byte`, `Char`, `DateTime`, `Decimal`, `Double`, `Int16`, `Int32`, `Int64`, `IntPtr`, `SByte`, `Single`, `TimeSpan`, `UInt16`, `UInt32`, and `UInt64`. In addition to these intrinsic types, you can also derive your own value types from the `ValueType` class. The CTS also provides support for enumerated types (enums) that are based on one of the integer types (`Int16`, `Int32`, or `Int64`).

NOTE Although every CLS-compliant language must externally support only the value types specified in the CLS, every language does *not* need to support all the value types. For instance, Visual Basic .NET does not support some of the value types that the CLS provides. In addition, not every CLS-compliant language uses the same nomenclature for every CLS value type.

Reference Types

Reference types are types that are passed by reference and not by value. They are created on the heap and not the stack, as in value types. Therefore, the memory address of the object is stored in the reference type's variable, not the actual value, as in value types. In addition, the garbage collector automatically cleans up reference type variables as needed. (Value type variables do not need garbage collection because they already carry the actual data around with them.)

Classes

If you've worked with Visual Basic or any other object-based language before, you're probably familiar with classes. Classes are like blueprints for objects that will be instantiated at runtime. They define the members of the class—that is, the methods, fields, properties, and events that are associated with an object. Optionally, classes also define the implementation of objects. Classes that do not provide implementation are called abstract classes.

Classes are the building blocks of the CTS and everything you will do in the .NET Framework. You will use classes to model the real objects and behaviors that exist within the domain of your application's environment. The .NET Framework provides thousands of classes for you to build your application on.

Those of you who are familiar with Visual Basic's earlier versions will know that prior to this version, VB was not truly object oriented. That is, until now, it did not have implementation inheritance. Previously, you could inherit only from an interface, and you had to recode all the relevant required implementation code. Now, thanks to the .NET platform, VB.NET has true implementation inheritance, helping it make the jump from just being an object-based language to a truly object-oriented language. This topic will be discussed further in Appendix A, "Migrating to Visual Basic .NET."

Interfaces

Interfaces are somewhat similar in concept to abstract classes; they define a class without an implementation. Therefore, although you can instantiate a class, you cannot instantiate an interface. Instead, you must create a class that implements an interface.

Delegates

Delegates are the equivalent of an object-oriented function pointer. A delegate points to the method of an object. Delegates are useful when you need to handle the events of an object—especially if you want to share event-handling code among different objects. Delegates will be discussed more as we dive into creating some object-oriented code in the Saturday Afternoon session, "Exploring the Visual Basic .NET Programming Language."

Garbage Collection

If you've used VB previously, you might be familiar with COM or COM+. With these technologies, reference counting handled object lifetimes. Now, with .NET, the CLR manages object lifetimes through a technology referred to as garbage collection. This process prevents you, the developer, from having to keep track of all the objects and resources that you have allocated in your applications and components. When you are finished with an object or resource, the garbage collector marks it for deletion and releases the object or resource at the optimum time. The garbage collection process is highly optimized and has many complex algorithms within it, allowing you to do what you do best (develop applications) while it takes care of cleaning up after you.

If you're a seasoned developer, you might find that this is an unusual programming practice. Personally, I've worked with lower-level languages such as C, C++, and Delphi quite a bit, and the idea of creating objects and resources and just leaving them there is sometimes a foreign concept and a hard habit to break. I find myself always wanting to deallocate what I've allocated somewhere else in the application. In addition, it might not be easy for low-level application developers to get used to the idea of giving up control to an entity like the CLR to do garbage collection. Traditionally, situations like this have implied less control for the developer in addition to somewhat of a performance hit. With .NET, however, this is not true: Having the garbage collector do the cleanup for you is actually faster than your doing it yourself.

Namespaces

Namespaces are a new entity with the .NET Framework, but they are an essential element. Namespaces are used to organize assemblies into hierarchical groups of common functionality and allow developers to itemize their utilization of those common groups of code at design time. Assemblies can have many namespaces, and namespaces can contain many classes and other namespaces.

Because you are new to this, you might tend to confuse assemblies and namespaces, so let's take a look at the difference between these.

◄◄

Assemblies are the physical grouping of different files used in a .NET application or component.

Namespaces are the logical grouping of different classes used in a .NET application or component.

◄◄

Namespaces, therefore, can span multiple assemblies. We will create our own assemblies and namespaces throughout this book, so you will become more comfortable with these concepts as you read on.

Take a Break

Okay, so you've just read all about the CLR, CLS, and CTS, and you have a gazillion Three-Letter Acronyms (TLAs) running through your head. Some of you might feel like your head is going to explode. But before your head blows up (remember the old horror movie *Scanners?*), get up, stretch, take a short walk around the house, and start thinking about all that is .NET and what it could mean for you. Then, get a fresh cup of whatever you've been drinking (Java!?!) and buckle yourself up for another round of .NET Framework technotalk. Next, we'll be learning about what the .NET platform means to developers and why it is needed.

Why Do We Need the .NET Framework?

Having read this far, you might be thinking to yourself, "Well, this is all great and wonderful, but why do I need it?" To appreciate all that .NET brings to the table, we must first establish a baseline by examining what programming for Microsoft Windows was like before the introduction of the .NET platform.

A Brief History of Windows Programming

I have always subscribed to the idea that to truly appreciate what you have, you need to try to live a while without it. For example, do you truly appreciate your car? Try living for a while either without a car or with a much less flashy or less dependable car. Then, get your regular car back. See how you feel—I guarantee you'll appreciate your car much more. Those of us who were involved at the beginning of the Windows programming evolution back in the late 1980s and early 1990s remember what it was like to drive applications back then, and we perhaps are the ones who most appreciate what .NET has to offer.

Depending on your age, you might recall how painful Windows programming was at the beginning. You pretty much had only one language choice (the C programming language), and you had to code your applications using low-level and complex APIs. In addition, your programs had to take care of all event-driven operations within one large event loop, which often became tedious if not almost impossible to maintain. Those of us who remember clenching our fists in frustration while desperately combing through a well-used copy of Charles Petzold's *Programming Windows* book are probably having flashbacks right now, perhaps starting to get the shakes and go into convulsions.

Fortunately, relief eventually came with the introduction of C++ and object-oriented programming with frameworks. Using C++ and frameworks such as

MFC, OWL, Zinc, or Zapp, you could create Windows applications with much greater ease than before. Gone were the days of long event loops, and gone were the large spaghetti-code infested program listings. Instead, we had cleaner code that was better organized both physically and logically.

In 1991, Microsoft introduced Visual Basic 1.0, and the programmers of the world gasped. Those of us who had programmed Windows for years had one of two reactions: "Thank God! It's about time!" or "BASIC? Who the heck wants to program Windows with BASIC?" Well, regardless of the typical C/C++ programmer's reaction to Basic as a language, VB took the world by storm. No longer did programmers have to learn complex APIs or frameworks—they could simply drag and drop their way into a Windows application with ease. Visual Basic represented a truly revolutionary step in the evolution of Windows programming.

Soon after, other companies followed suit. PowerSoft, the creator of Power-Builder, created a product that was loosely modeled around the same concept of VB. PowerBuilder geared itself toward the everyday business user, and the PowerSoft marketing arm went to work and successfully marketed the product to enterprise organizations all over the world. Other similar environments (Gupta's SQLWindows, for instance) also had varied success in providing 4GL solutions for Windows programming needs.

In 1995, Borland introduced Delphi, which was another revolutionary step in Windows development. With Delphi, Windows programmers could create their own applications and components with the same language (Object Pascal). VB developers could create their applications with VB, but they had to create their components in C or C++. Not only that, but the applications and components created with Delphi were compiled natively for the Windows platform. VB (at the time) was interpreted and required a runtime module to be distributed with each application.

At about the same time, a group of developers at Sun were coming up with a new language that is now known as Java. Java was supposed to be the single solution to all developmental needs, allowing developers to "write once, run everywhere." Java took off faster than greased lightning in the mid-1990s, and it seemed that new Java titles flooded bookstores every week. At a conceptual level, the idea of a virtual machine that ran on multiple platforms indeed had merit, and many corporations quickly took a serious look at Java. However, Java suffered heavily in the performance department, and people also realized that it had serious interface issues—the GUI transported from platform to platform was not quite native enough for the most demanding developers. Therefore, in the late 1990s, Java found its true home—as a server-based platform. Here, with the advent of J2EE and technologies such as Java Server Pages and Servlets, Java has proven itself to be an enterprise solution. Today, Java stands as one of the major competitors of the .NET platform.

I can safely argue that a lot of the improvements made in VB during subsequent years were due to increased competition from Borland, PowerSoft, and Sun. Microsoft learned from Borland's innovation with Delphi, PowerSoft's marketing prowess with PowerBuilder, and Sun's enterprise goals of Java and began to push VB as more than just a Windows development toy and more of an enterprise solution. In fact, Delphi's chief architect, Anders Hielsberg, left Borland in the late 1990s and joined Microsoft, becoming the primary architect of the .NET platform. Those of us who have used Delphi or Java recognize many features carried over from these environments into the new .NET architecture.

What Microsoft .NET Provides

Microsoft .NET represents a revolutionary step in modern programming, allowing developers to create applications that are more robust, reliable, and secure in much less time than was previously possible in other environments. It brings together all the necessary elements to create a single, unified application development platform that is a Windows developer's dream.

The developer stands to benefit from the improvements brought on by .NET because he can now focus on doing his job of creating applications instead of lamenting the choice of a particular programming language, tool, component set, or technology. The developer can program in the language of his choice and leverage the full power of .NET to create applications in record time. All of the necessary elements are in place—true object-oriented features, exception handling, security, garbage collection, Windows (OS) services, and Web services. All of these and more are at the developer's disposal. The developer now can focus on the business logic and business-related features instead of focusing on the implementation headaches of yesterday.

The user stands to benefit from .NET's improvements because the applications that .NET developers create will be more reliable, more secure, and easier to deploy. If the user already has the .NET distributable installed on his machine, then new copies of the application can be deployed with ease and should be small. Users can run .NET applications with the assurance that the applications will be more secure and that the instances of renegade virus-laden programs will be kept to a minimum. Users won't have to put up with the aftereffects of DLL Hell; they will be able to install and upgrade applications with more reliable results than before.

Ultimately, corporations that adopt .NET will stand to benefit in many ways from all of the features provided. Whether it be increased developer productivity, better application reliability and deployment, or greater user satisfaction and security, corporations will most likely find themselves better off by adopting the .NET platform.

Comparing .NET to Sun's Java

Of course, unless you've been locked away in the Pit of Despair for the past five years, you're probably familiar with Sun's Java initiative and Java 2 Enterprise Edition (J2EE). Although both environments (J2EE and .NET) have similar goals and features, their implementations are quite different under the hood, and there are some compelling reasons that I personally believe that .NET is a better choice.

First, there is the language issue. With .NET, you can choose the language you want to work with. With Java, you do not have this choice. However, with Java, you have the choice of which platform to use; with .NET, you must use the Windows platform. However, the .NET platform is prime for porting to other platforms, so this might not be an issue in the future. So, with .NET, you have your choice of multiple languages on one platform. With Java, you have one language on your choice of multiple platforms.

Second, there is the framework. Although Java's framework currently might be slightly more broad than what .NET offers, it is by no means better organized. The .NET Framework is well organized and encompasses most of what every developer would ever want to develop enterprise applications.

Third, there are the development tools. Microsoft provides Visual Studio .NET, a highly productive Integrated Development Environment (IDE) that is a dream come true for developers. This IDE integrates everything from designing UML diagrams to creating and managing databases to rapidly developing applications and Web services. All of this is provided in one environment. With Java, no single tool encompasses all of this functionality under one roof. Borland's JBuilder is the only one that comes even remotely close.

Next, there is the productivity. Microsoft's Visual Basic and C# are easier to learn and use than Java, and developers can often get their job done in less time and with less code using VB.NET or C# than Java. Ultimately, this can save a ton of money on enterprise-scale projects.

Finally, there is the speed issue. Because of the highly intelligent design and optimization techniques of the .NET platform, applications that are created to run with .NET will be much faster than those that are created with Java. The .NET JITing process ensures that your applications will always run at the speed of native machine code and will never be interpreted. Java code, by default, is interpreted in nature and relies heavily on the Java Virtual Machine (JVM) for its implementation. Although some Java compilers exist on the market today, a Java compiled program is not as fast as a .NET compiled program.

To prove all this, Microsoft recently took Sun's "model" Java application (an implementation of an online pet store) and ported it to the .NET platform. The results were amazing. They showed that the .NET solution performed 28 times faster than the Java solution, was created with 1/4 the amount of code, and was 7 times more scalable. The results of this case study can be found on Microsoft's Web site.

NOTE You can see for yourself the full results of Microsoft's port of the "Pet Store" Java application and more comparisons to Java online at http://www.gotdotnet.com/team/compare/default.aspx.

The choice between .NET and Java is yours. If you're already knee-deep into Java in your organization, you are probably going to be okay because Java provides all the necessary tools to get the job done. In many cases, it might not be cost effective (in the short run) to make a move to .NET right away. However, you might want to look at J# (Microsoft's Java-like language implementation) if you have a relatively small Java code base or if you're just starting a new Java project. I believe that you will come out ahead in the long run by choosing to base your application development endeavors on .NET technologies.

What Is Visual Basic .NET?

Microsoft Visual Basic .NET is one of the premier languages with which you can develop applications for the .NET platform. Visual Basic .NET is loosely based on the legacy BASIC (Beginner's All-purpose Symbolic Instruction Code) language, although many of its legacy features are now finally removed.

In its current form, Visual Basic .NET represents a language that has matured in its 10+ years of existence and is now fully object oriented. In essence, this is not "your father's" Visual Basic. VB.NET can now be used to code all portions of an enterprise application—client components, server components, Windows services, Web services, the client interface, and the database and middle-tier layers. VB.NET has all the features of an enterprise-scale application development language.

A Brief History of Visual Basic

If you're new to the Visual Basic language, you might be wondering how we got here in the first place. It's a long story, but I'll attempt to give you a brief history of how the language started and how we got here.

Back in the mid-1960s, a new language was invented at Dartmouth College— BASIC. The syntax was loosely based on ALGOL and FORTRAN. The idea was that this simple language could be taught to students as an introductory programming language. Then, the students could move on to more complex programming languages.

BASIC was then ported to many various platforms throughout the 1960s and 1970s. It was in the late 1970s that Microsoft created its first BASIC adaptation called GW-BASIC (GW stood for Gee Whiz). GW-BASIC was interpreted and included in early versions of DOS. Anyone who started out programming on the PC back then inevitably remembers writing at least a few GW-BASIC applications.

As the popularity of GW-BASIC grew, Microsoft realized the potential of the language and enhanced it with every new version of DOS. Then, in the 1980s, Microsoft came out with what was then a somewhat revolutionary step in the BASIC language—QuickBasic. This was a new "visual" DOS-based environment that supported the integrated development of BASIC applications. For anyone who was used to GW-BASIC, it was a dream come true. Additional compiler and environment features were added with each release, making the product better and better.

In the summer of 1991, with the aid of Alan Cooper, Microsoft released Visual Basic 1.0—a truly revolutionary step in BASIC development. This tool, known as "VB," was the first to support true Rapid Application Development (RAD) for Windows. Although VB 1.0 contained many cool features, it did not catch on with the programmers of the world right away. The next year, Microsoft released version 2.0, with added features like database support.

In 1993, Microsoft released VB 3.0, and the popularity of the product started to boom. The BASIC language, and even Visual Basic, had always been thought of as a "toy" and not a "real" language or development tool. C/C++ programmers had always poked fun at the language and tool, claiming that it was good only for simple projects or prototyping, but when you needed a real application, you had to go to a lower-level language. I know this because I was one of those people. Back then, I was a C/C++ application programmer.

It wasn't until one of my friends, Bill Hatfield, purchased VB 3.0 and showed it to me that I truly understood the implication of how much it brought to the table. I already had VB 2.0, but after looking at it for a week, I put it on the shelf and dismissed it as "toyware." After seeing what Bill was doing, I went out the very next day and upgraded to VB 3.0. Thus began my adventure with Visual Basic.

In what seemed like an eternity, Microsoft spent many years developing VB 4.0. Finally, in late 1996, it was released and contained many new features such as enhanced bound controls and advanced OLE support. One year later, VB 5.0 was released with full ActiveX support. This release, along with the ActiveX "revolution," became very popular. The complexities of having to write COM objects in other languages such as C++ made it compelling for developers to use VB instead.

Finally, in 1998, version 6.0 was released with new object-oriented features and better support for enterprise development. It was right about this time that corporations around the world started rapidly adapting VB as an accepted development tool. No longer was VB thought of as a toy or a tool just for prototyping—real enterprise applications could be created with it.

Still, serious issues remained. VB still suffered from many angles. It still wasn't truly 100 percent object oriented (it didn't support implementation inheritance—a big drawback); deployment of VB applications was a nightmare due to the complexities of ActiveX deployment and DLL Hell; it couldn't be used to write truly multithreaded applications; and it wasn't used to create VB components (most of these were written in C++). For some companies, other development tools such as Java, Delphi, and PowerBuilder remained more attractive because of the deficiencies that still existed in the core VB language.

In its current incarnation, VB 7.0 (or VB.NET as it has become widely known) has taken care of most of the traditional complaints of low-level application programmers. It no longer suffers from the problems that have kept it tied down. Thus, many developers who previously balked at VB as a tool of choice now warmly welcome it into their personal or corporate toolset.

The next several sections will focus on the new features of VB.NET so that you can become more familiar with the product and the language.

Basic Language Features

Before learning about the features of Visual Basic .NET, you should know two things. Visual Basic .NET is a programming language based on the traditional VB language that Microsoft has developed over the past 10+ years. Visual Studio .NET is an Integrated Development Environment (IDE) that natively supports Visual Basic .NET development. In this book, you will learn both the features of VB.NET—the language—and Visual Studio .NET—the development environment.

This being said, here are some of the basic features of the Visual Basic .NET language:

➤ **Object-oriented.** At its core, Visual Basic .NET is an object-oriented programming language that supports the .NET platform. It supports all major facets of any OOP language—inheritance, encapsulation, and polymorphism. As I mentioned earlier, any deficiencies in Visual Basic's OOP features of yesterday have been eliminated with Visual Basic .NET.

➤ **Structured.** In addition to its OOP features, Visual Basic .NET supports typical structured programming constructs such as functions, procedures, conditional statements, loops, variables, arrays, and the like.

➤ **Visual.** Visual Basic .NET natively supports the creation and usage of visual objects such as forms and Windows controls. It also supports the visual drag-and-drop ease of many modern-day programming environments. Instead of having to code many items, object properties can be set visually. Visual Basic .NET makes event-driven programming easy.

➤ **Powerful.** Visual Basic .NET compiles to the same MSIL code that C# and Visual C++ .NET are compiled to, putting it on par with those two languages. No longer can the C/C++ techno-wizards claim that they are the true performers and that VB is an also-ran. Now, with the advent of native multithreading and JITing, your VB.NET code can and will do just as much or more than any other .NET language.

➤ **Enterprise ready.** Visual Basic .NET is a language for the enterprise. It includes native support for building all aspects of enterprise-scale applications, including the client-side GUI, the database layer, the transport and middle layers, and the core business objects that we base our applications on. In addition, Visual Basic .NET can be used to build Web services, Windows services, console applications, and even Web browser-based applications. It is truly an enterprise solution.

What Can You Do with Visual Basic .NET?

Visual Basic .NET, in conjunction with the Visual Studio .NET development environment, can tackle just about any programming task that comes your way. Here are a few of the things you can do with Visual Basic .NET:

➤ **Windows applications.** As with previous versions of Visual Basic, Visual Basic .NET can be used to produce "standard" Windows applications. The Windows applications you create will still require a runtime module, but not the traditional VB runtime. Instead, any application you create with Visual Basic .NET will be able to run only on host machines that already have the .NET redistributable installed on it. At press time, this redistributable package was just over 20 megabytes (MB) in size and was supported on Windows 98, 98 SE, Me, NT, 2000, and XP. Figure 1.3 shows a typical Windows application developed with Visual Basic .NET.

NOTE

Windows 95 is not supported for the deployment of .NET Windows applications.

➤ **Web applications.** New in this version of Visual Basic is the ability to create applications that run within a Web browser. Those of you who are familiar with the traditional Active Server Page model know that you could previously build Web applications with ASP, VB Script, and Visual InterDev. Now, with Visual Basic .NET and ASP.NET, you can build complete natively compiled (not interpreted!) Web applications from within Visual Studio .NET. What's more, you get to tap into the complete power of Visual Basic .NET and code your Web applications using "code behind" technology that mimics the way VB programmers have traditionally written regular Windows applications. Figure 1.4 shows a Web application developed with Visual Basic .NET.

BUZZ WORD

Natively compiled means that the program was compiled to run specifically with the machine's hardware and software without required intervention by a runtime interpreter or manager.

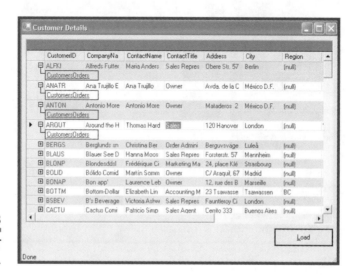

Figure 1.3

A Windows .NET application.

➤ **XML Web services.** Visual Basic .NET makes it easy to create and use XML Web services—that is, standalone, remotely callable procedures and functions that are platform independent and can be called via a standard Internet connection. Thus, you now have a new opportunity to create products and services built around an open service-based architecture. You can build programs that consume Web services that others have written and made available, and you can build your own Web services for others (possibly customers or vendors of yours) to utilize. Visual Basic .NET makes this easy to do. Figure 1.5 shows a Visual Basic .NET Web service test page in action.

➤ **Windows services.** Using Visual Basic .NET, it is easy to create Windows operating system services that run in the background under Windows NT, 2000, and XP. This can be useful for anyone who is developing server-side software that must remain active at all times, even when machines are left unattended for long periods.

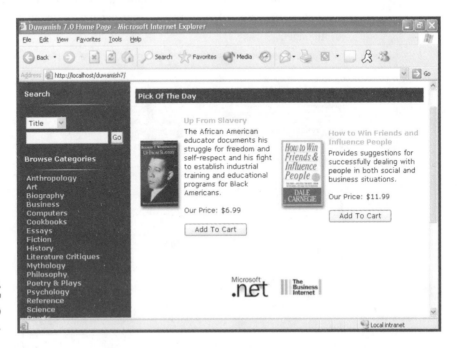

Figure 1.4

An ASP.NET Web application.

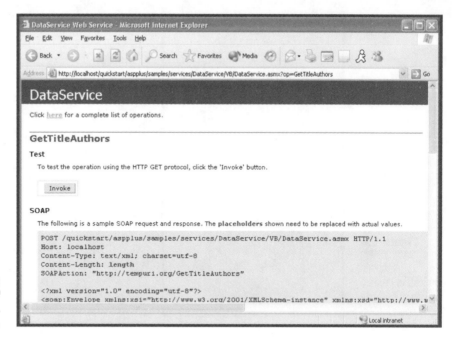

Figure 1.5

Testing an XML
Web service.

> ➤ **Console applications.** Another useful new feature of Visual Basic
> .NET is the ability to create console applications that have the old
> DOS-based utility program look and feel. This feature comes in handy
> for creating small utilitarian-type applications and batch-file operations
> and for writing "tester" programs to do regression testing.

> ➤ **Mobile applications.** Using the Mobile Internet Toolkit (a free down-
> load available from Microsoft), you can now create applications with
> Visual Basic .NET that target mobile devices such as mobile phones.
> This opens up a new and exciting opportunity for Visual Basic pro-
> grammers to enter into the mobile world of application development.
> Figure 1.6 shows a sample mobile application built with Visual Basic
> .NET and the Mobile Internet Toolkit.

> ➤ **Devices.** Visual Basic .NET is not limited to Windows and Web devel-
> opment; you can now program any device that supports the .NET
> platform. This means that as new programmable devices (such as
> refrigerators, televisions, microwaves, stoves, and so on) are introduced,
> you will be able to write applications to drive these devices using
> Visual Basic .NET.

Figure 1.6

A mobile application created with the Mobile Internet Toolkit.

➤ **Classes, components, and frameworks.** Of course, Visual Basic .NET is not limited to creating visual applications. You can also create your own classes and frameworks to use internally or sell to the general public. In addition, you can create your own set of components to use or sell as a third-party vendor.

➤ **COM components.** Although Visual Basic .NET can't create truly native COM components, it *can* create COM wrappers around your .NET components so that your Visual Basic .NET applications and components can be used in the COM world.

What's New in Visual Basic .NET?

To say that there are a lot of changes in Visual Basic .NET is a gross understatement. It's like saying that the world has changed a bit in the past 100 years. Take someone from 1900 and put him into the world of 2000, and chances are that person would be a bit scared, freaked out, and uneasy with his surroundings. It would take him a while to get used to things, like being able to call or instant message someone instead of having to send a telegram; being able to jump on a plane and be across the country in a matter of hours instead of months; and being able to get the news from around the world instantly instead of waiting for the next wire or Western Union transmission. The person who is transplanted from 1900 to 2000 would be equally filled with trepidation and excitement all at once.

Welcome to the world of the typical Visual Basic programmer who is migrating from an older version of Visual Basic to VB.NET. Like the person who instantly is transplanted a century from his current setting, the traditional VB programmer will most likely find himself equally concerned and excited about the new features of VB.NET.

What will be of concern for many of you who have been using VB to write applications is the notion that much of what you have been working on for years will need to be thrown away or rewritten significantly. Although it is true that Visual Basic .NET represents a significant change from previous versions, all is not lost. Microsoft, in part due to a strong resistance by existing VB developers, has worked hard to preserve existing VB development efforts and has provided an upgrade tool to help convert much of existing VB code to Visual Basic .NET. Although some developers of small applications might be able to migrate quickly, I expect that most enterprise applications will not port so easily. Generally speaking, the larger and more complex the application and the more variables (not program variables, but variables such as the number of third-party controls, middle-tier issues, database issues, and so on), the harder it will be to migrate.

At the heart of the migration issue is a core paradigm shift from what was traditional VB to the new Visual Basic .NET. Simply put, there are enough compelling reasons to make the migration worth it in the long run, but language enhancements such as true inheritance and multithreading make a good case for a fresh start at a new architecture. To tap into the full power of Visual Basic .NET, I recommend taking a long look at your current VB applications to determine whether your applications could benefit enough from a move to .NET. The advent of true inheritance capabilities in VB could cause you to rethink your internal classes and possibly come up with better underlying designs for your programs. The introduction of multithreading could cause you to rethink portions of your program that could use this technology to increase the efficiency and responsiveness of your applications. Whatever the case, the migration to .NET technologies is not simply one of having to deal with the syntactical changes, but one of contemplating the possibilities of redoing the underlying core architecture and design of your applications.

On the other side of the fence are those of us who have been screaming for changes to VB for many years. New features such as true inheritance and multithreading are a welcome addition to an already great and otherwise fully capable language. We look at all the changes in .NET and welcome them with open arms, excited about the possibility to use Visual Basic for all of our programming needs. No longer do we have to worry about having to program our low-level or performance-intensive code in C++; no longer do we need to rely on C++ for creating custom components; no longer do we have to design class hierarchies based on an interface inheritance model. With Visual Basic .NET, we can feel confident in using one language for all our programming needs and not have to worry that we're missing anything.

Language Changes

For those of you who are migrating to VB.NET, you're in for quite a change; you need to know about numerous language changes. Although covering all the changes in VB could easily fill an entire book, we are instead going to concentrate on the major changes in the language and forego examining every low-level change. This section will focus on presenting the changes in VB.NET from a 10,000-foot point of view; there won't be a lot of in-depth discussion here or a lot of code samples. Those will come later. For now, you can read this section and know some of the basics.

Here, then, is a list of the major changes in the VB language:

➤ **Everything is an object.** Yes, you read that right. The core `Object` class that is defined in the `System` namespace inherits `Integers`, `Longs`, `Strings`, and all other variable types. Thus, it is possible to do the following:

```
Dim str As String
str = 64.ToString()
MessageBox.Show(str)
```

Look strange? Get used to it!

➤ **String changes.** All strings in VB.NET are Unicode strings. Also, fixed-length strings are not supported. Thus, the following is impossible in VB.NET:

```
Dim str As String * 64
```

In addition, you can no longer carelessly convert numeric values to string values and back if Option Strict is turned on. Thus, the following is not possible:

```
Dim str as String
Dim int as Integer
int = 64
str = int
```

The Option Strict statement is new to VB.NET. It tells the VB.NET compiler to disallow automatic type conversions such as that listed in the preceding code.

■ ■

TIP I recommend that you always turn on Option Strict for the best possible quality assurance and control in your VB.NET applications.

■ ■

➤ **Integer changes.** In Visual Basic 6, an Integer was a 16-bit number and a Long was a 32-bit number. In Visual Basic .NET, an Integer is a 32-bit number and a Long is a 64-bit number. The VB.NET type Short is a 16-bit number. Thus, you should convert any existing Integer types to Short and any Long types to Integer when you're migrating to VB.NET.

➤ **Other type changes.** Other miscellaneous changes to data types have been made for VB.NET. First, the value of True has changed. In VB.NET, 0 is False and any non-zero value is True. In prior versions of VB, −1 was True and everything else was False. Second, the Decimal data type has replaced the Currency data type. Finally, the Object data type has replaced the Variant data type. Remember: Because everything in VB.NET is ultimately inherited from the Object data type, the Object type becomes the new catch-all instead of Variant. User-Defined Types (UDTs) have been replaced with structures. Structures are nothing more than a simple aggregate grouping of data (and optionally, methods). Here is a sample Structure in VB.NET:

```
Structure Point
    Dim x as Integer
    Dim y as Integer
End Structure
```

```
Dim TopLeft as Point
TopLeft.x = 10
TopLeft.y = 50
```

➤ **Array changes.** Prior versions of VB allowed you to declare arrays that had non-zero lower bounds. In addition, you could use the `Option Base` statement to declare the default lower bounds of an array to be 0 or 1. In VB.NET, these options are gone. All arrays in VB.NET have a lower boundary of 0. Also, assigning arrays to one another no longer creates a copy of the array; instead, it creates a reference to the original array.

➤ **Sub and function changes.** In VB.NET, all sub and function calls now require parentheses. This is a welcome change because it creates consistency within VB as well as other .NET languages. Perhaps one of the strangest changes in VB is that parameters are now passed `ByVal` instead of `ByRef` by default. I expect this to be one of the major sources of confusion and frustration for those of us migrating from older versions of VB to VB.NET. Other changes are also present: Optional arguments now require a default value; static subs and functions are no longer supported; and parameter arrays are now passed by value instead of by reference. A welcome addition to the VB.NET language is the `return` statement, which causes the execution of a sub or procedure to end and return to the caller immediately.

➤ **Error handling.** In one of my favorite changes, VB.NET finally has good structured error-handling mechanisms instead of relying on the old `On Error Goto` way of trapping errors. The old way still works, but the new way is much more flexible and structured. The new method involves the `Try…Catch… Finally` statement, which will be demonstrated in Saturday Afternoon's session.

➤ **Class changes.** VB.NET introduces the concept of constructors and destructors.

Constructors and destructors are similar in concept to the `Class_Initialize` and `Class_Terminate` events in VB 6.0. Of course, one major change that has already been discussed is that VB.NET now supports implementation inheritance. This means that you can inherit both the interface and the implementation from a class, saving a lot of recoding time and headaches. In addition, VB.NET supports overloading, which allows developers to use the same method name more than once in a class.

◄◄◄◄◄◄◄◄◄◄◄◄◄◄◄◄◄◄◄◄◄◄◄◄◄◄◄◄◄◄◄◄◄◄◄

A *constructor* facilitates the creation of aggregate items in an object upon creation of that object. Conversely, a *destructor* helps clean up aggregate items in an object upon destruction.

◄◄◄◄◄◄◄◄◄◄◄◄◄◄◄◄◄◄◄◄◄◄◄◄◄◄◄◄◄◄◄◄◄◄◄

➤ **Miscellaneous changes.** Default properties are no longer implemented. Instead, you should always fully qualify the property that you are working with. Also, VB.NET now natively supports multithreading, giving developers far greater flexibility for creating performance or process-intensive code.

Although the preceding list is by no means comprehensive, it gives you an idea of what high-level changes have been made to the VB.NET language. As we move through the book, we will point out each change and provide thorough examples.

Environment Changes

Along with the many other changes from previous versions, Visual Basic now has a new home: Visual Studio .NET. This new environment hosts many of the new .NET languages: VB.NET, C#, C++, J#, and more. Although it is not necessary to use Visual Studio .NET to create .NET applications, you might want to use this IDE as opposed to a regular text editor or some other tool for several reasons.

With Visual Studio .NET, you can build Windows applications, Web applications, mobile applications, Web services, and more within one unified environment. Most of the languages that support .NET have plug-ins that allow you to code, run, and test your applications from within VS.NET. This means that VS.NET supports the creation of mixed-language solutions. In fact, with the new environment, you can have all of the portions of your application integrated into one environment—everything from the client-side interface to the server-side business rules to the database SQL and stored procedures. You can integrate these easily into one cohesive project within the environment, allowing you to create, run, and test your entire enterprise applications from within one environment.

Numerous tools are included in the new environment to help speed up development. A new, well-structured "intelligent" code editor, a new server explorer that supports many different database packages, a solution explorer to help you organize and manage your projects, dynamic help to assist you as you develop your applications, the task list, the command window, and numerous additional debugging tools have been included in the new VS.NET to help make your job as a programmer much easier. In addition, VS.NET supports several third-party plug-ins that allow other vendors to create tools that plug in directly to the new IDE. Figure 1.7 shows just a few of the tools available within the new Visual Studio .NET environment.

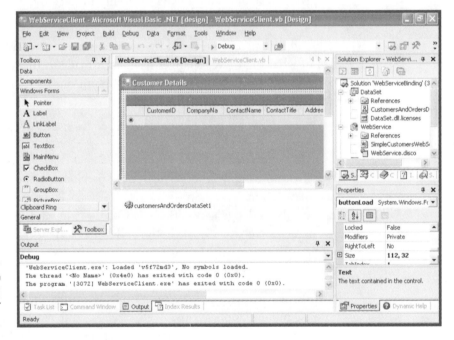

Figure 1.7

The new Visual Studio .NET environment.

We will talk about the new Visual Studio .NET environment in more detail in tomorrow morning's session.

What's Next

In the next session, you'll learn how to create Windows applications with the .NET Windows Forms architecture. You'll learn about forms, controls, graphics, and printing. In addition, you'll dive deeper into the Visual Studio .NET development environment.

Creating Windows Applications

- ➤ The Visual Studio .NET Integrated Development Environment
- ➤ Windows forms
- ➤ Controls
- ➤ Menus
- ➤ Graphics
- ➤ Printing
- ➤ Deploying Windows applications

Last night, I gave you a lot of background information and touched on the highlights of what .NET really is. Now it's time that I showed you how to use Visual Studio .NET. This morning, you will be jumping feet first into Windows application development.

Discovering the Visual Studio .NET Integrated Development Environment

The Visual Studio .NET Integrated Development Environment (VS.NET IDE) is your workroom for creating applications. Microsoft provides an excellent place to host all of the tools you will need while developing your applications. The all-in-one approach of the VS.NET IDE will save you a tremendous amount of time as you create and debug your applications. Microsoft threw in everything except the kitchen sink—with Web services, even the kitchen sink might soon be available to your .NET applications.

Overview of the Environment

Let's start by taking a quick tour of the VS.NET IDE. First, however, you need to make sure you've completed the Visual Studio installation. After you've installed Visual Studio, you need to run it. From the Start menu, click on Start, All Programs, Microsoft Visual Studio .NET, Microsoft Visual Studio .NET. Figure 2.1 shows how this looks on my computer.

You'll hear a lot of buzzing and whirring as Microsoft does its magic. Then, before your very eyes, Visual Studio will appear. Visual Studio presents several different areas to you:

➤ Menus

➤ Toolbars

➤ Tool windows

➤ Document windows

I have identified some of these areas of the VS.NET IDE for you in Figure 2.2.

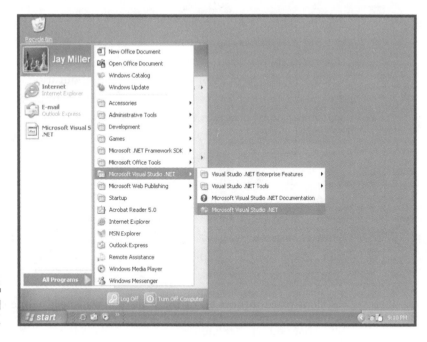

Figure 2.1

Launching Visual
Studio .NET.

Menu

Tool window

Toolbar

Document window

Tool window

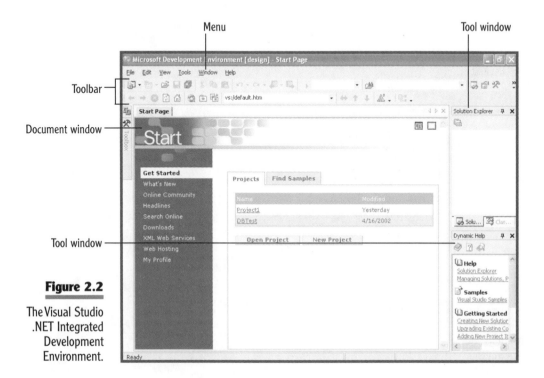

Figure 2.2

The Visual Studio
.NET Integrated
Development
Environment.

The menus and toolbars that the VS.NET IDE presents are similar to those that most windows applications use. I'll talk more about specific items on the menu and toolbars as you need to use them. Document windows are where you will do most of the work on your application. In this type of window, you can place or rearrange controls on a form or edit the source code that makes your program tick. Tool windows provide access to various parts of Visual Studio. The View menu shown in Figure 2.3 gives you access to a wide selection of tool windows.

You can display or hide each tool window depending on your current needs. Let me mention a few tool windows that I think you will find yourself using all the time. The first is the Solution Explorer. The Solution Explorer tool window shows a collapsible view of all the files that are part of your application. In the Solution Explorer, you also can find a list of all assemblies that your application references. Most of your applications will reference system assemblies that the .NET Framework provides. Your applications also can contain references to assemblies from third-party providers or other assemblies that you have created.

Figure 2.3

Tool windows are available from the View menu.

When you are working with forms, you'll want to have two tool windows readily available. The Toolbox window is the palette of controls that you choose from to place on your forms. The Properties window is where you set the properties of each control. With these two windows, you'll take care of the design-time settings for your application's user interface. Figure 2.4 shows the Toolbox window docked to the left side of the VS.NET IDE and the Solution Explorer and Properties windows docked to the right side.

When you start Visual Studio, you see the Start Page document window already open. Microsoft provides the Start Page as a resource for you to simplify finding the information you need. The Start Page has several sections:

➤ Get Started
➤ What's New
➤ Online Community
➤ Headlines
➤ Search Online

➤ Downloads
➤ XML Web Services
➤ Web Hosting
➤ My Profile

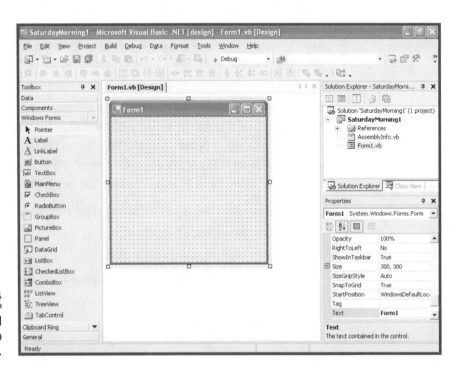

Figure 2.4

Three common tool windows docked to the VS.NET IDE.

CUSTOMIZING YOUR ENVIRONMENT

The VS.NET IDE is highly customizable. When you are comfortable moving around in the environment, you might want to play a little. You can move a tool window around onscreen by placing the mouse over the title bar for the window, holding down your left mouse button, and then dragging the mouse. An outline of the window follows your mouse as you move it. When the window is where you want it to be, release the left mouse button and the window reappears.

If you move your mouse near one of the borders of the IDE, the window outline snaps into a position along the border. This indicates that the window will be docked in that position when you release the left mouse button. A docked window is always visible while you are working in the IDE. Docking multiple windows in the same position causes tabs to appear that allow you to select among the windows that you've docked together.

Another feature of tool windows is their ability to hide themselves when you are not using them. When Auto Hide is enabled for a tool window, it collapses to show only its name and icon along the edge of the IDE when not in use. To access a hidden tool window, you simply place the mouse over the name or icon of the tool window and the window slides back in view for your use. You can enable or disable Auto Hide by clicking the right mouse button over a tool window and selecting Auto Hide from the menu that appears.

Tool windows are only one part of the VS.NET IDE that you can customize. Nearly every aspect of the IDE is customizable. To see just how many things you can change, select Options from the Tools menu. The Options dialog box appears, as shown in Figure 2.5. From the Options dialog box, the appearance and behavior of the IDE is at your command. You can do things like these:

➤ Change fonts and colors for almost every element in the IDE.

➤ Select the keyboard mapping.

➤ Assign shortcut keys to commands.

➤ Set Source Control options if you're using Visual SourceSafe.

➤ Enable automatic reformatting of your code.

➤ Set your debugging preferences.

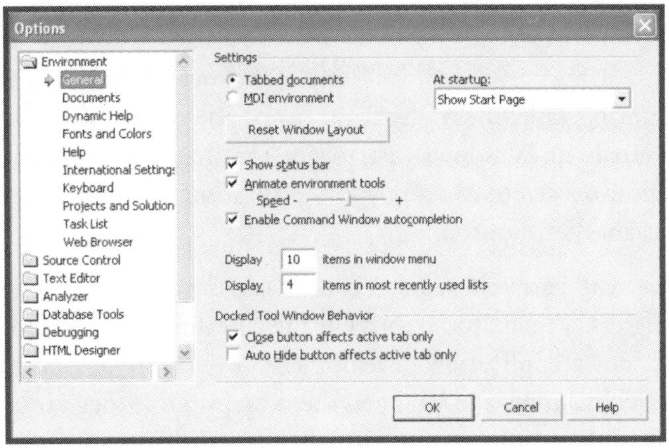

Figure 2.5

Making the IDE
bend to your will.

Figure 2.6 shows the Start Page. I won't be covering these sections in detail, so I suggest you take a couple minutes to see what each of them has to offer. When you are finished exploring the Start Page, come on back and I'll show you how to create your first Windows application using the VS.NET IDE and Visual Basic .NET.

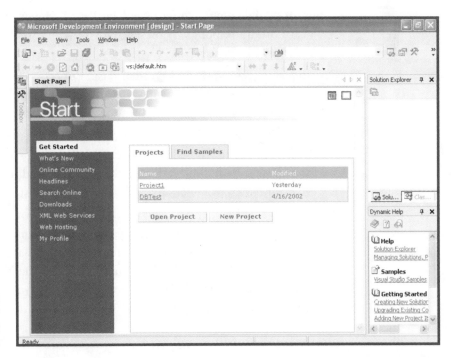

Figure 2.6

The Visual Studio
.NET Start Page.

Building Your First Visual Basic .NET Application

Only a few years ago, building Windows applications from scratch was a daunting task to say the least. You had to be intimately familiar with the internals of Windows just to get the first window of your application to appear onscreen. Making your application do something useful—well, that was another monster.

Over the past few years, Visual Basic developers have made quite a bit of progress. Visual Studio .NET is the culmination of Microsoft's efforts to ease Windows application development. Microsoft has taken the best of their individual tools and wrapped them up into one mega-tool. The result? Much less work for you and me. In just a moment, you are going to do in about a minute what used to take developers days to accomplish. No smoke, no mirrors, just Visual Studio. How, you ask? Templates.

Using a template, you can create the entire basic structure of an application in moments. Your application isn't very interesting at this point, but it is a Windows application and it will run. You seem skeptical, so I guess I'll have to prove it to you. Just follow these steps and you'll have a working Windows application.

1. From the File menu, choose New, Project, as shown in Figure 2.7. Visual Studio responds by presenting you with the New Project dialog box shown in Figure 2.8.

2. Under Project Types, select Visual Basic Projects. The Templates section now displays a variety of Visual Basic .NET application templates for you to choose from.

3. Under Templates, select Windows Application. If you don't see Windows Application immediately, you might need to scroll through the list of Visual Basic Project Templates until you find it. Whatever you do, don't click OK—yet. You still have one more step to complete.

4. In the Name field, enter ReverseMe, the name of your first test application. If you're feeling adventurous, you could name the application EmEsrever (for those of you who aren't dyslectic, that's ReverseMe spelled backward). The Application Wizard uses the Name and Location fields to create a directory where the files for your application are stored.

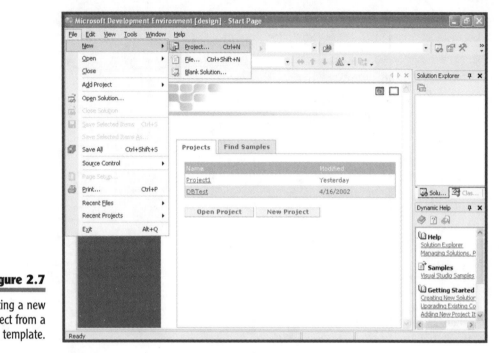

Figure 2.7

Creating a new project from a template.

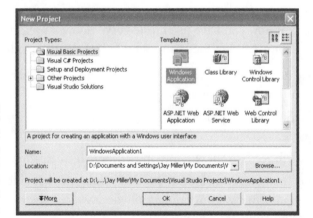

Figure 2.8

The New Project dialog box of the Application Wizard is your starting point for creating a new application.

5. Finally, click OK. When the commotion on your computer ends, Visual Studio presents you with a blank Form1 document window. Figure 2.9 shows you what the VS.NET IDE might look like after creating the application.

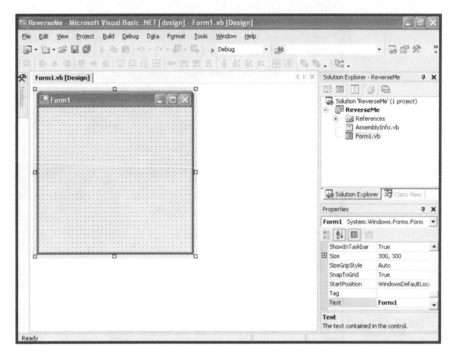

Figure 2.9

The ReverseMe
application as
generated by the
Application Wizard.

Believe it or not, you have just created a Windows application. Take another
look at Figure 2.9. Let me point out a few of the things there:

➤ One document window has a blank form, Form1, that is the basis of
the user interface for your application.

➤ The Solution Explorer tool window shows the files that the template
created.

➤ The Properties tool window shows some of the properties of Form1.

➤ The Toolbox tool window is hidden along the left side of the IDE. For
more information on hiding tool windows, see the earlier sidebar titled
"Customizing Your Environment."

Running Your Application

Okay, are you ready to take your application for a test drive? First, you need
to make sure that your application doesn't contain errors. When you're sure
it doesn't, you can build your application. Select the Build menu, and then
choose Build Solution.

TIP You might have noticed that some menu items have a keyboard shortcut displayed next to them. If you like to keep your hands on the keyboard all the time, you will find these shortcuts a huge time saver. The Build Solution item on the Build menu, for example, has a keyboard shortcut of Ctrl+Shift+B. This means that if you hold down the Ctrl and Shift keys while you press the letter B, Visual Studio builds your application. In addition to the keyboard shortcuts that Visual Studio defines, you can define your own keyboard shortcuts to perform just about any action in Visual Studio.

Visual Studio then begins its work. It takes the source files for your application and processes them with the Visual Basic .NET compiler. Visual Studio displays an Output window that shows the result of compiling your application (see Figure 2.10). The Output window should indicate that one build succeeded. If it does, then Visual Studio has given your application its blessing and you are free to run your application.

BUZZ WORD *Compilers* bring together the source files for a project and produce a single executable file that you can run as an application.

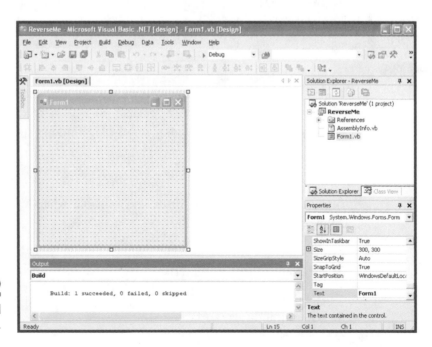

Figure 2.10

Results of the build process.

To run your application, click on Start Without Debugging from the Debug menu. After a moment, a window appears that looks just like the Form1 document window, but without the grid of spots. You should see something similar to Figure 2.11. To close your application, click on the Close button in the upper-right corner of the application window.

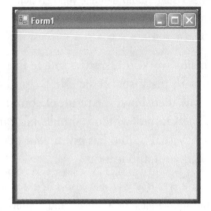

Figure 2.11

Your first Windows application.

See, I told you it wouldn't be hard to create a Windows application. I wouldn't update your résumé yet to say that you're a Windows applications programmer, but by the end of the weekend, you'll be well on your way.

Forms

Forms represent the screen real estate that your application lays claim to. Windows Forms provide an extensible, object-oriented set of classes that allow you to develop great-looking, flexible Windows applications.

Overview

Several different types of forms are available when you're creating your application:

➤ Standard windows
➤ Multiple Document Interface (MDI) windows
➤ Dialog boxes
➤ Graphical display surfaces

To define the user interface for your application, you place controls onto forms. A little later this morning, in the "Controls" section, I'll go into more detail about how to use controls. Forms have properties that define their appearance, events that define their interactions with users, and methods that define their behavior. To make a form respond the way you want, you set the form's properties and respond to its events.

You can use the Code Editor to create an entire form—if you like torturing yourself. Or, and this would be my suggestion, you can use the Windows Forms Designer. Visual Studio provides the Windows Forms Designer to prevent you from pulling your hair out. If only this had been available when I started writing Windows applications, I wouldn't be keeping the makers of Rogaine in business. Anyway, the Windows Forms Designer gives you a graphical means of creating your application's user interface.

You have already seen the Windows Forms Designer, and I bet you didn't even notice it. Look at Figure 2.12. See the document on the Form1.vb[Design] tab? Well, that's the designer. The Windows Forms Designer is a What You See Is What You Get (WYSIWIG) tool for user interface creation.

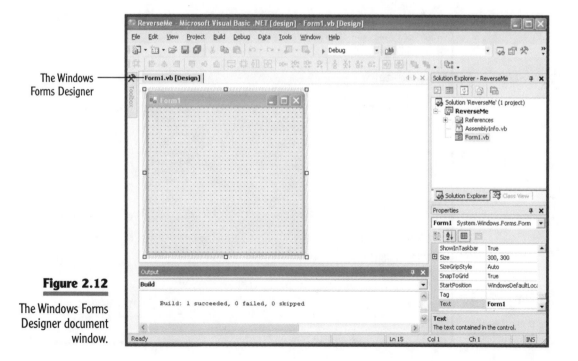

Figure 2.12

The Windows Forms Designer document window.

The Windows Forms Designer

TIP The Visual Studio IDE gives you access to both code document windows and designer document windows in the same environment. When you're working with both types of document windows, look for the [Design] indicator to distinguish a designer document window from another type of document window.

Form Properties

Form properties define the state, appearance, and behavior of a form. To view or modify a form's properties, you use the Properties tool window. Figure 2.13 shows the form from your first Windows application with the Properties tool window enlarged so that you can get a better look at it.

The top portion of the Properties window lets you know for which item you are displaying properties. Next comes a row of buttons that let you change how you view properties. Then you see the list of properties and their values followed by an area that shows a brief description of the currently selected property.

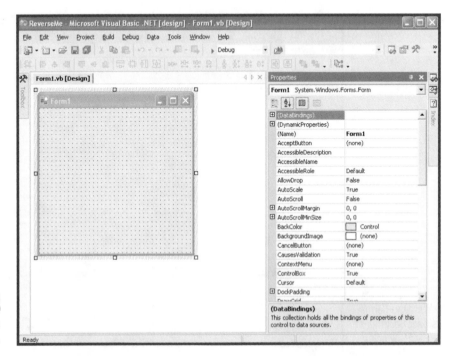

Figure 2.13

The properties of a form revealed.

The default behavior of the Properties tool window is to display the list of properties in alphabetical order. Notice that some of the properties are enclosed in parentheses. Parentheses are used to force those properties to appear at the beginning of the alphabetical list. You can also view properties sorted by category if you click on the leftmost button that appears directly above the property list. The category view is beneficial when you are working with an object that has several properties.

Because forms have quite a few properties, I generally use the Category view when working with a form. Select the Categorized button that appears just above the list of properties to change to the Category view. A form's properties are broken down into the following categories:

➤ Accessibility

➤ Design

➤ Appearance

➤ Focus

➤ Behavior

➤ Layout

➤ Configurations

➤ Misc

➤ Data

➤ Window Style

In the Category view of properties, you can expand or collapse an entire category. You will have a much easier time setting related properties by getting all of the other properties out of your way. Figure 2.14 shows how the

Figure 2.14

I'll take Properties for $500, Alex.

category view of properties looks with some categories expanded and others collapsed.

Take some time to explore the Form's properties. If a property's function isn't obvious from its name, click on it and read the description that appears at the bottom of the Properties window.

You set the value of a property by selecting the value that appears next to its name. Some properties, such as Text, you set by selecting its value and typing the new value. Other properties don't allow you to just enter any value that you like. Instead, these properties provide you with a drop-down list of values to select from. The FormBorderStyle property shown in Figure 2.15 is an example of selecting a value from a drop-down list.

Some properties, such as the Font property, can't easily display their possible values in a drop-down list. A complex property like this displays an Ellipsis button in its value. When you click on the button, a dialog box opens that allows you to set the value of the property. Figure 2.16 shows the Font dialog box that you use to set the different parts of the Font property.

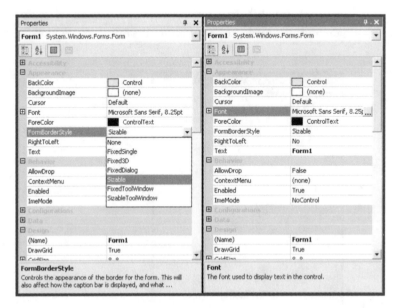

Figure 2.15

Setting different types of properties.

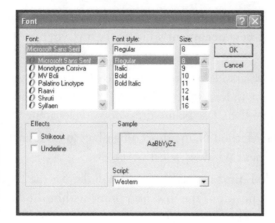

Figure 2.16

The dialog box that
is used to set the
Font property.

Form Events

Forms can receive events from user actions, program code, or the system. An
event is an action that you can respond to in code. You define event handlers
to respond to events that your form receives. You can use the Windows
Forms Designer to create event handlers.

◄◄◄

Events are messages sent by objects announcing that something important has
happened.

Event handlers are procedures in your code that determine the actions to be performed
when an event occurs. When an event is raised, the event handler that receives the event
is executed.

◄◄◄

You use the Code Editor to create event handlers in Visual Basic. Let me
show you how to create an event handler that does something when the user
clicks on a form with the left mouse button.

■ ■

If you don't know what an area of the Visual Studio IDE is called or if it isn't obvious what
a button does by the icon displayed, just place your mouse over the item and wait. A small
window, or ToolTip, will appear that describes the item your mouse is pointing to.

■ ■

1. Right-click on the form and choose View Code from the menu that appears. A new document window, Form1.vb, opens allowing you to modify the code for your form.

2. From the Class Name drop-down box located at the top left of the document window, select (Base Class Events). You can see on Figure 2.17 where the Class Name drop-down is located.

3. From the Method Name drop-down box located at the top right of the document window, select Click.

4. The Code Editor inserts the event handler for the Click event of Form1 and positions the insertion point within the method.

```
' Visual Basic
Private Sub Form1_Click(ByVal sender As Object, ByVal e _
                        As System.EventArgs) Handles MyBase.Click


End Sub
```

5. Add this code to the Form1_Click event handler. The code changes the background of the form to a random color.

```
Me.BackColor = Color.FromKnownColor(CInt(Int(150 * Rnd()) + 1))
```

Class name   Method name

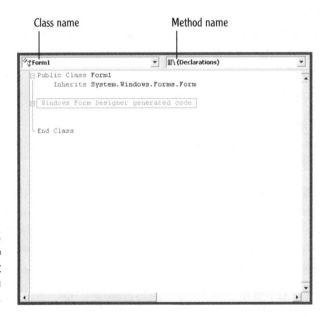

Figure 2.17

Defining event handlers for form events.

6. From the Debug menu, select Start Without Debugging. Visual Studio builds your application, which eventually appears onscreen.

7. Click on the background of your application using the left mouse button. Each time you click, the background color changes.

Use the Method Name drop-down box of the Code Editor document window to browse the events that a form can receive. You might be surprised by the number of events that your forms have the opportunity to respond to.

CAUTION Be careful when browsing events in the Method Name drop-down. Remember: Each time you click on an event, the Code Editor inserts an event handler into your application. Sometimes, you can end up with a lot of unnecessary event handlers that have no functionality.

Working with Multiple Forms

So far, your application has only a single form. One form doesn't provide you with much space to create an interesting Windows application. To fit everything that you want into your application, you have two basic choices: Put a bazillion tabs on a single form, or use multiple forms. Although I like tabs, using multiple forms is usually a much more flexible solution, so that is what I'll show you next.

You really don't have to do much work to use multiple forms. It's as simple as 1, 2, 3.

1. Add another form to your application.
2. Modify the form to your heart's content.
3. Connect the form to the rest of your application.
4. Run your application.

Okay, so it took four steps. I was close, though. Your application can have as many forms as you want. If your application uses multiple forms of the same type, such as a word processing program that supports editing multiple documents at the same time, you'll find the next section on "Multiple Document Interface" helpful. For now, though, I'll discuss applications that only let the user work with one form at a time. I'll continue by having the form you have been working with display a new form when the mouse is clicked.

1. Begin by right-clicking on the project name, ReverseMe, in the Solution Explorer tool window.
2. Click on Add to display the Add submenu.
3. Select Add New Item to display the Add New Item dialog box.
4. In the Templates pane, choose Windows Form.
5. In the Name field, enter Output.vb.
6. Click on Open.

Visual Studio churns away while it adds the new form to your application. When it has finished, a new Windows Forms Designer document window is opened for your form. The form also appears in the list of your application's files in the Solution Explorer, as you can see in Figure 2.18.

Why don't you put a Label control on your new form? Later, in the "Controls" section, I'll show you how to use Form1 to change the content of the label you place on Output. Placing the label is fairly quick and easy. Here is how you do it:

1. Make sure that the Toolbox window is visible in the IDE. If you can't see the Toolbox anywhere, then choose Toolbox from the View menu. If the Toolbox is in Auto Hide mode, see the "Customizing Your Environment" sidebar for information on how to display it.
2. Click on the Windows Forms tab in the Toolbox to display the controls that you can place on your form.
3. Double-click the left mouse button on the Label control in the list. Visual Studio places a new label control on your form.
4. Using the mouse, drag Label1 to the middle of the Output form.
5. Change the Text property of Label1 to Output goes here! Visual Studio should now look something like Figure 2.19.

NOTE Remember how you used the Properties tool window to change Form properties? Well, you can do the same thing with controls. When you select a control on a form, such as Label1 that you just added, the Properties window displays the properties for that control. To display Form properties again, just click anywhere on the background of the form. The Properties window updates to display only your Form properties.

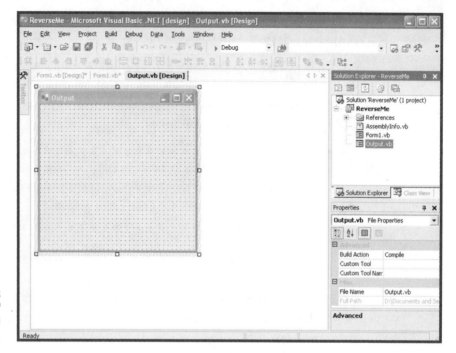

Figure 2.18

Creating multiple forms.

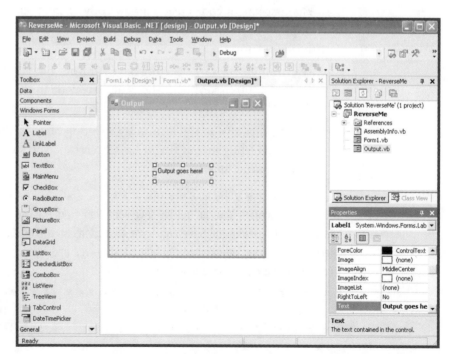

Figure 2.19

Your completed Output form.

Now all you have to do is hook the Output form up to Form1. With a few more quick steps, you'll be ready to go.

1. Switch back to the Code Editor window for Form1. You do this either by clicking on the Form1.vb document window tab if it is visible or by right-clicking on Form1.vb in the Solution Explorer and selecting View Code from the shortcut menu.

TIP To make it easier to see what is in the Code Editor window, you might want to get rid of the Toolbox window. You can close the window or enable Auto Hide. Either way, you'll have an easier time working with the Code Editor window.

2. Find the Form1_Click procedure where you added the code to change the form's background color.

3. Add the following lines of code immediately before the line of code that changes the background color:

```
Dim frmOutput As New Output()
frmOutput.ShowDialog()
```

The first line of code creates a new copy of the Output form and assigns it to the frmOutput variable. The second line of code displays the Output form.

4. Save your changes by selecting Save All from the File menu or using the Ctrl+Shift+S keyboard shortcut. The code in the Form1.vb document window should now resemble Figure 2.20.

5. Build and run your application by selecting Start Without Debugging from the Debug menu. If you have no errors, you should see your Form1 window appear.

TIP Save your work often! You can quickly save your work from the File menu, using the keyboard shortcut, or with the Save and Save All buttons on the toolbar. I recently felt the effects of not saving often when my home lost power, and I lost several hours of work. Trust me on this one—save often!

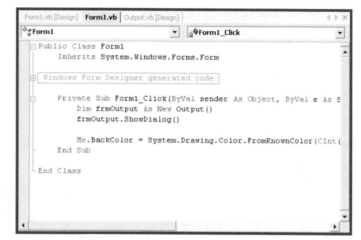

Figure 2.20

Connecting your forms.

What you see now doesn't look any different than before. To display the Output form, click anywhere on Form1. When you do so, the Output form appears in front of Form1. If you can't see Form1, move the Output form by dragging its title bar. You should now be able to see Form1 as well. Figure 2.21 shows what my screen looks like when I have both forms displayed.

You might have noticed that you can't do anything with Form1 while Output is still displayed. That is because Output is modal. First, you must close Output, and then you can close Form1. For more information on what modal means, see the following sidebar "Focusing on Modes."

You can add any number of forms to your application using the method I have shown you with the Output form. I'll come back to the ReverseMe example in a little bit, but first, let me introduce you to another type of Windows application interface—the Multiple Document Interface described in the next section.

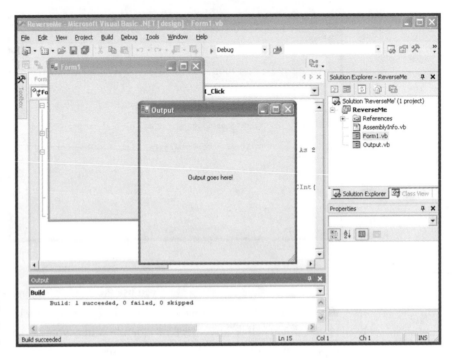

Figure 2.21

Displaying two forms at once.

Multiple Document Interface

Before I dig into Multiple Document Interface (MDI) applications, make sure you save the ReverseMe application. I'll be coming back to it, but for this section, you'll be creating a new application.

As I mentioned earlier this morning, an MDI application allows you to display multiple documents at the same time, each in its own window. The starting point for an MDI application is the MDI parent form. The MDI parent form contains the MDI child forms. The MDI child forms are normally where the user does most of the interacting with your application.

You'll start creating an MDI application just like you did the ReverseMe example. Here again are the steps you take to create a new Windows application:

1. From the File menu, choose New, Project.
2. Under Project Types, select Visual Basic Projects.
3. Under Templates, select Windows Application.

FOCUSING ON MODES

Forms are either modal or modeless. A modal form must be closed or hidden before you can work with the rest of an application. Forms that display important information or require immediate user interaction should be modal. You should use modal forms to display error messages or prompt the user to log in to your application.

A modeless form lets you change focus to another form while still displaying your original form. You can move back and forth between modeless forms at will without having to close them. You should use modeless forms to display frequently used commands or information. The tool windows in Visual Studio are a good example of modeless forms.

You determine whether a form is modal or modeless when you display the form. To display a form modally, you use the ShowDialog method. To display a modeless form, you use the Show method. In the ReverseMe example, the Output form is displayed modally using ShowDialog.

```
frmOutput.ShowDialog()
```

To display the Output form as modeless, you would use this line of code:

```
frmOutput.Show()
```

NOTE

When a form is displayed as modal, the code after the call to ShowDialog is not executed until the modal form is closed. On the other hand, if a form is shown as modeless, the code after the call to Show is executed immediately after the modeless form is displayed.

4. In the Name field, enter Multiple.

5. Click on OK.

When Visual Studio is finished with its work, you should have a new project with one form that looks like Figure 2.22.

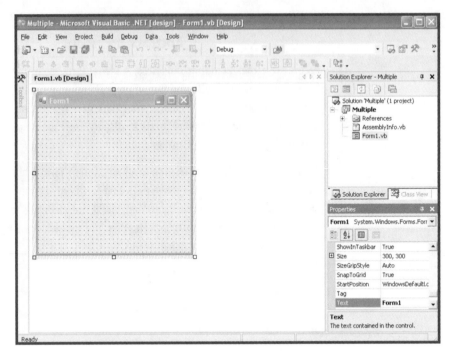

Figure 2.22

The start of an MDI
application.

Now you need to make the form able to contain other forms. It's really as
simple as setting a property. First, though, rename the initial form so that
you can easily tell which is the parent and which is the child.

1. Right-click on Form1.vb in the Solution Explorer window.

2. Select Rename from the menu.

3. Change the name of the form to Parent.vb.

4. Select the form again so that its properties are displayed in the Properties window.

5. Find the IsMdiContainer property and set its value to True. If you
have the Properties window categorized, IsMdiContainer appears in
the Window Style section.

6. Change the Text property in the Appearance section to Multiple
Parent.

■■■

TIP You might also want to set the WindowState property to Maximized. You can find WindowState in the Layout section. By doing this, you make the most screen space available for the child windows.

■■■

You need to do one more thing to the parent form: Add a menu. The application needs a way to open and close child windows. You need to perform only a few more steps before you can move on to the child form.

1. Add a MainMenu control to the parent form from the Toolbox. You can either drag the MainMenu from the Toolbox to the form, or you can double-click MainMenu to add it to the form.

2. In the area that says Type Here, add menus named &File and &Window.

3. Under the File menu, add the items &New and &Close.

4. Select the Window menu item.

5. Set the MdiList property to True in the Properties window.

● ●

NOTE The ampersand (&) in the menu name indicates which letter to use as the keyboard shortcut for the menu item. The ampersand does not appear in the text displayed on the menu.

● ●

Your form should look like Figure 2.23 when you have added the menu items. Go ahead and test the application to make sure that everything is

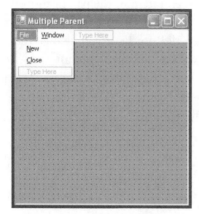

Figure 2.23

Adding a menu to your application.

working all right. Select Start Without Debugging from the Debug menu to run your application. Take a quick look at the menus to make sure they are correct.

Before going any further with the parent window, you need to add a child form to your project. I'm going to show you how to create a child form and add a RichTextBox control to the form. The RichTextBox control is a full-featured text-editing control. Follow these steps to add the child form to your application:

1. Right-click the project in Solution Explorer to display the context menu.
2. Select Add Windows Form from the Add menu.
3. Enter Child in the Name field.
4. Click on Open. A new form is added to your project and the form is displayed.
5. Add a RichTextBox control from the Toolbox to the child form.
6. Select the new RichTextBox control so that its properties are displayed in the Properties window.
7. Set the Anchor property to Top, Left.
8. Set the Dock property to Fill.
9. Save your changes!

That's all there is to the child form. Figure 2.24 shows how Visual Studio looks when you complete these steps.

You can now go back to the parent form and connect it to the new child form. Double-click on the New menu item of the parent form. Visual Studio opens a Code Editor window for your parent form and adds an event handler for the New menu item. Because I did not have you change the name of the menu item, the event handler should be called MenuItem2_Click. If you created your menu items in a different order than I did, the 2 might be a different number. Add this code to the MenuItem2_Click procedure to enable the parent window to create new child windows.

```
'Declare a variable to hold the Child window.
Dim NewMDIChild As New Child()
'Set the Parent Form of the Child window.
NewMDIChild.MDIParent = Me
```

```
'Display the new form.
NewMDIChild.Show()
```

Each time the user selects New from the File menu, a new copy of the child form is created. The Window menu lists all of the child windows. You can switch between child windows by clicking on the window you want or choosing the window from the Window menu. You have just one final piece of code before your MDI application will be complete. Create an event handler for the Close item on the File menu and add this code to it:

```
If Not Me.ActiveMdiChild Is Nothing Then
    Me.ActiveMdiChild.Close()
End If
```

If a child window is active, this code closes the child window. Run your application using the keyboard shortcut Ctrl+F5, which is the same as Start Without Debugging on the Debug menu. Use the menus on the parent window to open and close several child windows. Figure 2.25 shows what your application might look like after opening and closing a bunch of windows.

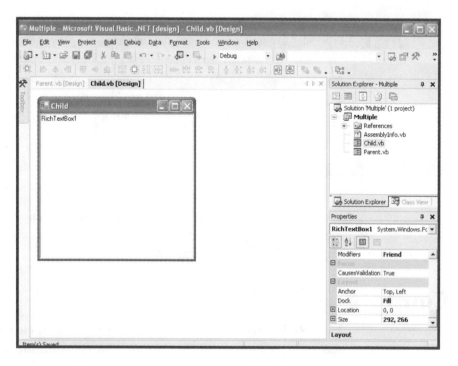

Figure 2.24

An MDI child form.

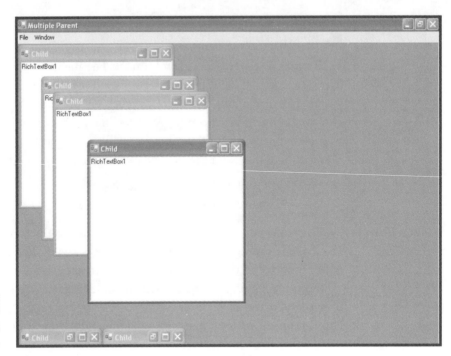

Figure 2.25

An MDI application in action.

NOTE In addition to opening and closing child windows, you can minimize and maximize them just like you can Windows applications. Figure 2.25 includes a couple child windows that have been minimized. The minimized child windows appear along the bottom left of the parent window and show only the window's title bar.

Take a Break

It's time to take a break. I know you're excited about developing Windows applications, but step away for a few minutes. When you come back, I'll introduce you to more of the controls that Visual Studio provides for you to use in building your applications.

Controls

You have already seen a few controls in action, but these are only the tip of the iceberg. The controls that Visual Studio provides are the basic building blocks that you use to create a user interface for your application. In addition, third parties produce a wide variety of controls that you can purchase to enhance your applications. For now, let's stick with what comes with Visual Studio out of the box.

Before I show you the controls, let's switch back to the ReverseMe application. Make sure you have saved your changes to the Multiple application. When you have, go to the File menu and select Recent Projects. Find ReverseMe and choose it. Visual Studio should then reload your ReverseMe application. Make sure that the designer window for Form1 is shown and that the Toolbox window is visible.

Common Controls

Visual Studio includes a wide variety of controls for you to use. Figure 2.26 shows all of the controls included in the Toolbox. You'll find controls for labels, text, radio buttons, check boxes, lists, grids, tabs, images, menus, and much more.

To introduce you to working with controls, I want to finish work on the ReverseMe application. You'll add Label, TextBox, and Button controls to the main form. When that is completed, you'll hook up the Button control to display the Output form when clicked. Ready? Let's get started.

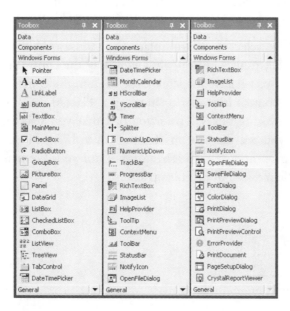

Figure 2.26

The Toolbox and all of its controls.

TIP
There are too many controls to display in the Toolbox all at once. You can use the up and down arrows that appear on the other tabs of the Toolbox to scroll through the controls until you find the one you want.

1. Add a Label control to Form1 by double-clicking Label in the Toolbox.
2. Add a TextBox control to Form1.
3. Add a Button control to Form1.

Now the stage is set. It's time to move on and make this look a little more presentable.

Moving and Sizing Controls

How do you think your Form1 looks? A little cluttered maybe? When you double-click a control in the Toolbox, the control is added to the top-left corner of your form. The more controls you double-click, the more layers of controls that pile up. This probably isn't what your users are going to want to see.

To start, move the controls so that they are not sitting on top of each other. When you select a control, a shaded box surrounds the control to let you know which control is selected. Select the button on Form1 now. Around the shaded box are eight small white sizing boxes. You can see what the button you added to Form1 looks like when it is selected in Figure 2.27.

To move the selected control, place the mouse over the control and hold down the left mouse button while you drag the control to its desired location. When you release the left mouse button, the control remains in place. Resizing a control is similar to moving it. Place the mouse over one of the eight white sizing boxes. The sizing box that you select determines which direction you will be able to size the control. Again, hold down the left mouse button and drag the sizing box until your control is the right size. Release the mouse button to stop sizing.

Figure 2.27

A selected Button control.

Here is what I want you to do with the controls you added to Form1:

1. Move the Button control to the bottom, center area of the form.

2. Move the TextBox control to the center, right area of the form.

3. Move the Label control so that it is immediately to the left of the TextBox control.

4. Resize the Label control by dragging its left sizing box until it is near the left side of the form.

You can see where I placed the controls in Figure 2.28.

Figure 2.28

Positioning controls on a form.

Control Properties

Controls have properties just like forms do. When you select a control, the Properties window displays all the properties for the control. You set control properties like you set form properties. Follow these instructions to set some of the properties for the three controls that you added to Form1.

1. Change the Label control's (Name) property to lblInputPrompt.

2. Change the Label control's Text property to Enter something to reverse:.

3. Change the Label control's TextAlign property to MiddleRight.

4. Change the TextBox control's (Name) property to txtInput.

5. Delete the contents of the TextBox control's Text property.

6. Change the Button control's (Name) property to btnReverse.

7. Change the Button control's Text property to Reverse.

NAMING CONVENTIONS FOR CONTROLS

You might want to spend some time thinking about the names you give to your controls. The names your choose can have a dramatic impact on how easy it is to read and maintain your application. When you add a control to a form, the control's default name will be the type of control followed by a sequential number, such as Button1, Button6, or Label4. Although these names tell you what type the control is, they do not relay the use of the control. It would be difficult to determine just from looking at your code that Button1 is supposed to save a document and Button6 is supposed to cancel all changes made to a document.

To avoid such situations, you should define a standard naming convention for controls and then be consistent in using that convention. Your naming convention should indicate at least the type of the control and its purpose. A naming convention that I came across and adopted a long time ago has served me well. Each control name begins with an abbreviated version of the control type in lowercase. The control type is followed by a noun(s) for controls that store data or by a verb(s) for controls that indicate action. I have included a few examples of this convention in Table 3.1.

TABLE 3.1 CONTROL NAMES

Type	Abbreviation	Example
Label	lbl	lblCutomerID
Button	btn	btnSave, btnSaveDocument
TextBox	txt	txtFirstName
CheckBox	chk	chkMale
PictureBox	pct	pctLogo
ListBox	lst	lstProducts
TreeView	tvw	tvwOrders
RichTextBox	rtb	rtbDocument
ToolBar	tlb	tlbEdit
OpenFileDialog	ofdlg	ofdlgOpenDocument

Controls aren't the only things that I would suggest you define naming conventions for. Variables also benefit greatly from using a standard name structure. I recommend that you spend a little time searching through Visual Studio's help. Search on "naming conventions" to see what Microsoft has to say. You can adopt Microsoft's conventions, or at least use them as a guideline in developing your own naming conventions.

When you have finished setting the control properties, your form should look similar to Figure 2.29. Take a little time to look through the properties of each of the three controls on the form, as well as the properties of the form. Notice which properties are common across the controls and form and which properties are unique to each.

Figure 2.29

The new and improved ReverseMe main form.

Control Events

Remember when you added the event handler for a mouse click on Form1? Then you spent some time looking at the events that a form can receive. Controls can receive events as well. Just like with control properties, some events are common among most controls, and some are unique to a specific control. I am going to show you the events that the controls you added to Form1 can process. Then you will add an event handler for the Click event of btnReverse.

To see the events that are available to a control, you need to switch to the Code Editor window for Form1. You can do this by right-clicking on Form1 and selecting View Code from the menu. The Class Name drop-down list shows all of the objects in Form1 that can receive an event. Find the name of one of the controls you added to Form1 and select it. Then, display the list of events in the Method Name drop-down list. Do this with each of the controls you added to get a better feel for what the controls can do.

When you are finished exploring, you'll add code to respond to the click of btnReverse. Select btnReverse from the Class Name drop-down list, and then choose Click from the Method Name drop-down list. Figure 2.30 shows what Visual Studio should look like as you choose Click from the Method Name drop-down list.

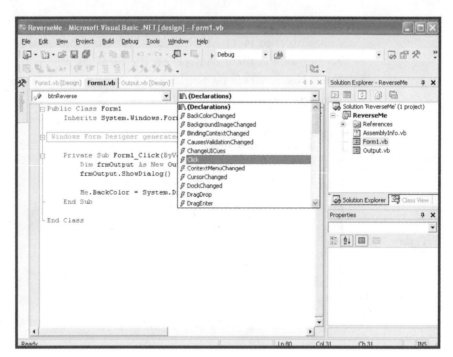

Figure 2.30

Choosing to respond to a control event.

After you choose the event, Visual Studio adds an event handler procedure to your code. You still need to fill in the implementation details, but Visual Studio takes care of hooking into the event and calling your event handler at the appropriate time. In this case, the btnReverse_Click() procedure has been created. Insert the following code into the btnReverse_Click() procedure:

```
Dim frmOutput As New Output()
Dim i As Integer
Dim output As String

'Loop through the input text and store the reverse of
'the input in output.
For i = 1 To txtInput.TextLength
    output = Mid(txtInput.Text, i, 1) & output
Next
'Set the value of the label on the output form
```

```
'to the reversed input string.
frmOutput.Label1.Text() = output
'Display the form.
frmOutput.ShowDialog()
```

This bit of code first declares variables for the Output form, a loop control, and an output string. The For loop iterates over the length of the input string, adding each letter to the output string in reverse order. Next, the text of the label on the Output form is set to the value of the output string. Finally, the Output form is displayed.

Build and run your application by choosing Start Without Debugging from the Debug menu. Test the application by entering something into the text box and then selecting the Reverse button. The Output form is displayed with the reverse of your text. Figure 2.31 shows an example of the ReverseMe application.

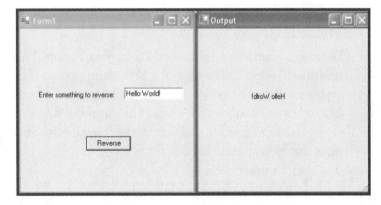

Figure 2.31

Running the ReverseMe application.

Copying and Deleting Controls

If you have several of the same type of control on a form, all with similar property settings, it can become quite time consuming to set all of the properties on each control. One way to simplify your life is to add one control to your form and get all of the properties set exactly the way you would like. After you have one control finished, you can copy it to the Clipboard and then paste it onto the form as many times as you want. At that point, all you need to do is change each control's properties that differ from the initial control you created.

Using this method, you can also copy a control from one form to another. The first thing to do when you want to copy a control is to select the control to use as the template. Make sure all of the properties are set appropriately, and then copy the control to the Clipboard. You can copy the control to the Clipboard using either the Copy item on the Edit menu or the Ctrl+C keyboard shortcut. Select the form that you want to add a copy of the control to. Add it to the form using the Paste item on the Edit menu or the Ctrl+V shortcut. At this point, it is just as if you created a new control on the form and set all of the properties individually.

TIP

■ ■

If you already have a group of controls on a form and you need to set the same property on all of the controls, you have another option. You can use the Ctrl and Shift keys in combination with the mouse to select more than one control. When more than one control is selected, the Properties window shows only those properties that are common to all selected controls. Setting the value of a property in the Properties window sets that value for all selected controls.

■ ■

Deleting a control is even easier than copying a control. You simply select the control and select Delete from the Edit menu or press the Delete key on your keyboard. What if you want to move the control to another form? In this case, select the control and choose Cut from the Edit menu. Cut copies the control to the Clipboard and deletes the control from the form. You can now paste the control onto another form.

CAUTION

◆ ◆

Always be careful when you are deleting items. Make sure that you do not need the control you are deleting. Check your code to ensure that other procedures are not using the control. If the control you delete has event handlers defined, you need to make sure you delete them and remove the control from the form.

◆ ◆

Anchoring Controls

The way a control is anchored determines the way it positions itself when a form is resized at runtime. The Anchor property lets you define how a control resizes dynamically. When you anchor a control to a side of the form, the control resizes as the form is resized so that the distance remains the same between the control and the side of the form where it is anchored. If you don't anchor a control and the form is resized, the position of the control relative to the edges of the form changes.

Run your application and try resizing Form1 in each direction. Pay attention to how the controls move when you resize the form. By default, each control is anchored to the top and left edges of the form. Let me show you what happens when you change a control's anchor points:

1. Select the btnReverse control.

2. Click on the arrow to the right of the Anchor property in the Properties windows. Visual Studio displays an editor that shows a cross. The dark gray boxes show which edges are anchored. Figure 2.32 shows what the anchor editor looks like.

3. Click on the top box to deselect anchoring to the top edge of the form.

4. Click on the bottom and right boxes to anchor those sides of the button.

Figure 2.32

Setting a control's anchor points.

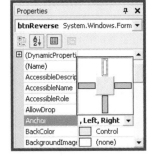

Docking Controls

Docking a control permanently attaches it to an edge of a form. Using the Dock property, you can also tell a control to completely fill its container. A text editor is an example of an application in which the editing control normally fills the entire window. Let me show you how docking works in the ReverseMe application:

1. Select the btnReverse control.

2. Click on the arrow to the right of the Dock property in the Properties windows. Visual Studio displays the Docking Editor.

3. Click on the bottom box to anchor the button to the bottom of the form.

You can see the Docking Editor as well as the docked btnReverse control in Figure 2.33. Notice how the button is attached to the bottom of the form and has expanded to fill the entire width of the form. Run the application again and see how the button behaves when you resize the form.

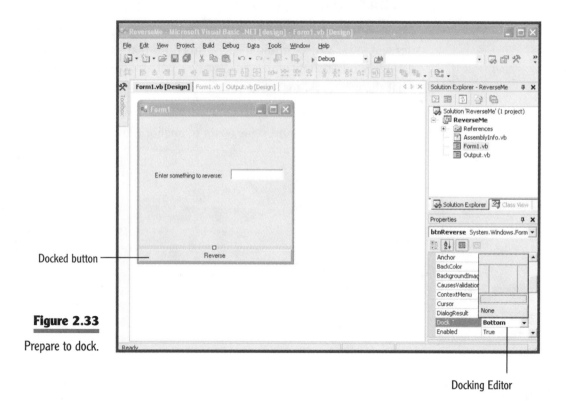

Docked button

Figure 2.33

Prepare to dock.

Docking Editor

Common Dialog Boxes

Common dialog boxes allow you to perform some common, but complex, functions in a standard way. You have several common dialog boxes at your disposal. Using these dialog boxes saves you a lot of time and energy. In addition, your application will look and feel like most other Windows applications, making the user feel more at home. These are the common dialog boxes that Visual Studio provides:

➤ OpenFileDialog   ➤ ColorDialog

➤ SaveFileDialog   ➤ PrintDialog

➤ FontDialog   ➤ PrintPreviewDialog

Let me show you how to use the FontDialog. Follow these steps to get the basics of a new project in place:

1. Create a new project by selecting Project from the File menu's New submenu.

2. Choose Windows Application and name it `CommonDialog`.

3. Click on OK.

4. Add a button and a FontDialog to the form.

5. Make the button taller and wider.

6. Change the `Name` property of the button to `btnChangeFont`.

7. Change the `Text` property of the button to `Change Font`.

NOTE Some controls do not have a normal visual presence on a form. The common dialog boxes, for example, do not display anything directly on your form. Instead, when you access them, they display their own window. Other controls, such as data access controls, might not have a graphical interface at all. These controls appear in a pane below the form. You can still select them and set their properties just like any other control. They just do not appear on your form because they don't have a normal visual element.

Your form should now appear similar to Figure 2.34.

What you want to have happen now is to display the Font common dialog box whenever `btnChangeFont` is clicked. I'm going to let you do a little more on your own here. I'll give you the basic steps to perform, but if you need more details, look at previous examples:

1. Create an event handler for the `Click` event of `btnChangeFont`.

2. Add this code to the `Click` event handler:

```
'Display the Font dialog box.
FontDialog1.ShowDialog()
```

```
'Change the font of the button to the selected font.
btnChangeFont.Font = FontDialog1.Font
'Show the name of the font on the button.
btnChangeFont.Text = FontDialog1.Font.Name
```

3. Run your application.

4. Click on the button.

5. Change some of the font properties and click OK.

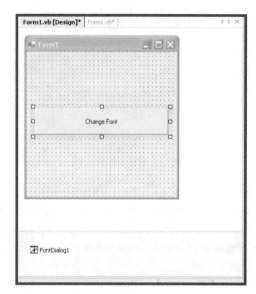

Figure 2.34

Using the
FontDialog
common dialog
box control.

The code that you added to the Click event handler performs three actions. First, it displays the Font common dialog box so that the user can make changes to the font. Next, it changes the font of the button text to the font selected in the Font common dialog box. Finally, it displays the name of the selected font on the button. You can see an example of this application running in Figure 2.35. Explore the Font common dialog box to see what fonts you have available. I think you'll be surprised by some of the fonts you find.

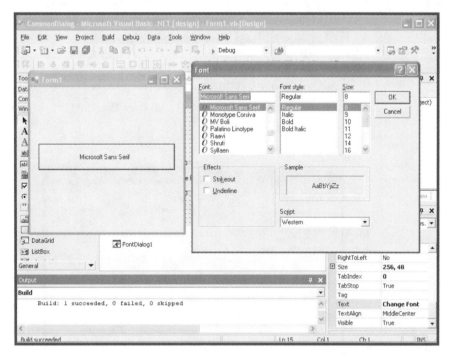

Figure 2.35

Displaying the
Font common
dialog box.

Deploying Windows Applications

◄◄

Deployment is the process by which you distribute your application to be installed on a user's computer.

◄◄

Visual Studio .NET uses the Microsoft Windows Installer to deploy applications. To deploy your application, you need to add a Setup Project to your application and configure it to install your application. Although this process is not that complex, it is a little lengthy. I'll use the CommonDialog application as an example.

To create the deployment project, follow these steps:

1. Select New Project from the Add Project submenu of the File menu.

2. Select Setup and Deployment Projects in Project Types.

3. Choose Setup Project from the Templates section.

4. Change the Name to `My Common Dialog Installer`. Figure 2.36 shows the completed New Project dialog box.

5. Click on OK.

6. Select My Common Dialog Installer in the Solution Explorer.

7. In the Properties window, change the `Product Name` property to `Common Dialog`.

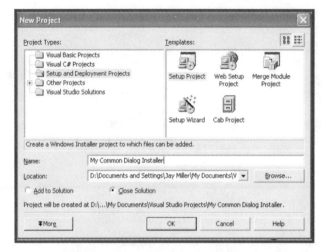

Figure 2.36

Adding a Setup
Project for the
Common Dialog
application.

Visual Studio adds the setup project to the Solution Explorer. A document window for the setup project is also displayed. You can see the different parts of the setup project in Figure 2.37.

To add the Common Dialog application to the My Common Dialog Installer, follow these steps:

1. Select My Common Dialog Installer in the Solution Explorer.

2. Under File System on Target Machine in the document window, choose Application Folder.

3. On the Action menu, select Project Output from the Add submenu.

4. Select CommonDialog from the Project drop-down list on the Add Project Output Group dialog box.

5. Select Primary Output from the list. Figure 2.38 shows the completed Add Project Output Group dialog box.

6. Click on OK.

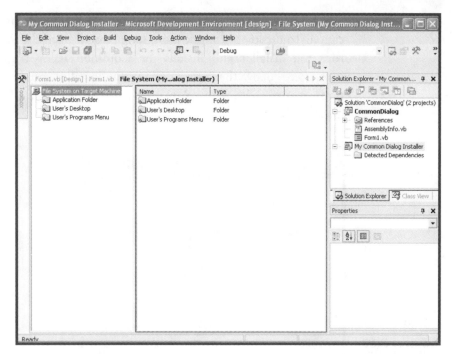

Figure 2.37

The My Common Dialog Installer document window.

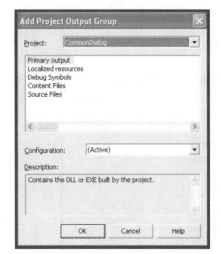

Figure 2.38

Adding a project output group to the installation.

7. Choose Build My Common Dialog Installer from the Build menu.

8. Check the Output window to ensure that the build completed without errors.

9. Save your changes!

You now have a complete installation project for the CommonDialog application. To deploy the application, select Install from the Project menu. This runs the installer and installs the CommonDialog application on your computer. Follow the instructions in the installer to complete the installation. Figures 2.39, 2.40, 2.41, and 2.42 show some of the steps of the installation.

Figure 2.39

The Common Dialog Installer welcome screen.

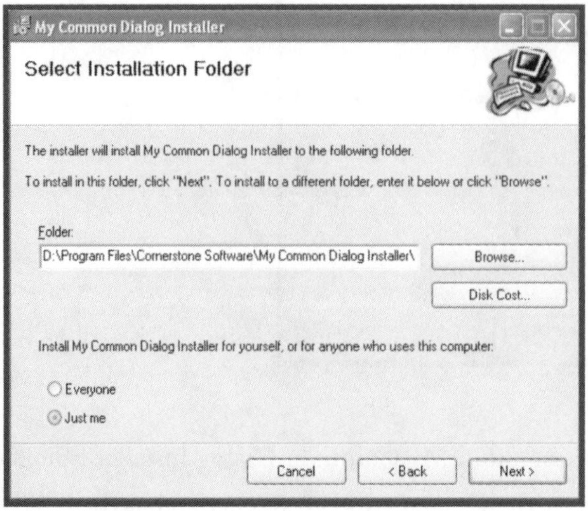

Figure 2.40

Selecting where to install the application.

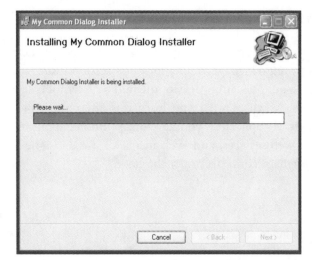

Figure 2.41

The installation
working away.

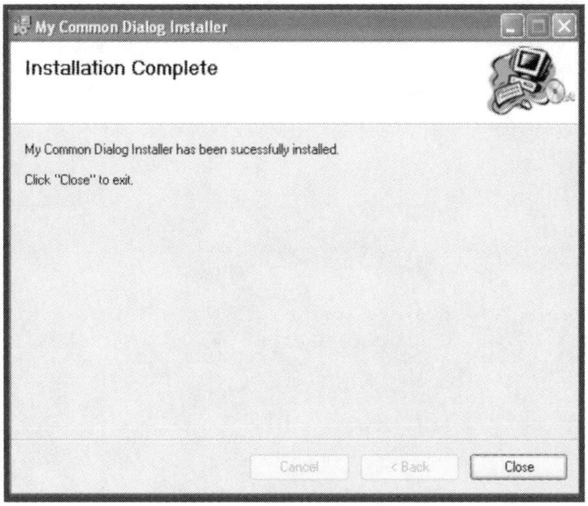

Figure 2.42

A successful
installation!

To test the installation, use Windows Explorer to browse to the directory
where you installed the application. Run CommonDialog.exe and the application should appear just as it did when you ran it from Visual Studio. Make
sure that it behaves the same as when you tested it earlier.

That's all there is to it. You now know how to create a Windows application
and how to create an installation for the application. By combining multiple
forms and taking advantage of the wide array of controls that are available,
you can create just about any type of Windows application that you desire.

What's Next

In the next session, I'll introduce you to the guts of the Visual Basic .NET programming language. This morning's session dealt with the visual aspect of Windows application development. The afternoon session is really about raw code. Much of what you learn this afternoon will apply regardless of what type of application you develop. Windows applications, console applications, Web services, and Web forms all use the same VB.NET programming language concepts under the hood.

Exploring the Visual Basic .NET Programming Language

- ➤ Data types
- ➤ Operators and expressions
- ➤ Control flow
- ➤ Procedures
- ➤ Error handling
- ➤ Classes and objects

It's Saturday afternoon and time to dig into the core of the Visual Basic .NET programming language. In this session, you'll gain a solid understanding of the VB.NET programming language. I've included plenty of example code to get you started. You'll be declaring variables, defining procedures, and creating classes before you know it.

Language Features

To get started, you need to know the syntax of the VB.NET programming language. The samples in this chapter, as well as the code that is available from the companion Web site, provide you with examples and explanations of the basic syntax. Don't worry too much about remembering everything on your first pass through. The Visual Studio Integrated Development Environment is very helpful when it comes to making sure your application's syntax is correct. Are you ready to see what makes a VB.NET application tick? I am, so let's get started.

Variables and Constants

The fundamental container in programming is the variable. Variables can hold all sorts of things. One variable might hold a number, another a string, and yet another a reference to an object. Let's start by looking at how variables are declared:

```
Dim n As Integer
```

This statement declares the variable n as an Integer data type. The Dim keyword tells VB.NET to allocate space for a new variable, whereas the As keyword indicates the type of the variable. From that point on in the program, the variable n can be used to store an integer value. You can assign a variable an initial value when it is declared. You can assign static values or the value of another variable to a variable.

```
Dim m As Integer      'Declare m as an integer.
Dim n As Integer = 3  'Declare n as an integer and initialize it to 3.
```

```
m = 1                    'Assign m the value 1.
m = n                    'Assign m the value of n.
```

The declaration of n sets its initial value to 3. The first assignment statement sets the value of m to 1. The second assignment statement sets the value of m to the value that n holds—in this case, 3.

You can also declare constants for use in your program. The value of a constant must be set when it is declared. You cannot change the value of a constant.

```
Const Pi As Single = 3.1415
```

This statement declares a constant of type Single, Pi, and sets its value to 3.1415. The Const keyword acts much like the Dim keyword, except that it tells VB.NET that the program cannot change its value.

Variables and constants can be declared just about anywhere within your program. Normally, variables and constants are declared at the beginning of a class or procedure. You cannot use variables or constants in your application until they are declared.

Data and Object Types

All variables fall into one of two classifications: value types or reference types. Value type variables are stored on the stack, accessed directly, and always contain a value of the declared type. Reference type variables are stored on the heap, accessed indirectly, and contain either a reference to a value of the declared type or a null reference. I have included a summary of VB.NET's main data types in Table 3.1.

Value types include the following:

➤ All numeric data types
➤ Boolean, Char, and Date
➤ All structures, even if they contain reference types
➤ Enumerations, because their underlying type is always a value type

Reference types include the following:

➤ String
➤ All arrays, even if they contain value types
➤ VB.NET class types, such as Form
➤ User-defined class types

TABLE 3.1 VISUAL BASIC .NET DATA TYPES

VB.NET Type	Type	Size	Range
Boolean	Value	2 bytes	True or False
Byte	Value	1 byte	0–255
Char	Value	2 bytes	0–65,535
Date	Value	8 bytes	January 1, 0001–December 31, 9999
Decimal	Value	16 bytes	10^{-28}–10^{28} *
Double	Value	8 bytes	10^{-324}–10^{308} *
Integer	Value	4 bytes	-2,147,483,648–2,147,483,647
Long	Value	8 bytes	-10^{20}–10^{20} *
Object	Reference	4 bytes	Any type can be stored in a variable of type Object
Short	Value	2 bytes	-32,768–32,767
Single	Value	4 bytes	10^{-45}–10^{38} *
String	Reference	Varies	0–2 billion Unicode characters *

*Approximate range

Data Conversion

When I look at 12 or 34.56, all I see are numbers. VB.NET, however, sees two very distinct types of numbers. The second number has a decimal; the first does not. Even though VB.NET recognizes these as different data types, it also realizes that both are numbers that share some common characteristics. With this knowledge, VB.NET will attempt to coerce any type mismatches it identifies in your program. Sometimes, you will get the results you expect, and other times you will not. You need to be aware of how and when VB.NET will make these conversions. You are not at the mercy of VB.NET, though. You can take full control of data type conversions.

There is also an element of direction when data conversion takes place. If the range of the data type that holds the result of the conversion includes the entire range of the original data type, it is a widening conversion. If the range of the data type that holds the result of the conversion does not include the entire range of the original data type, it is a narrowing conversion. Let me show you an example to make this clear:

```
Dim b As Byte
Dim s As Short
s = b     'Widening conversion
b = s     'Narrowing conversion
```

THE STACK AND HEAP

The stack is the working area of memory for your program. As your program runs, the stack grows and shrinks dynamically with the demands of your program. The stack is a part of the memory that is allocated to your program when it is executed. All value type variables are stored on the stack, as are parameters that are passed to procedures. Accessing data on the stack is fast because it is within the area of memory that is allocated to your program. The down side of the stack is that the amount of memory available for its use is determined when your program starts.

The heap is a part of memory that is not initially allocated to your program, but which your program can use. When you create a new reference type variable, the memory for the actual data is allocated from the heap. Only enough memory to point to a location on the heap is allocated on the stack. That is why these variables are called reference types. Instead of storing the actual data, the variables point to the location on the heap where the data is stored. Because of this setup, accessing data on the heap is slower than accessing data on the stack. The advantage the heap has is that there is much more memory available to draw upon.

Other features of the stack and heap can affect your program, but you won't need to worry about them until you have a firm grasp on VB.NET programming.

This snippet of code includes both a widening and a narrowing conversion of data. I show in Table 3.1 the ranges of the various VB.NET data types. For b, type Byte, the range of valid values is 0–255. For s, type Short, the range of valid values is -32,768–32,767. When s is assigned the value of b, a widening conversion takes place. It is a widening conversion because s includes all possible values that b could hold. On the other hand, when b is assigned the value of s, a narrowing conversion takes place. s can store possible values that would be outside the range of values that b supports. Because it's not guaranteed that a narrowing conversion will succeed, an error could occur.

If you're ready, let's look at how VB.NET makes these conversions and what you need to do to take control for yourself.

 TIP

To eliminate the chance of performing a conversion that could cause an error, add the Option Strict On statement at the beginning of each of your source files. Option Strict On forces VB.NET to generate an error when you attempt to compile code with a dangerous conversion instead of when you run the program. With this option turned on, all dangerous conversions must be explicit for your code to compile.

Implicit Conversions

Implicit conversions happen when your application does not tell VB.NET how to handle mismatched data types. Implicit conversions don't require you to do anything—VB.NET simply does the work for you. Sometimes you don't even realize that an implicit conversion is taking place. The most common place I have found this is when passing arguments to procedures. If you do not pay close attention to the types of each argument, you might find yourself facing runtime errors.

Explicit Conversions

Explicit conversions happen only when you tell VB.NET how to handle mismatched data types by using one of VB.NET's type conversion keywords. These keywords allow you to tell VB.NET exactly how to handle your data. When used with a widening conversion, you make clear your intent. When used with a narrowing conversion, you show that you recognize the need to convert the data. If Option Strict is turned to On, then you have to use explicit conversions for all narrowing conversions. Even with Option Strict turned On, you are not forced to explicitly convert a widening conversion. Table 3.2 lists the functions you can use to perform explicit conversions.

TABLE 3.2 TYPE CONVERSION FUNCTIONS	
Function Name	**Return Type**
CBool(expression)	Boolean
CByte(expression)	Byte
CChar(expression)	Char
CDate(expression)	Date
CDbl(expression)	Double
CDec(expression)	Decimal
CInt(expression)	Integer
CLng(expression)	Long
CObj(expression)	Object
CShort(expression)	Short
CSng(expression)	Single
CStr(expression)	String

Arrays

Most variables contain a single value. Sometimes, however, it would be nice for a variable to contain a set of related values. This is where arrays come in. You use arrays to reference a set of variables of the same type by a single name, telling them apart by use of an index or subscript. Many times, an array can make your program shorter and simpler. Arrays can have one or more dimensions. An array has a subscript for each of its dimensions. Normally, you won't find an array that has more than two or three dimensions, although they can have as many as 32. The following example declares a single dimension string array and assigns values for the names of the days of the week:

```
Dim DayNames() As String = {"Sunday", "Monday", "Tuesday", _
    "Wednesday", "Thursday", "Friday", "Saturday"}
```

In this case, the number of items on the right side of the equal sign determines the number of elements in the DayNames array. If you want to retrieve a value from the array, you use a subscript to choose which item to access. Remember: The first element of an array is always number 0. So, if I wanted to access Tuesday, I would use DayNames(2). To declare an array but fill in its values later, your code might look something like this:

```
Dim MyArray(10) As Integer
Dim i As Integer
For i = 0 To 10
    MyArray(i) = i + 100
Next I
```

MyArray is defined to have 11 elements with subscripts of 0–10. A For loop is then used to set the value of each element to its subscript plus 100. You can declare and access multidimensional arrays in a similar manner. The declaration needs to indicate the number of dimensions, and each time an element is accessed, you must include a subscript for each dimension of the array:

```
Dim Array2D(4, 9) As Byte
Dim Index1, Index2 As Integer   'Note that two variables are
                                'declared at once.

For Index1 = 0 To 4
    For Index2 = 0 To 9
        Array2D(Index1, Index2) = Index1 * Index2
    Next Index2
Next Index1
```

Here, Array2D is defined with two dimensions, and the value of each element is set to the product of the subscripts for each dimension.

You need to make sure you are aware of the amount of space needed to store the values of your array. The total number of elements in an array is the product of the sizes of all dimensions. For most arrays, space is allocated for each element when the array is declared, not when values are assigned to each element. The amount of space required to store a multidimensional array can increase quickly if you don't use care.

The arrays I have shown you so far have been fixed length. The number of elements in each of the arrays is determined when the array is declared. You also have a means to resize arrays after declaring them by using the ReDim keyword. Normally, when you ReDim an array, its existing values are lost. You can retain them by using the Preserve keyword when you ReDim the array. When you use Preserve with a multidimensional array, you are only able to change the last dimension. Let's look at how you can resize the array in the previous example. The first line is the original declaration of the array. The second line doubles the number of elements in the last dimension of the array, but the values stored in the array are lost. The third line again doubles the number of elements in the last dimension, but this time the existing data is not lost.

```
Dim Array2D(4, 9) As Byte
ReDim Array2D(4, 19)
ReDim Preserve Array2D(4, 39)
```

Changing the dimension of an array can be a slow and memory-consuming operation. When you use the ReDim keyword, VB.NET creates a new array with the dimensions indicated. If the Preserve keyword has been used, a copy of the values from the original array is moved into the new array. The space that the original array used is then released. Enough space must be available to store both the original array and the new array. If you happen to be using a large multidimensional array, the amount of space needed can be large. Copying the values if Preserve is used can also be time consuming if the array has many elements.

Enumerations

You use enumerations to associate a set of related constant values with names. I have used enumerations to represent status, months of the year, or days of the week. Any time that you have a group of numeric constant values that would be easier to deal with by name, you will find enumerations helpful. Enumerations can only be defined in the declarations section of a class or module. You cannot define an enumeration within a procedure. Here is a sample enumeration for the days of the week:

```
Public Enum DayOfWeek
        Sunday = 1
        Monday = 2
        Tuesday = 3
        Wednesday = 4
        Thursday = 5
        Friday = 6
        Saturday = 7
End Enum
```

 NOTE   You can initialize constants in an enumeration in a manner similar to variables, as seen in the previous example. If you don't initialize the first item in an enumeration, then VB.NET assigns it a value of zero. Each subsequent item in the enumeration is assigned the next sequential value. Any time that an item in the enumeration is initialized to a specific value, the numbering of the following items is based on the value of the most recently initialized item.

This defines an enumeration with the name DayOfWeek. Now you can declare a variable of type DayOfWeek and use the constants Sunday–Saturday to set its value:

```
Dim Day As DayOfWeek
Day = DayOfWeek.Thursday
```

You use the name of the enumeration in the Dim statement just as you would use any of VB.NET's basic data types. Then, to assign a value to a variable of an enumerated type, you use the name of the enumeration followed by a . (period) and the name of one of the constants in the enumeration.

TIP

■■■

Microsoft's Intellisense technology makes it easy to access enumerated types. When you are making an assignment to a variable that is an enumerated type, a small window appears when you type the equal sign. The window shows all of the possible values for the enumerated type. You simply have to select the value you want to use. Intellisense does not apply only to enumerated types. You will see the Intellisense window appearing many times during your development. You can reduce your development time and avoid many errors by taking advantage of this feature of the Visual Studio IDE. Figure 3.1 is an example of an Intellisense window.

■■■

```
Dim Day As DayOfWeek
Day =
    ▣ DayOfWeek.Friday
    ▣ DayOfWeek.Monday
    ▣ DayOfWeek.Saturday
    ▣ DayOfWeek.Sunday
    ▣ DayOfWeek.Thursday
    ▣ DayOfWeek.Tuesday
    ▣ DayOfWeek.Wednesday
```

Figure 3.1

Intellisense at work.

Structures

A structure allows you to combine elements of different types. Your structures become data types that you can use just like VB.NET's built-in data types. To create a variable of your new data type, you simply use the `Dim` keyword. After you define your structure, you can create an array of your structure type, pass your structure as an argument to a procedure, or even include your structure in another structure definition.

In addition to combining data elements in your structure, your structure can define procedures and events as well as implement interfaces. I will discuss these features later in this session in the "Procedures" section. For now, let me show you a sample structure definition:

```
Structure ContactInfo
    Public FirstName As String
    Public LastName As String
    Public Age As Integer
```

```
    Public Function FullName() As String
        Return (FirstName & " " & LastName)
    End Function
End Structure
```

Here, I have defined a structure called `ContactInfo`. The structure stores values for `FirstName`, `LastName`, and `PhoneNumber`. I have included a procedure in the structure, `FullName`, which returns the `FirstName` and `LastName` values concatenated with a space between them. This is what your code looks like when you use the structure:

```
Dim Contact As ContactInfo
Contact.FirstName = "Jay"
Contact.LastName = "Miller"
MsgBox(Contact.FullName)
```

First, a variable of type `ContactInfo` is declared. The declaration is the same as it would be for any other VB.NET type. After the variable is declared, the values of the `FirstName` and `LastName` elements are set. Finally, the `FullName` procedure is called, and the result, `"Jay Miller"`, is displayed in a message box.

NOTE Unlike VB.NET's built-in data types, structure elements might not be initialized when they are defined. When a variable of a structure type is declared, the values of the elements are initialized to the default value for each element type. You then can set the values of each of the elements in the structure.

Collections

A collection is a way of grouping related items. VB.NET uses collections extensively, such as the `Controls` collection of a form that provides access to all controls on that form. The `Collection` object has methods to `Add` items to and `Remove` items from the collection. Each item stored in a collection is actually a variable of type `Object`, allowing the collection to store items of any type. Your collection can store value types, reference types, or a combination of both value and reference types.

CAUTION

◆◆

Although they're similar to collections you can declare in your programs, some of VB.NET's collections support different features than the `Collection` object that VB.NET supplies.

◆◆

When you add an item to a collection, you can include a text string as a key that can be used later to retrieve the item from the collection. Collections support a `Count` property that returns the number of items in the collection as well as an `Item` property. The `Item` property retrieves a specific item from the collection. You pass the `Item` property either the string that was used for the key of an item or a number that indicates the ordinal position of the item within the collection. Let me show you how to declare a collection and then access each item in the collection:

```
Dim Numbers As New Collection()
Dim i, Total As Integer

'Add the numbers 1 - 5 to the collection.
For i = 1 To 5
    Numbers.Add(i, "Item" & CStr(i))
Next

'Add up the values of all items in the collection.
For i = 1 To Numbers.Count
    Total = Total + Numbers.Item(i)
Next
```

At the end of this section of code, `Total` will have a value of 15, the sum of each item in the collection. VB.NET provides a more efficient way to examine each item in a collection. You can use `For Each` to cycle through a collection, assigning the next item to the variable you provide each time through the loop. Because integers are stored in the collection, I have provided `i`, an integer, to the `For Each` loop to use. If you replace the `For` loop with the `For Each` loop, the resultant value of `Total` remains the same:

```
For Each i In Numbers
    Total = Total + i
Next
```

NOTE The example `For Each` loop works only if `Option Strict` is `Off`. Remember: Collections store each item they hold in an `Object` type, so any item retrieved from a collection is an `Object` type as well. Because `i` is an integer and each of the items in the collection is a number, VB.NET coerces the object that is returned from the collection into an integer. Anything other than a valid integer being stored in the collection causes an error when the `For Each` loop tries to assign it to the variable `i`.

Controlling Flow

You will find several of VB.NET's control statements helpful in your programs. VB.NET provides all the tools you need for making decisions and looping through data. You will also find statements that allow you to exit from the middle of loops and procedures.

Before looking at controlling the flow of your program, let's look at a simple console application. The following program prompts the user to enter a number, waits for the user to enter a number, and then displays what the user entered. It's pretty straightforward.

```
Module ConsoleTest
    Sub Main()
        Dim Num As Integer

        'Prompt the user to enter a number.
        Console.WriteLine("Enter a number from 1 - 10: ")
        'Read the number and store it in an integer variable.
        Num = CInt(Console.ReadLine())
        'Display the number the user entered.
        Console.WriteLine("You entered: " & CStr(Num))
        'Wait for the user to press Enter before exiting.
        Console.WriteLine("Press Enter to quit...")
        Console.Read()
    End Sub
End Module
```

Decision Statements

Decision statements test a condition to determine whether a block of code will execute or be skipped. The two most common decision statements are If…Then…Else and Select…Case. Let's start by giving the user a little feedback. How about if I tell the user whether the number he entered was greater than 5? To do that, I add an If statement to the preceding program. If statements evaluate an expression to determine whether it is True or False. The code inside the If will only execute if the expression is True. A message will only display if the number that the user enters is greater than 5. This is what the body of the program should look like:

```
'Prompt the user to enter a number.
Console.WriteLine("Enter a number from 1 - 10: ")
'Read the number and store it in an integer variable.
Num = CInt(Console.ReadLine())
'Display the number the user entered.
Console.WriteLine("You entered: " & CStr(Num))
'Decide if the number is greater than 5.
If Num > 5 Then
    Console.WriteLine("Your number was > 5")
End If
'Wait for the user to press Enter before exiting.
Console.WriteLine("Press Enter to quit...")
Console.Read()
```

If the number the user enters is greater than 5, an additional message is displayed. If the number entered was not greater than 5, then no additional message is displayed. Suppose you want to display a message either way. That's no problem. You just add the Else part to the If statement. Now the code between the If and Else is executed when the expression is True, and the code between the Else and End If is executed when the expression is False. Here is the updated code listing with the Else included:

```
'Prompt the user to enter a number.
Console.WriteLine("Enter a number from 1 - 10: ")
'Read the number and store it in an integer variable.
```

```
Num = CInt(Console.ReadLine())
'Display the number the user entered.
Console.WriteLine("You entered: " & CStr(Num))
'Decide if the number is greater than 5.
If Num > 5 Then
    Console.WriteLine("Your number was > 5")
Else
    Console.WriteLine("Your number was <= 5")
End If
'Wait for the user to press Enter before exiting.
Console.WriteLine("Press Enter to quit...")
Console.Read()
```

■ ■

If your If statement does not have an Else part, and there is only one line of code to execute if the expression is True, then you can use a shortened version of the If statement. You can leave off the End If and put the code to execute immediately after the Then, like this:

```
If Num > 5 Then Console.WriteLine("Your number was > 5")
```

■ ■

The other decision statement that you will use regularly is the Select…Case statement. Whereas the If statement determines only whether an expression is True or False, the Select statement compares an expression against specific values or ranges of values. You include a Case clause for each set of values that the expression is compared with. Continuing with the preceding example, you can tell the user whether the number entered is odd or even. You can accomplish the same result with a series of If statements, but the Select statement makes it easy. Here is the Select statement in action:

```
'Prompt the user to enter a number.
Console.WriteLine("Enter a number from 1 - 10: ")
'Read the number and store it in an integer variable.
Num = CInt(Console.ReadLine())
'Display the number the user entered.
Console.WriteLine("You entered: " & CStr(Num))
'Decide if the number is greater than 5.
If Num > 5 Then
    Console.WriteLine("Your number was > 5")
```

```
Else
    Console.WriteLine("Your number was <= 5")
End If
'Determine if the number is odd or even.
Select Case Num
    Case 1, 3, 5, 7, 9
        Console.WriteLine("You entered an odd number")
    Case 2, 4, 6, 8, 10
        Console.WriteLine("You entered an even number")
End Select
'Wait for the user to press Enter before exiting.
Console.WriteLine("Press Enter to quit...")
Console.Read()
```

Looping Statements

Whereas decision statements let you execute a section of code based on an expressions value, looping statements allow you to execute a section of code in an iterative manner. Looping is simply executing the same section of code multiple times. VB.NET provides several different looping statements for you to choose from. You can repeat the statements until a condition is True, until a condition is False, for a specified number of times, or once for each object in a collection.

The first looping statement I'll show you, the While statement, executes a section of code while a condition is True. Returning to the preceding example, I will use a While loop to continue asking for a number until one within the range is entered:

```
'Prompt the user to enter a number.
Console.WriteLine("Enter a number from 1 - 10: ")
'Read the number and store it in an integer variable.
Num = CInt(Console.ReadLine())
'Display the number the user entered.
Console.WriteLine("You entered: " & CStr(Num))
'Continue asking for a number if it is not in 1 - 10.
While Num < 1 Or Num > 10
    'Prompt the user to enter a number.
    Console.WriteLine("Enter a number from 1 - 10: ")
    'Read the number and store it in an integer variable.
```

```
        Num = CInt(Console.ReadLine())
        'Display the number the user entered.
        Console.WriteLine("You entered: " & CStr(Num))
End While
'Decide if the number is greater than 5.
If Num > 5 Then
    Console.WriteLine("Your number was > 5")
Else
    Console.WriteLine("Your number was <= 5")
End If
'Determine if the number is odd or even.
Select Case Num
    Case 1, 3, 5, 7, 9
        Console.WriteLine("You entered an odd number")
    Case 2, 4, 6, 8, 10
        Console.WriteLine("You entered an even number")
End Select
'Wait for the user to press Enter before exiting.
Console.WriteLine("Press Enter to quit...")
Console.Read()
```

The next looping statement to take a look at is the Do…Loop statement. A While expression is included to determine when the section of code inside the loop is executed. If you place the While with the Do portion, the expression is checked before the code inside the loop is executed. If the expression is False to begin with, the code inside the loop will never execute. If you place the While with the Loop portion, the expression is checked after the code inside the loop is executed. This means that the code inside the loop will always execute at least one time. When you place the While with the Do portion, the Do statement and the While statement exhibit the same behavior. The listing that follows changes only the looping lines while maintaining the same functionality.

```
'Prompt the user to enter a number.
Console.WriteLine("Enter a number from 1 - 10: ")
'Read the number and store it in an integer variable.
Num = CInt(Console.ReadLine())
'Display the number the user entered.
Console.WriteLine("You entered: " & CStr(Num))
```

```
'Continue asking for a number if it is not in 1 - 10.
Do While Num < 1 Or Num > 10
    'Prompt the user to enter a number.
    Console.WriteLine("Enter a number from 1 - 10: ")
    'Read the number and store it in an integer variable.
    Num = CInt(Console.ReadLine())
    'Display the number the user entered.
    Console.WriteLine("You entered: " & CStr(Num))
Loop
'Decide if the number is greater than 5.
If Num > 5 Then
    Console.WriteLine("Your number was > 5")
Else
    Console.WriteLine("Your number was <= 5")
End If
'Determine if the number is odd or even.
Select Case Num
    Case 1, 3, 5, 7, 9
        Console.WriteLine("You entered an odd number")
    Case 2, 4, 6, 8, 10
        Console.WriteLine("You entered an even number")
End Select
'Wait for the user to press Enter before exiting.
Console.WriteLine("Press Enter to quit...")
Console.Read()
```

If you include the While with the Loop portion, then the code inside the loop will always execute once. To prevent the user from initially being prompted to enter a number twice, you need to remove the code outside of the loop that prompts the user. The resultant code looks like this:

```
'Continue asking for a number if it is not in 1 - 10.
Do
    'Prompt the user to enter a number.
    Console.WriteLine("Enter a number from 1 - 10: ")
    'Read the number and store it in an integer variable.
    Num = CInt(Console.ReadLine())
    'Display the number the user entered.
    Console.WriteLine("You entered: " & CStr(Num))
```

```
Loop While Num < 1 Or Num > 10
'Decide if the number is greater than 5.
If Num > 5 Then
    Console.WriteLine("Your number was > 5")
Else
    Console.WriteLine("Your number was <= 5")
End If
'Determine if the number is odd or even.
Select Case Num
    Case 1, 3, 5, 7, 9
        Console.WriteLine("You entered an odd number")
    Case 2, 4, 6, 8, 10
        Console.WriteLine("You entered an even number")
End Select
'Wait for the user to press Enter before exiting.
Console.WriteLine("Press Enter to quit...")
Console.Read()
```

Instead of including a While expression in the Do statement, you can include an Until expression. In this case, the code within the loop will repeatedly execute until the expression is True. Like the While expression, the Until expression can be included either on the Do portion or the Loop portion. This is how the last example looks when the While expression is changed to an Until expression.

```
'Continue asking for a number if it is not in 1 - 10.
Do
    'Prompt the user to enter a number.
    Console.WriteLine("Enter a number from 1 - 10: ")
    'Read the number and store it in an integer variable.
    Num = CInt(Console.ReadLine())
    'Display the number the user entered.
    Console.WriteLine("You entered: " & CStr(Num))
Loop Until Num >= 1 And Num <= 10
'Decide if the number is greater than 5.
If Num > 5 Then
    Console.WriteLine("Your number was > 5")
Else
```

```
        Console.WriteLine("Your number was <= 5")
End If
'Determine if the number is odd or even.
Select Case Num
    Case 1, 3, 5, 7, 9
        Console.WriteLine("You entered an odd number")
    Case 2, 4, 6, 8, 10
        Console.WriteLine("You entered an even number")
End Select
'Wait for the user to press Enter before exiting.
Console.WriteLine("Press Enter to quit...")
Console.Read()
```

The last looping statement that I want to introduce you to is the For…Next statement. While and Do loops are appropriate when you do not know how many times a loop needs to be executed. When your loop needs to be executed a specific number of times, however, a For loop is a better choice. Instead of evaluating an expression to determine whether it is True or False, like While and Do loops, For loops use a counter to determine when to stop looping. The counter is set to an initial value and compared against the ending value. If the counter does not exceed the ending value, the code inside the loop executes once. The counter is then incremented and compared against the ending value. If the counter does not exceed the ending value, the loop is executed again and the counter is incremented. This process continues until the counter exceeds the ending value.

My final addition to our beloved example is to display a message a number of times equal to the number the user entered. I do this by using a For loop to repeatedly display the message:

```
Dim c As Integer

'Continue asking for a number if it is not in 1 - 10.
Do
    'Prompt the user to enter a number.
    Console.WriteLine("Enter a number from 1 - 10: ")
    'Read the number and store it in an integer variable.
    Num = CInt(Console.ReadLine())
    'Display the number the user entered.
```

```
        Console.WriteLine("You entered: " & CStr(Num))
Loop Until Num >= 1 And Num <= 10
'Decide if the number is greater than 5.
If Num > 5 Then
        Console.WriteLine("Your number was > 5")
Else
        Console.WriteLine("Your number was <= 5")
End If
'Determine if the number is odd or even.
Select Case Num
    Case 1, 3, 5, 7, 9
        Console.WriteLine("You entered an odd number")
    Case 2, 4, 6, 8, 10
        Console.WriteLine("You entered an even number")
End Select
'Display a message Num times.
For c = 1 To Num
    Console.WriteLine("This message is in a For loop")
Next
'Wait for the user to press Enter before exiting.
Console.WriteLine("Press Enter to quit...")
Console.Read()
```

NOTE The default increment value of a For loop is 1. You can change the increment value by including a Step expression with the For loop like this:

```
For c = 1 To Num Step 3
```

Here the counter i will be incremented by 3 each time through the loop.

NOTE One additional looping statement is available: the For Each...Next statement. You only use this particular statement with collections. You will find an example of a For Each statement in the prior section on collections.

EXITING CONTROL STATEMENTS

You can exit a control statement in three ways: when an expression evaluates to True, when an expression evaluates to False, or when a specific condition is met. Sometimes, however, you might need to exit a control statement because the expression that controls it will never cause it to terminate. An endless loop could occur that causes your program to appear to be frozen. To avoid such situations, VB.NET includes Exit statements that immediately transfer control to the first statement after the end of the control statement. If you have nested control statements, be aware that an Exit statement will only break out of the closest level of control statement. Here is a list of Exit statements for control structures:

➤ Exit Select

➤ Exit While

➤ Exit Do

➤ Exit For

In addition, VB.NET provides Exit statements that immediately transfer control to the end of a procedure. These Exit statements break out of any level of nested control structures. The procedure Exit statements are as follows:

➤ Exit Sub

➤ Exit Function

➤ Exit Property

Take a Break

I've thrown a lot at you so far this afternoon. You are being exposed to the core of the VB.NET language. I know it is a lot to digest, but take heart because the best is yet to come. So, take a break, stretch your legs, and come back when you're ready to continue with the adventure.

Operators and Expressions

When you combine operators and variables, you form expressions, or in the case of the assignment operator, statements. I will show you several different types of operators: arithmetic operators, comparison operators, concatenation operators, and logical operators.

Arithmetic Operators

You use arithmetic operators when you want to perform normal math functions on your data. Table 3.3 summarizes VB.NET's arithmetic operators. You will find yourself using these operators all the time. Because most of these operators are the same ones you learned in grade school, you shouldn't have a hard remembering them.

TABLE 3.3 ARITHMETIC OPERATORS

Operator	Meaning	Example
^	Raises a number to a power	x = 2 ^ 2 'Returns 4
*	Multiplies two numbers	x = 3 * 4 'Returns 12
/	Divides two numbers	x = 10 / 4 'Returns 2.5
\	Divides two numbers	x = 11 \ 4 'Returns 2
Mod	Calculate the remainder	x = 11 / 4 'Returns 3
+	Adds two numbers	x = 4 + 3 'Returns 7
-	Subtracts two numbers	x = 4 - 3 'Returns 1

Comparison Operators

Comparison operators compare two expressions and return a boolean value that represents the result of the comparison. You will find yourself comparing numbers, strings, and even objects. Numbers are compared using the numeric comparison operators. As with the arithmetic operators, the numeric comparison operators are the same ones you learned in math class. The numeric comparison operators are found in Table 3.4.

TABLE 3.4 NUMERIC COMPARISON OPERATORS

Operator	Meaning
=	Equality
<>	Inequality
<	Less than
>	Greater than
<=	Less than or equal to
>=	Greater than or equal to

You can also compare String values using the numeric comparison operators. The numeric comparison operators return results based on the sort order of the strings compared. Here are some examples of String comparisons:

```
"45" < "9"          'True
"d" > "a"           'True
"hello" = "hello" 'True
```

In addition to the numeric comparison operators, you can use the Like operator to compare String values. The Like operator lets you compare a string to a pattern. If the string matches the pattern, the result is True; otherwise, the result is False.

```
If "hello" Like "h??l*" Then
    '...
End If
```

Here, I am comparing the "hello" with the pattern "h??l*". Each question mark in the pattern represents a single character. Each asterisk in the pattern represents any number of characters. So, to match this pattern, the String must start with an h followed by any two characters. It then must have an l. After the l, the string can have any number of characters, or the l might be the last character.

The last thing you are likely to compare are objects. Objects have two comparison operators. First, you can check to see whether two objects reference to the same instance of an object using the Is operator:

```
Dim object1 As SomeClass
Dim object2 As New SomeClass()
Object1 = object2
If object1 Is object2 Then
    '...
End If
```

In this example, object1 and object2 are of type SomeClass. A new SomeClass object is created and assigned to object2. Next, object2 is assigned to object1. Because object1 and object2 both refer to a single copy of SomeClass, the If statement will be True. In the following code, the If statement will be False because object1 and object2 do not refer to the same copy of SomeClass.

```
Dim object1 As New SomeClass()
Dim object2 As New SomeClass()
If object1 Is object2 Then
    '...
End If
```

The other object operator tests whether an object is of a particular type. You should use the TypeOf…Is operator to determine whether a variable is of a specific type. Let's look at an example of the TypeOf operator:

```
Dim object1 As New SomeClass()
Dim object2 As New SomeOtherClass()
If TypeOf object1 Is SomeClass Then
    'True
End If
If TypeOf object2 Is SomeClass Then
    'False
End If
```

This time, object1 and object2 are of different types: SomeClass and SomeOtherClass, respectively. The first If statement checks to see whether object1 is of type SomeClass. It is, so the code inside the If will execute. The second If statement checks to see whether object2 is of type SomeClass. Because object2 is actually a SomeOtherClass type, the If will be False and the code inside the If will not execute.

Concatenation Operators

VB.NET supports two operators for concatenating, or joining, strings. The two operators are + and &. These operators will join string variables and literal strings as seen here.

```
Dim x As String = "Visual Basic .NET"
Dim y As String = "a Weekend"
Dim z As String
z = "Learn " & x & " in " & y
'z equals "Learn Visual Basic .NET In a Weekend."
z = "Learn " + x + " in " + y
'z equals "Learn Visual Basic .NET In a Weekend"
```

When Option Strict is On, both the + and & operators accept only string expressions for concatenations and behave the same. If Option Strict is Off, however, the + operator performs implicit conversions on expressions that are not String. For example, you could concatenate a string and a number without explicitly converting the number, like this:

```
Dim z As String
z = "Some text " + 123   'z equals "Some text 123"
```

Logical Operators

Logical operators compare boolean expressions and return a Boolean result. Table 3.5 shows the main logical operators and the values they return.

TABLE 3.5 LOGICAL OPERATORS	
Operator	**Returns**
And	True if both expressions are true
Or	True if either expression is true
Xor	True if one expression is true and one is false
Not	Opposite of expression

Let's look at some examples to make it clear how logical operators work:

```
Dim x As Boolean
x = 56 > 34 And 34 > 6    ' x = True
x = 34 > 56 And 34 > 6    ' x = False
x = 45 > 34 Or 6 > 34     ' x = True
x = 45 > 67 Or 6 > 34     ' x = False
x = 45 > 67 Xor 34 > 6    ' x = True
x = 45 > 34 Xor 34 > 6    ' x = False
x = 34 > 45 Xor 6 > 34    ' x = False
x = Not 45 > 34    ' x = False
x = Not 45 > 89    ' x = True
```

All expressions in the example statements are evaluated to determine whether the logical operation will return True or False. Sometimes, you might not want this behavior. VB.NET provides two logical operators that stop evaluating expressions as early as possible. AndAlso corresponds to And, whereas OrAlso corresponds to Or. For the AndAlso operator, expressions are only evaluated until one is False or all expressions are evaluated. Evaluation of expressions using the OrElse operator stops as soon as an expression is True. The difference is most obvious when one of the expressions is a procedure call that returns a boolean value. Using And or Or, the procedure is always called. Using AndAlso or OrAlso, the procedure is only called if necessary.

```
34 > 67 And SomeProcedure() ' SomeFunction is called.
34 > 67 AndAlso SomeFunction()   ' SomeFunction is not called.
67 > 34 Or SomeFunction()   ' SomeFunction is called.
67 > 34 OrElse SomeFunction()   ' SomeFunction is not called.
```

Keywords

Keywords are words that VB.NET has reserved for its own use. You might have noticed that when I use a keyword in the text, it is represented in a monospace font, such as Dim. Because VB.NET uses these words, if you choose to use keywords for variables, procedures, or classes, you must do a little extra work to ensure that VB.NET understands how to treat them. Let's suppose that I want to declare a variable called Loop. I want to use this variable to determine whether the program should perform a loop operation. Here is how I would declare the variable:

```
Dim [Loop] As Boolean
```

The brackets let VB.NET know that I am using a reserved keyword as a variable in my program. When I want to access the value of the variable `Loop`, I also have to use the brackets:

```
[Loop] = False
If [Loop] Then
    '...
End If
```

An error is generated if I attempt to use `Loop` without the brackets. VB.NET thinks I am trying to use the `Loop` keyword in the wrong context.

✦✦

CAUTION It is easy to forget to use the special syntax and inadvertently introduce an error into your program. For this reason, I recommend that you do not use VB.NET keywords as elements in your programs.

✦✦

Handling Exceptions

You will receive an exception when an unexpected situation occurs while your program is running. Exceptions come in a variety of shapes and sizes depending on the cause of the situation. If you do not handle the exceptions that come your program's way, they could cause it to crash—something users tend not to like. So, to keep your users happy, I'll show you what you can do to trap exceptions that your program encounters.

◀◀

BUZZ WORD *Structured error handling* is code designed to detect and respond to errors during execution by combining a control structure with exceptions, protected blocks of code, and filters.

◀◀

VB.NET provides a method to detect and respond to exceptions while your program is running. This method is called structured error handling. When you detect an exception, you have several options. You can choose to ignore the exception if it doesn't impact your program, you can handle the exception yourself, or you can pass the exception to another part of the program and let it decide what to do with the exception. You can also generate your own exceptions for other programs or other parts of your program to process.

Using the `Try...Catch...Finally` statement, you can isolate sections of code that have a potential to raise errors. Let me quickly show you the structure of the `Try...Catch...Finally` statement:

```
Try
    'Some code that might fail
Catch 'Optional filter
    'Code to handle an exception
[More Catch blocks]
Finally
    'Code that always executes
End Try
```

The `Try` block is where you put your code that might generate an exception. If an error occurs while code inside the `Try` block is executing, VB.NET examines each of the `Catch` statements until it finds one whose condition matches the error. If a matching condition is found, your program begins executing the code inside that `Catch` block. If VB.NET does not find a matching `Catch` condition, then an error is produced. The code in the `Finally` block is always executed, either after the code in the `Try` block finishes or after the code in a `Catch` block executes if an exception occurs.

`Catch` blocks allow you to filter exceptions by their class or by using a conditional expression. Let me show you another console application to demonstrate exactly how the `Try...Catch...Finally` statement works. This program prompts the user to enter two numbers, divides the first number by the second number, and then displays the result:

```
Module ExceptionTest
    Sub Main()
        Dim Num1, Num2 As Integer
        Dim Result As Decimal

        Console.WriteLine("This program divides two numbers " & _
                          "that you enter.")
        'Prompt the user to enter numbers.
        Console.WriteLine("Enter your first number:")
        'Read the first number and store it in an integer variable.
        Num1 = CInt(Console.ReadLine())
```

```
        Console.WriteLine("Enter your second number:")
        'Read the second number and store it in an integer variable.
        Num2 = CInt(Console.ReadLine())

        Result = Num1 / Num2
        'Display the result.
        Console.WriteLine("The result of " & CStr(Num1) & "/" & _
            CStr(Num2) & " is " & CStr(Result))

        'Wait for the user to press Enter before exiting.
        Console.WriteLine("Press Enter to quit...")
        Console.Read()
    End Sub
End Module
```

First, this program declares two integers to store the numbers that the user enters and a decimal to store the result of the division. Next, the user is prompted to enter the two numbers. Now—and here comes the dangerous part—the first number is divided by the second number and the result is displayed. What is so dangerous about division, you say? Well, on paper, nothing. To your program, however, unknowns could cause errors. Let me show you how to catch one of the most common math errors: division by zero. To ensure that division by zero does not crash your program, you need to enclose that section of code in a `Try...Catch...Finally` statement. You can use two types of filters to determine when the code in a `Catch` block will be executed. You can filter based on any expression that returns a boolean value, or you can filter based on the type of the exception.

```
Try
    Result = Num1 / Num2
    'Display the result.
    Console.WriteLine("The result of " & CStr(Num1) & "/" & _
        CStr(Num2) & " is " & CStr(Result))
Catch e As Exception When Num2 = 0
    'Display an error message.
    Console.WriteLine("Denominator cannot be 0!")
    Console.WriteLine(e.Message)
Catch e As OverflowException
```

```
        'Display an error message.
        Console.WriteLine("Overflow exception caught!")
        Console.WriteLine(e.Message)
Finally
        'Display an error message.
        Console.WriteLine("Look ma, I didn't crash.")
End Try
```

This example has two `Catch` blocks—one for each type of filter. When an exception is generated within the `Try` block, the code in the first `Catch` block executes only when the second number entered—`Num2`—is 0. In this case, a message is displayed and control moves to the code in the `Finally` block. If an exception occurs but `Num2` is not 0, then the second `Catch` block checks to see whether the exception is of type `OverflowException`. If the exception is not an `OverflowException`, then other structured error handlers in effect get a chance to process the exception. Even if the `Try` block doesn't generate exceptions, the code in the `Finally` block will be executed.

NOTE In addition to structured error handling, VB.NET supports unstructured error handling using the `On Error` statement. With `On Error`, you can instruct VB.NET to ignore errors, resume executing code with the line immediately following the line that generated the error, or have control branch to a label in the same procedure. Unstructured error handling is more limited than structured error handling, so make sure you use structured error handling whenever possible. Prior versions of Visual Basic supported only unstructured error handling.

Procedures

A procedure is a section of code that is given a name. To declare a procedure, you use the `Sub`, `Function`, or `Property` keyword. Table 3.6 explains the differences in procedure types. This named section of code can then be invoked from another location in your program.

BUZZ WORD *Invoking*, or calling, a procedure transfers control to the procedure. When the procedure finishes executing, control returns to the code that called it.

TABLE 3.6 PROCEDURE TYPES	
Type	**Description**
Sub	Performs actions but does not return a value to the calling code. (All event-handling procedures are Subs.)
Function	Performs actions and returns a value to the calling code.
Property	Returns or assigns values to properties on objects or modules.

Every line of code in your program must be within a procedure. Dividing your program into small, manageable procedures will make your program much more readable and easy to maintain. Procedures allow you to perform repeated tasks easily. They are great for implementing a calculation or processing text or data. Procedures are quick and easy to access; you can call a procedure from just about anywhere in your program. Because of this ease of use, procedures will probably form the building blocks of your program. In addition, procedures make your program easier to debug if you don't find yourself writing perfect programs the first time. Finally, procedures allow you to use code in one program that was developed in another program.

That's enough talk. Let me show you a couple sample procedures. In the previous section on handling exceptions, you were introduced to procedures and probably didn't even realize it. I have included that example again to illustrate:

```
Module ExceptionTest
    Sub Main()
        Dim Num1, Num2 As Integer
        Dim Result As Decimal

        Console.WriteLine("This program divides two numbers " & _
                        "that you enter.")
        'Prompt the user to enter numbers.
        Console.WriteLine("Enter your first number:")
        'Read the first number and store it in an integer variable.
        Num1 = CInt(Console.ReadLine())
```

```
        Console.WriteLine("Enter your second number:")
        'Read the second number and store it in an integer variable.
        Num2 = CInt(Console.ReadLine())

        Try
            Result = Num1 / Num2
            'Display the result.
            Console.WriteLine("The result of " & CStr(Num1) & _
                "/" & CStr(Num2) & " is " & CStr(Result))
        Catch e As Exception When Num2 = 0
            'Display an error message.
            Console.WriteLine("Denominator cannot be 0!")
            Console.WriteLine(e.Message)
        Catch e As OverflowException
            'Display an error message.
            Console.WriteLine("Overflow exception caught!")
            Console.WriteLine(e.Message)
        Finally
            'Display an error message.
            Console.WriteLine("Look ma, I didn't crash.")
        End Try

        'Wait for the user to press Enter before exiting.
        Console.WriteLine("Press Enter to quit...")
        Console.Read()
    End Sub
End Module
```

Here, Main() is a Sub. It happens to be the point where execution of the program begins. The procedure begins with the Sub Main() line and ends with the End Sub line. Because Main() is where execution of this program begins, when the End Sub line is reached, the program terminates. Your procedures can have no arguments, like Main(), but many times, it is useful to pass arguments to a procedure. You declare arguments just like you do variables, except that you place them with the procedure declaration. I'll show you by taking the lines from the example, which get the numbers from the user, and placing them in their own procedure:

```
Module ExceptionTest
```

```
Sub Main()
    Dim Num1, Num2 As Integer
    Dim Result As Decimal

    Console.WriteLine("This program divides two numbers " & _
                        "that you enter.")
    GetNumbers(Num1, Num2)

    Try
        Result = Num1 / Num2
        'Display the result.
        Console.WriteLine("The result of " & CStr(Num1) & _
            "/" & CStr(Num2) & " is " & CStr(Result))
    Catch e As Exception When Num2 = 0
        'Display an error message.
        Console.WriteLine("Denominator cannot be 0!")
        Console.WriteLine(e.Message)
    Catch e As OverflowException
        'Display an error message.
        Console.WriteLine("Overflow exception caught!")
        Console.WriteLine(e.Message)
    Finally
        'Display an error message.
        Console.WriteLine("Look ma, I didn't crash.")
    End Try



    'Wait for the user to press Enter before exiting.
    Console.WriteLine("Press Enter to quit...")
    Console.Read()
End Sub

Sub GetNumbers(ByRef Input1 As Integer, ByRef Input2 As Integer)
    'Prompt the user to enter numbers.
    Console.WriteLine("Enter your first number:")
    'Read the first number and store it in an integer variable.
    Input1 = CInt(Console.ReadLine())
```

```
        Console.WriteLine("Enter your second number:")
        'Read the second number and store it in an integer variable.
        Input2 - CInt(Console.ReadLine())
    End Sub
End Module
```

Notice the new procedure: GetNumbers(ByRef Input1 As Integer, ByRef Input2 As Integer). The Sub line declares a new procedure with the name GetNumbers. It expects two integer arguments called Input1 and Input2. The code inside the procedure is the same as before, except Num1 and Num2 have been changed to Input1 and Input2, respectively. The lines that gather the two numbers from the original version are then replaced with the following line:

```
GetNumbers(Num1, Num2)
```

When this line of code is reached in the Main() procedure, control transfers to the GetNames() procedure. When the GetNames() procedure finishes executing, control returns to Main() on the line of code following the call to GetNames().

■ ■

For a procedure to be able to modify any of its arguments, the arguments must include the ByRef keyword in their declaration. If an argument is declared ByVal instead of ByRef, then the procedure can use the value of the argument but cannot change its value.

■ ■

To show you a little more about procedures, I'll make another change to the example. This time I am going to take the code that performs the division, along with the error handling code, and move it to a procedure. This new procedure will not need to modify the values that are passed as arguments, so I will declare them using ByVal. Also, this procedure will return the result of the division as a decimal number. Because the procedure returns a value, I will use a function instead of a sub:

```
Module ExceptionTest
    Sub Main()
        Dim Num1, Num2 As Integer
        Dim Result As Decimal
```

```vb
        Console.WriteLine("This program divides two numbers " & _
                            "that you enter.")
        GetNumbers(Num1, Num2)

        Result = DoDivide(Num1, Num2)

        'Wait for the user to press Enter before exiting.
        Console.WriteLine("Press Enter to quit...")
        Console.Read()
    End Sub

    Sub GetNumbers(ByRef Input1 As Integer, ByRef Input2 As Integer)
        'Prompt the user to enter numbers.
        Console.WriteLine("Enter your first number:")
        'Read the first number and store it in an integer variable.
        Input1 = CInt(Console.ReadLine())

        Console.WriteLine("Enter your second number:")
        'Read the second number and store it in an integer variable.
        Input2 = CInt(Console.ReadLine())
    End Sub

    Function DoDivide(ByVal Num1 As Integer, _
                        ByVal Num2 As Integer) As Decimal
        Dim Result As Decimal

        Try
            Result = Num1 / Num2
            'Display the result.
            Console.WriteLine("The result of " & CStr(Num1) & _
                "/" & CStr(Num2) & " is " & CStr(Result))
        Catch e As Exception When Num2 = 0
            'Display an error message.
            Console.WriteLine("Denominator cannot be 0!")
            Console.WriteLine(e.Message)
        Catch e As OverflowException
            'Display an error message.
```

```
        Console.WriteLine("Overflow exception caught!")
        Console.WriteLine(e.Message)
    Finally
        'Display an error message.
        Console.WriteLine("Look ma, I didn't crash.")
    End Try


    Return (Result)
  End Function
End Module
```

This time, a new procedure, DoDivide(), has been added. DoDivide() takes two numbers as arguments, divides them, and then returns the result as a decimal. The code inside the Try...Catch...Finally block is exactly as before. The only additions to the procedure are the declaration of the variable Result and the Return(Result) statement. A Return statement sets the return value of a function. Take a look back at the Main() Sub. Do you notice anything different? It is much easier to understand, isn't it? With the code to get the numbers from the user and the code to do the division—along with handling exceptions—moved into procedures, the main body of the program is much simplified. You can now tell just by skimming over Main() what the program does. If getting numbers from the user returns an error, it will be much easier to debug the GetNumbers() procedure than to determine which code is gathering input and which code is not. The same holds true for the DoDivide() procedure.

I hope you can see the benefits that using procedures brings to your program. As you create more programs, it will become second nature to look for sections of code that would benefit from being turned into procedures. Your programs will quickly become a collection of subs and functions.

TIP   There is a good rule of thumb to use when creating a procedure. As a general rule, a procedure should not be more than one screen long. That is, you should be able to see the entire procedure on the screen at once. In addition to making it easier to debug a procedure because you can see everything, keeping your procedures short forces you to think about your program's design.

Scope

The scope of an element is the set of all code that can access it without having to qualify its name or import it. The four levels of scope are as follows:

➤ **Block.** The element is only available within the code block in which it is declared.

➤ **Procedure.** The element is only available with the procedure in which it is declared.

➤ **Module.** The element is available to all code within the module, class, or structure in which it is declared.

➤ **Namespace.** The element is available to all code in the namespace.

◀◀

Blocks are sets of statements terminated by an `End`, `Else`, `Loop`, or `Next` statement. An element declared within a block can be used only within that block.

Namespaces organize the objects that are defined in assemblies. They prevent ambiguity and simplify references to objects when you are accessing a large group of objects or a third-party class library.

◀◀

The block is the smallest set of code that can access the element without qualification, and the namespace is the largest set of code that can access the element without qualification. The scope of an element is set when you declare it. An element's scope can be affected by the location in your code where you declare the element, the namespace where the element belongs, and the accessibility that you specify for the element. Both variables and procedures have scope.

Block Scope

A block is a section of code that an `End`, `Else`, `Loop`, or `Next` statement terminates. An element declared within a block is only available to code that is also within that block. For example, if you declare a variable inside a `For` statement, that variable can only be accessed from other code that is within the `For` statement.

NOTE Even when you declare a variable in a block, VB.NET keeps it around for the duration of the entire procedure. You can't access it outside the block, but it is still there. This means that if the block in which it is declared is entered more than once, such as inside another loop, the variable maintains the value it had on the last iteration of the loop. For this reason, you should always initialize a variable that has block scope after it is declared.

Procedure Scope

An element that is declared within a procedure cannot be used outside of that procedure. You will normally hear variables with procedure scope called local variables. Any variable that is declared within a procedure but outside of all blocks that are within the procedure has procedure scope. Local variables are probably the most common scope of variable that you will use in your programs.

Module Scope

To use a variable with module scope, you declare it outside of all procedures within the module. Module-level scope applies to VB.NET modules, classes, and structures.

Although you can freely use an element with module scope anywhere within the module that declares it, you can also make an element available to other modules if you choose. This is called the element's accessibility. When you use the Dim statement to declare a variable at the module level, the variable's scope defaults to private accessibility. Private accessibility means that the variable is available only to procedures within the module. To make your intentions clear, you can replace the Dim keyword with the Private keyword for elements that have module scope.

BUZZ WORD *Accessibility* refers to the set of all declaration spaces in which the declared element is accessible. The five accessibility types are Public, Protected, Friend, Protected Friend, and Private. Public is the most permissive and Private is the least permissive.

Your code would look like this:

```
Private MyVar As String
```

instead of:

```
Dim MyVar As String
```

Both of these lines of code declare the variable MyVar with private module scope.

CAUTION

◆ ◆

The Private keyword applies only to elements with module scope. If you try to replace the Dim keyword with the Private keyword for a variable with procedure or block scope, it will generate an error.

◆ ◆

Procedures can also have module scope. Unlike variables of module scope that default to private accessibility, however, procedures default to public accessibility. To make a procedure private to the module where you declare it, you must include the Private keyword. Let me use the DoDivide() procedure from earlier as an example. The original declaration of the procedure was as follows:

```
Function DoDivide(ByVal Num1 As Integer, _
                  ByVal Num2 As Integer) As Decimal
    'The body of the function was here.
End Function
```

When you declare the function in this manner, it defaults to Public, meaning that other modules have access to it. To make the function accessible only to other procedures within the same module, you need to include the Private keyword:

```
Private Function DoDivide(ByVal Num1 As Integer, _
                          ByVal Num2 As Integer) As Decimal
    'The body of the function was here.
End Function
```

Now, code outside the module that declares DoDivide() will not be able to call that function.

Namespace Scope

Module-level elements that are public have namespace scope. If you do not specify Namespace statements, then everything in your project is in the same namespace. Again, both variables and procedures can have namespace scope. Here is how you can declare the variable and procedure so that they have namespace scope:

```
Public MyVar As String
Public Function DoDivide(ByVal Num1 As Integer, _
                         ByVal Num2 As Integer) As Decimal
    'The body of the function was here.
End Function
```

Because these declarations include the Public keyword, you can access them from any part of your project. Any public elements in your modules, classes, or structures are also available to any other project that references your project.

Modules

A module is a reference type that can include variables, procedures, enumerations, and structures. Modules are an exception, however, in that you do not declare a variable of a module type. Public elements in a module are shared; that is, they are available to any other part of your project. Any code in your program can retrieve or change the values of these public variables. Because the variables are available to your entire program, if code in one module sets the value of a variable, then code in another module will see that change when it accesses the variable. Also, all public procedures can be called from anywhere within your program.

◀◀

Modules are reference types whose members are shared and scoped to the declaration space of the module's containing namespace, rather than just to the module declaration itself.

◀◀

You will use modules to declare variables that you want to be global to your program. You should also put general-purpose procedures into modules so that they can be accessed from anywhere within your program. You can have multiple modules in your project. I would suggest that you group similar procedures into a module of their own. This makes it easy for you to include the module in another project.

CAUTION Because public elements of modules are accessible to your entire program, you need to be careful when you define elements with the same name in different modules. When you access an element from the module where it is declared, you can simply use the name of the element. If, however, you want to access an element that has a duplicate in another module, you must qualify the element by including the module name when you reference it.

Classes and Objects

Classes are blueprints that define objects that your program uses while it is running. Classes describe the properties, fields, procedures, and events that make up objects. They are the templates that VB.NET uses when it creates the object you request. You can use a class to create as many objects as your program needs.

Many times, the terms "class" and "object" are used interchangeably. They are, however, two distinct entities. Classes describe the structure of objects and objects are instances of classes. Creating an instance of a class for use by your running program is called instantiation. Every instance is an exact copy of its class, yet each instance is independent of any other instances of its class. This means that you can have two instances of the same class that contain completely different data.

BUZZ WORD
Instantiation is the process of allocating and initializing memory for a reference type variable.

NOTE   Classes can contain elements that are declared with the Shared keyword. Instead of each instance of the class having its own copy of an element, a shared element has the same value for all instances of its class. These elements exist independently of any instance of the class. If one instance of a class changes a shared element, all other instances of that class will see the change made to the shared element.

Being the blueprints for objects, classes are an important aspect of VB.NET's support of object-oriented programming. Classes allow you to group related items and control how they are accessed. Classes can also inherit behavior from other classes and allow you to easily reuse the code you have worked so hard to produce.

Prior to VB.NET, Visual Basic was really an object-based language. It supported classes, but you could not take advantage of all the benefits that truly object-oriented languages could provide. Microsoft has remedied that with VB.NET. With this newfound robustness come some concepts that might be new to you if you have not worked with an object-oriented language before. I'll start by explaining what these concepts are and how you implement them in VB.NET.

If you worked with prior versions of Visual Basic and caught a lot of flack from your C++ programming buddies, then things are about to change. You now have access to all of the features that your C++ programming buddies have had for a long time. It's time to turn the tables and leave them in your dust as you take off with VB.NET.

These are the classes I will use as examples to demonstrate the concepts that follow. Refer back to this listing as you read the rest of the chapter.

```
Public Class Automobile
    Public NumDoors As Integer
    Protected Color As String
    Private GallonsOfGas As Integer
    Public Sub StartEngine()
        'Put code here to make the car use gas.
    End Sub
    Public Sub StopEngine()
        'Put code here to make the car stop using gas.
    End Sub
```

```
      ReadOnly Property OutOfGas() As Boolean
          Get
              Return (GallonsOfGas = 0) 'Returns whether the car
                                        'is out of gas
          End Get
      End Property

End Class

Public Class DumpTruck
    Inherits Automobile
    Public Sub DumpLoad()
        'Dump the load.
    End Sub
    Property TruckColor() As String
        Get
            Return Color
        End Get
        Set(ByVal NewColor As String)
            Color = NewColor
        End Set
    End Property
End Class
```

Encapsulation

Encapsulation describes the ability to contain and control access to a group of related items. In the preceding example, the Automobile class encapsulates the data and procedures that describe an automobile. If you did not have encapsulation available, you would have to declare separate procedures and variables to track the data for an automobile. You would have much more work to do if you needed to track multiple automobiles at once. Encapsulation lets you deal with everything associated with an automobile in one nice package. Each instance of the Automobile class has everything it needs, so it is easy to work with more than one automobile at a time.

With encapsulation, you also gain the ability to better control how data and procedures are used. When you use the Public, Private, and Protected accessibility modifiers, you can prevent outside procedures from accessing your class' procedures and data. You should declare all internal details of your class as `Private`. This prevents any code that is outside your class from using these details in an undesirable way. It also allows you to change the internal implementation details of your class later without having to worry about compatibility problems. A general rule to follow is to declare all data in the class as `Private`. To access the data, your class then should use either `Property` procedures or other `Public` procedures. By doing this, you control exactly how the outside world gets to your data. I'll go into more detail on `Property` procedures and the `Protected` modifier in the sections that follow.

Properties

You use `Property` procedures to access the data of a class, module, or structure. You could make your variables public to allow outside access to them instead of using a `Property` procedure, but as I just discussed, using `Property` procedures is a much safer way to provide access to your data. By using `Property` procedures, you can make access to your data read-only, write-only, or read/write. When your property is accessed, you can define the code that is executed, both when a value is retrieved and when it is set. This allows you to do much more than just return or set the value of a variable.

`Property` procedures use `Get` statements to return a value and `Set` statements to set a value. The `OutOfGas` property of the `Automobile` class is an example of a read-only property. It has a `Get` statement but no `Set` statement, so it's not possible to update the amount of gas in an `Automobile` from outside the class. The `TruckColor` property of `DumpTruck` is an example of a read/write property. `Get` and `Set` statements provide access to the property.

Code outside of your class accesses properties in the same way that it accesses `Public` variables. Let me show you how you might access the `NumDoors` variable and `TruckColor` property of a `DumpTruck`. First, you need to declare the variables that you will be using:

```
Dim Truck As New DumpTruck()
Dim Doors As Integer
Dim Color As String
```

Now I'll show you how to retrieve some data about a `DumpTruck`. When you access the `NumDoors` variable, its value is simply returned because it is a `Public` variable. When you access the `TruckColor` property, however, the

Property procedure's Get section is executed, returning the value for the color. Although returning the values happens in different ways because of how the data is defined in DumpTruck, to outside code, NumDoors and TruckColor look the same. Retrieving the values looks like this:

```
Doors = Truck.NumDoors
Color = Truck.TruckColor
```

Setting the values of NumDoors and TruckColor is identical. The Set section of TruckColor is executed while the value of NumDoors is set directly. Again, to outside code, NumDoors and TruckColor look the same.

```
Truck.NumDoors = 4
Truck.TruckColor = "Blue"
```

Methods

You might hear another term when someone is talking about object-oriented programming: methods. Sometimes, "method" and "procedure" are used interchangeably like "object" and "class." They are different, though. A method represents an action that an object can perform. You define a method by adding a procedure—either a Sub or a Function—to your class. That's really all there is to it. Just be aware that technically speaking, a method applies to an object, whereas a procedure applies to a class.

An instance of a DumpTruck that your program uses while running has methods to start the engine, stop the engine, and dump the load. These are defined in the DumpLoad procedure of DumpTruck and the StartEngine and StopEngine procedures of Automobile.

Inheritance

Classes let you define data types that encapsulate a group of related items. What happens when you come across a new data type and you find that you already have a class that is *almost* what you need? Well, if you aren't using an object-oriented language, you would probably cut and paste the code from the existing class into the new one and start hacking away to make it what you need. Not anymore! With an object-oriented language, you can inherit all of the functionality of another class. Unlike characteristics that you inherited from your parents, you can get rid of, change, and add to the class that you inherit from. Classes that you inherit from are called base classes. Your new class that inherits from a base class is called a derived class. A derived class inherits all of the data and procedures that are defined in the base class. This means that after you have debugged a class, you can use it over and over again as a base class.

◄◄

Inheritance is the ability to define base classes that serve as the basis for derived classes that can extend the properties, methods, and events of the base class.

◄◄

• •

NOTE A class can only inherit from one other class. VB.NET does not support multiple inheritance.

• •

In the previous example, `Automobile` is a base class. The derived class is `DumpTruck`. This means that `DumpTruck` inherits the functionality of `Automobile`. Therefore, a `DumpTruck` can use the `Start` and `Stop` procedures that `Automobile` defines. `DumpTruck` also has a property called `NeedsGas`. In addition to these inherited features, `DumpTruck` defines a new procedure, `DumpLoad`, and a property that is used to set the color of the truck. Note that the variable to store the color is defined in `Automobile`, but access to it is given in `DumpTruck`.

The accessibility modifiers you use for the variables and procedures in a base class have an effect on the accessibility of those elements in a derived class. Table 3.7 gives a summary of how accessibility is handled in derived classes.

TABLE 3.7 INHERITED ACCESSIBILITY	
Accessibility in Base Class	**Accessibility in Derived Class**
Public	Public—Available to all outside code
Protected	Private—Available only in the derived class
Private	Not available to the derived class

Abstraction

You use abstraction to encapsulate common functionality for inherited classes. VB.NET supports abstraction with abstract classes. An abstract class is a class that cannot be instantiated; it must be inherited from. This is accomplished by using the `MustInherit` keyword in VB.NET.

An abstract class can include all of the same types of variables and procedures that a normal class includes. Usually, but not always, an abstract class will not be fully implemented. It is intended that the class that inherits from it will fill in the missing details. Abstract classes allow you to set an unchangeable level of functionality in some methods but leave the implementation of other methods until a specific implementation of the class is needed.

Look at the classes in the following example. Two classes are defined. The first, `Television`, is an abstract class because it includes the `MustInherit` keyword. `Television` defines a common implementation of the procedure `TurnOn`. All classes that inherit from `Television` will have the same implementation of the `TurnOn` procedure. `ChangeChannel`, on the other hand, is given no implementation in `Television`. In fact, the `MustOverride` keyword tells VB.NET that any class that inherits from `Television` must define the implementation of `ChangeChannel`.

Now look at the `MyTV` class. `MyTV` inherits from `Television`, so it gets the implementation of `TurnOn` from the `Television` class. `MyTV` then has to include an implementation of `ChangeChannel` because `ChangeChannel` must be overridden based on its definition in `Television`. Any other class that inherits from `Television` will also have to include an implementation of `ChangeChannel`.

```
Public MustInherit Class Television
    Public Sub TurnOn()
        'Put code here to make the car use gas.
    End Sub
    Public MustOverride Sub ChangeChannel()
End Class

Public Class MyTV
    Inherits Television
    Public Overrides Sub ChangeChannel()
        'Put code here to make the car stop using gas.
```

```
      End Sub
End Class
```

Overloading

Overloading is when you declare two or more procedures in your class that have the same name but different argument types. This is especially useful when you want to use one procedure name to operate on different types of data. Suppose you have a class that includes a procedure called `Display` that displays a string that you pass to it as an argument. The procedure might look something like this:

```
Sub Display(ByVal SomeString As String)
    'Code to display a string goes here.
End Sub
```

Great! Now you can display a string and move on to the next part of your program. That's when your manager calls you in to inform you that the requirements for your program have changed—and believe me, they will change! Your class now has to be able to display integers as well as strings. You can handle that, you say. I'll just change my procedure to display a string from `Display` to `DisplayString` and add a `DisplayInteger` procedure. There is one catch, though, your manager informs you. The developers who will be using your class have already changed their code and they kept the procedure name the same. They are calling `Display` for both strings and integers. Instead of having a feeling of dread come over you at having to tell your manager it won't work that way, you can tell him no problem; if that's what they need, that's what I'll give them. How? By using the `Overloads` keyword with your procedures.

Including the `Overloads` keyword allows you to define more than one copy of the `Display` procedure. You can define one that accepts a string and another that accepts an integer. The following listing shows the `Display` procedure from earlier with the `Overloads` keyword added as well as a `Display` procedure for integers:

```
Overloads Sub Display(ByVal SomeString As String)
    'Code to display a string goes here.
End Sub
Overloads Sub Display(ByVal SomeInteger As Integer)
```

```
        'Code to display an integer goes here.
End Sub
```

You are not limited to having only two procedures with the same name. You can have a virtually unlimited number as long as the arguments to the procedure vary by type or by the number of arguments. You could easily add Display procedures for Short, Long, Decimal, Boolean, and even your own class types.

Interfaces

Interfaces are similar to abstract classes. They define a set of properties and procedures. Unlike abstract classes, however, interfaces do not provide implementation. An interface is a contract that another class agrees to implement exactly. You declare interfaces using the Interface...End Interface statement.

```
Public Interface SomeInterface
    Property SomeProperty(ByVal SomeString As String)
    Function SomeFunction(ByVal SomeInteger As Integer) As Integer
End Interface
```

Here, an interface named SomeInterface is defined. It includes a property named SomeProperty and a function called SomeFunction. Any class that implements SomeInterface is required to implement SomeProperty and SomeFunction exactly as they appear in the interface.

When using abstract classes, your new class is inherited from the abstract class. However, your new class implements an interface. The Implements keyword is used to tell VB.NET that your class has agreed to implement the specified interface. When your new class declares a procedure that is going to implement a procedure from an interface, you have to indicate its intent in the declaration statement.

TIP

■ ■

Although the name you give the procedure in your new class does not have to be the same name used in the interface, the number of argument types does have to match exactly. It is common practice to use the same name for the procedure in the new class to avoid possible confusion.

■ ■

Now let's look at a class that implements `SomeInterface`. You will see how to indicate that a class plans to implement an interface and how to declare procedures to support the interface's procedures:

```
Public Class Implementor
    Implements SomeInterface
    Property SomeProperty(ByVal SomeString As String) Implements _
        SomeInterface.SomeProperty
        Get
            'Return a property.
        End Get
        Set(ByVal Value)
            'Set a property value.
        End Set
    End Property
    Function SomeFunction(ByVal SomeInteger As Integer) _
        As Integer Implements SomeInterface.SomeFunction
        'Do something interesting here.
    End Function
End Class
```

NOTE Unlike inheritance where a class can only inherit from a single base class, a class can implement any number of interfaces.

Events

An event is a message that an object sends to let other objects know that something interesting has taken place. Events are implemented by using delegates. Before Windows came along, most programs were a series of instructions that were executed in sequence. Few programs blindly run from start to finish anymore. Most programs are event driven, which means that external events determine the order of execution. Forms use events that your code can handle to indicate that the user has clicked a button or entered some text.

Your program can broadcast these types of messages using the `RaiseEvent` statement. Just about any type of object can raise an event. You can also define procedures to handle events that might come your program's way.

VB.NET uses a standard naming convention for event handlers. Although you are not forced to use this convention, doing so certainly makes your programs easier to read. The convention is to use the name of the event sender, an underscore, and then the name of the event. Therefore, the `Click` event of `Button1` on a form would be `Button1_Click`.

To hook up an event handler to an event, you use the `WithEvents` and `Handles` statements. In this example, the first line declares a variable of type `Button` and indicates that events from the button will be processed. Then the `Handles` keyword is used on a procedure to indicate that the procedure will process all `Click` events that `Button1` generates. You simply add the `Handles` keyword to other procedures to process other events.

NOTE

VB.NET handles the plumbing of events from forms for you. When you double-click on a control in the designer, VB.NET creates the event handler for you and connects it to the control on the form.

```
WithEvents Button1 As System.Windows.Forms.Button
Sub Button1_Click(ByVal sender As System.Object, _
    ByVal e As System.EventArgs) Handles Button1.Click
End Sub
```

This method of handling events is set at compile time. That is, the procedures that will handle the events have been predetermined in your program. VB.NET also provides a means to associate event handlers with events at runtime. To do this, you use the `AddHandler` and `RemoveHandler` statements. Using AddHandler, it is also possible to associate multiple event handlers with a single event. The example that follows shows how you can use `AddHandler` to attach a procedure to an event as an event handler.

```
Private Button2 As System.Windows.Forms.Button
Sub Button2_Click(ByVal sender As System.Object, _
    ByVal e As System.EventArgs)
End Sub
```

After the object that generates the events and the procedure to handle them have been declared, you can hook them together.

```
AddHandler Button2.Click, AddressOf Me.Button2_Click
```

NOTE The AddressOf statement always returns a reference to a delegate.

Delegates

A delegate is an object-oriented function pointer that allows a function to be called indirectly through a reference to the function. From a data standpoint, a reference data type is a parallel idea to the delegate. Reference data types and delegates both provide indirect access. You will use delegates primarily in two situations: to handle events, and to provide callback functions when using system classes. Less frequently, you might use a delegate to make an indirect call to another function.

◄◄

BUZZ WORD *Delegates* are reference types that refer to a shared method of a type or to an instance method of an object.

◄◄

Here is an example from the online help that shows creating and using your own delegate.

```
Delegate Sub MySubDelegate(ByVal x As Integer)
Protected Sub Test()
    Dim c2 As New class2()
    ' Test the delegate.
    c2.DelegateTest()
End Sub

Class class1
    Sub Sub1(ByVal x As Integer)
        MessageBox.Show("The value of x is: " & CStr(x))
    End Sub
End Class

Class class2
    Sub DelegateTest()
        Dim c1 As Class1
        Dim msd As MySubDelegate
```

```
        c1 = New Class1()
        ' Create an instance of the delegate.
        msd = AddressOf c1.Sub1
        msd.Invoke(10) ' Call the method.
    End Sub
End Class
```

In this example, class2 uses the delegate MySubDelegate to make an indirect call to Sub1 in class1.

Reflection

The Reflection namespace has classes and interfaces that give you a view of loaded types, methods, and fields, along with the ability to create and invoke them. Reflection provides objects that encapsulate assemblies, modules, and types, much like classes encapsulate data and procedures. Table 3.8 includes some of the typical uses of Reflection.

TABLE 3.8 TYPICAL REFLECTION USES

Class or Interface	Typical Use
Assembly	Define and load assemblies.
Module	Determine which assembly contains the module and the classes in the module. Get methods defined in the module.
MethodInfo	Determine the name, return type, parameters, access modifiers, and implementation details of a method.
EventInfo	Determine the name, event-handler data type, attributes, and declaring type of an event. Add or remove event handlers.
PropertyInfo	Determine the name, data type, and read/write status of a property. Get or set property values.
ParameterInfo	Determine the name, data type, direction, and position of a parameter in a method signature.

What's Next

In the next session, you'll learn how to work with files and folders. You'll also learn about manipulating database information using ADO.NET and learn how to write reports for your applications. Enjoy a good meal and come back refreshed to tonight's session.

Working with Files, Databases, and Reports

➤ Writing data to a file
➤ Reading data from a file
➤ Using a database
➤ Binding data to controls
➤ Creating reports
➤ Displaying reports

Congratulations! This afternoon, you made it through the most grueling session of the weekend. This evening, you'll learn how to work with data. I'll show you how to store and retrieve data from both files and databases. You'll also learn how to easily create reports for displaying data.

Working with Files

In the past, Visual Basic developers had to do a lot more work to read or write to a file. First, it was necessary to obtain a file number, or handle. Then you could open a file using the file handle. Every operation you performed on the file required a different function and file handle. When you were finished with the file, you closed it by using the file handle.

Luckily, the .NET Framework has simplified file access immensely. The System.IO namespace provides a wide range of classes and objects for you to use in manipulating files.

Files are nothing more than a collection of bits of data. The data could represent a picture, the text of a document, or even the source code for your program. Visual Studio .NET uses streams to access the data that is contained in a file.

◄ ◄

BUZZ WORD   *Streams* are abstractions that represent a sequence of bytes. You can read from a stream, write to a stream, or modify the current position in a stream.

◄ ◄

Let's look at some of the stream classes from the .NET Framework that you might use:

➤ **BinaryReader.** Reads primitive data types as binary values.

➤ **BinaryWriter.** Writes primitive types in binary to a stream and supports writing strings.

➤ **File.** Provides static methods for the creation, copying, deletion, moving, and opening of files.

➤ **FileInfo.** Provides instance methods for the creation, copying, deletion, moving, and opening of files.

➤ **FileStream.** Exposes a stream around a file, supporting both synchronous and asynchronous read and write operations.

➤ **TextReader.** Represents a reader that can read a sequential series of characters.

➤ **TextWriter.** Represents a writer that can write a sequential series of characters.

➤ **StreamReader.** Implements a TextReader that reads characters from a byte stream.

➤ **StreamWriter.** Implements a TextWriter for writing characters to a stream.

From these descriptions, it might appear that the functionality of some of the stream classes has some overlap. Well, in fact, it does. The .NET Framework provides you with multiple ways to accomplish the same task. As an example, I will show you how to use the `StreamReader` and `StreamWriter` classes.

TIP Although the various stream classes are similar in many ways, they are also different in several subtle ways. Some classes work with bytes, some with characters, and others with entire strings. Take advantage of the help in Visual Studio to make sure you use the stream class that best suits your needs.

1. Create a new Windows Application project and name it `File Access`.

2. Rename `Form1.vb` to `FileAccess.vb`.

3. Change the forms `(Name)` property to `FileAccess` and its `Text` property to `File Access`.

4. Add a label to the form and set its `Text` property to `Contents:`.

5. Add a text box below the label. Set its `(Name)` property to `txtContents` and delete the text in its `Text` property. Set its `Multiline` property to `True` and resize it to fill most of the form.

6. Add another label to the form and set its `Text` property to `File Name:`. Place it below the Contents text box.

7. Add another text box next to the File Name label. Change its (Name) property to txtFileName and delete the text in its Text property. Widen the text box until it reaches the right side of the form.

8. Add a button to the bottom of the form. Set its (Name) property to btnSave and its Text property to Save.

9. Add another button to the bottom of the form. Set its (Name) property to btnLoad and its Text property to Load.

That takes care of the user interface for this example. You can see what my completed form looks like in Figure 4.1.

To display the code for the form, right-click anywhere on the form and choose View Code from the menu. The first thing you need to do is add a line of code at the top of the code window. The stream classes are located in the System.IO namespace. To simplify the syntax of accessing these classes, add the following line of code at the top of the code window:

```
Imports System.IO
```

TIP If you find yourself using several classes from a namespace, you should include an Imports command for that namespace. By importing the namespace, you gain access to all elements in the namespace without having to include the name of the namespace every time you reference an element. For example, I am showing you how to access a file using the StreamWriter class from the System.IO namespace. If I do not import the namespace, I have to use System.IO.StreamWriter instead of just StreamWriter.

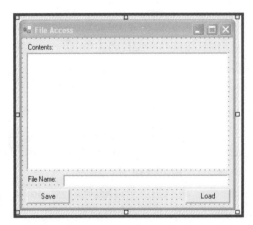

Figure 4.1

The user interface for the File Access example.

Build your application to ensure that you don't have errors. You can type whatever you want into the Contents text box and the File Name text box. So that you can learn how to use streams, you'll add some functionality to the buttons to save and then load a file.

1. Create an event handler for the Click event of btnSave.

2. Add this code to the Click event handler for btnSave:

```
'Declare a variable to use in writing to a file.
Dim OutputFile As StreamWriter

'Create a new StreamWriter object to access the file.

'Use the value of txtFileName as the name of the file.
OutputFile = New StreamWriter(txtFileName.Text)

'Write the contents of txtContents to the file.
OutputFile.Write(txtContents.Text)

'Close the file and release the memory used by OutputFile.
OutputFile.Close()
OutputFile = Nothing

'Clear txtContents.
txtContents.Clear()
```

3. Create an event handler for the Click event of btnLoad.

4. Add this code to the Click event handler for btnLoad:

```
'Declare a variable to use in reading from a file.
Dim InputFile As StreamReader

'Create a StreamReader object to access the file.
'Use the value of txtFileName as the name of the file.
InputFile = New StreamReader(txtFileName.Text)

'Read the contents of the file and put it into txtContents.
txtContents.Text = InputFile.ReadToEnd()

'Close the file and release the memory used by InputFile.
InputFile.Close()
InputFile = Nothing
```

That's all there is to it. The Save button takes whatever is in txtContents and stores it in the file listed in txtFileName. The Load button takes the contents of the file listed in txtFileName and displays it in txtContents.

CAUTION

For simplicity sake, I did not add error handling to this example. If you do not enter a valid path and file name when saving or loading, you will receive an error. I've been using C:\TestFile.txt while testing.

Let me step you through the code for this example in a little more detail. I'll start with the Click event for btnSave because you need to save something to a file before you can load it. The first line of code simply declares a variable of type StreamWriter for accessing a file:

```
Dim OutputFile As StreamWriter
```

The second line creates a new instance of the StreamWriter class and assigns it to the variable OutputFile. The name of the file is taken from the contents of the txtFileName text box. If the file doesn't exist, then it is created. Then it is opened and ready for writing to.

```
OutputFile = New StreamWriter(txtFileName.Text)
```

The next line writes the contents of txtContents to the file:

```
OutputFile.Write(txtContents.Text)
```

NOTE

In this case, I am writing the entire contents of a text box to the file at one time. If necessary, you can call the Write method multiple times to add more data to the file.

Now that I'm done writing to the file, I can close the file and release the reference to the StreamWriter:

```
OutputFile.Close()
OutputFile = Nothing
```

The last thing I do is to clear txtContents:

```
txtContents.Clear()
```

Run your application and enter several lines of text in the Contents text box. Enter a valid path and file name, and then click on the Save button. Your text is saved to the file, and the text box is cleared. Figure 4.2 shows the File Access application running.

Now let me show you the code to load text from a file. This code is similar to the code to save text to a file. The first line of code simply declares a variable of type `StreamReader` to access a file:

```
Dim InputFile As StreamReader
```

The second line creates a new instance of the `StreamReader` class and assigns it to the variable `InputFile`. Again, the name of the file is taken from the contents of the `txtFileName` text box. The file is opened and ready for reading from:

```
InputFile = New StreamReader(txtFileName.Text)
```

The next line reads the entire contents of the file and assigns it to the `Text` property of `txtContents`:

```
txtContents.Text = InputFile.ReadToEnd()
```

Now that I'm finished reading from the file, I can close the file and release the reference to the `StreamReader`:

```
InputFile.Close()
InputFile = Nothing
```

Figure 4.2

The File Access application in action.

To test loading from a file, run your application again. Enter the name of the file that you saved earlier into the File Name text box, and then select the Load button. Your application reads the file and displays the contents in txtContents.

I've really only scratched the surface of what you can do with files. As I mentioned earlier, the .NET Framework provides a wide variety of classes for working with files. Spend some time exploring the Visual Studio help system to find more information on what the System.IO namespace has to offer.

Working with Data

If you are developing anything but a trivial application, you are probably going to have to figure out how to access corporate data. Whether the data is stored in Access, SQL Server, Oracle, or some other database, you need to get at it. Never fear: Microsoft has incorporated tools into Visual Studio to ease accessing your data.

Overview

In Visual Studio, you use ADO.NET to get to your data. ADO.NET allows you to connect to your database, read data, and update data. ADO.NET is part of the Microsoft Data Access Components (MDAC). When you deploy your application that uses ADO.NET, you need to be sure that the user's computer has version 2.6 or later of MDAC installed.

 NOTE   If you don't have MDAC, you can download it from Microsoft's Web site. Browse to http://www.microsoft.com/data/download.htm to see a list of all MDAC components available. Make sure you download and install version 2.6 or later.

ADO.NET

ADO.NET works in a disconnected manner. This means that you only keep a connection open to your database long enough to perform an action; then you disconnect. Traditionally, databases were accessed in a connected manner. Your application would connect to the database when it started and not close the connection until the application ended. Although at times this might have been convenient for a stand-alone application, there are many advantages to a disconnected architecture, such as ADO.NET:

➤ Valuable system and database resources are not consumed to maintain an open connection.

➤ Applications can scale up to more users easily.

➤ Web applications are disconnected by their very nature, so they are more easily supported with a disconnected database model.

➤ Sharing data among applications is simplified when applications don't have to stay connected to their data source.

Data Adapters, Connections, and Datasets

The first thing that you need to do is make a connection to your database. If you can't connect to your database, then you're just out of luck. So, let's get past the first hurdle and get you access to your database.

 NOTE Within your company, you might need to take several steps outside of Visual Studio to access your corporate data. Talk to your database administrators and network technicians to ensure that you have the appropriate access to your database server. They also can help you address any security or performance requirements for your application.

Visual Studio provides the data adapters to ease working with databases. I'll show you how to step through a wizard for the data adapter that will set up the connection to your database and let you create a dataset to work with your data. First, though, you need to create a project to work in. To get started, follow these steps:

1. Create a new Windows Application project and name it Data Access.

2. Rename Form1.vb to Data Access.vb.

3. Change the forms (Name) property to DataAccess and its Text property to Data Access.

4. Make sure that the Toolbox window and the Properties window are visible.

5. Select the Data tab of the Toolbox. Figure 4.3 shows how my Visual Studio IDE looks at this point.

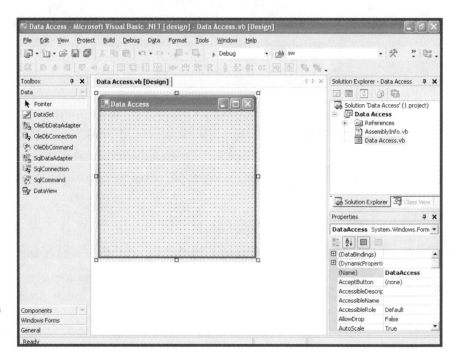

6. Drag an OleDbDataAdapter control from the toolbox and drop it onto the form. This starts the Data Adapter Configuration Wizard.

7. Select Next at the welcome screen. You should see the Choose Your Data Connection screen shown in Figure 4.4.

8. The wizard displays a list of available connections in the drop-down list. Select the connection you want to use and click Next.

9. Choose Use SQL Statements and click Next.

◄◄

BUZZ WORD

SQL stands for Structured Query Language, the language used to work with the data in your database. You use SQL statements to retrieve data, update data, gather summary information, or perform an action on your database.

◄◄

NOTE

In addition to specifying the SQL statements directly, you can have the data adapter use stored procedures. The wizard can create new stored procedures for you, or you can specify existing stored procedures to use.

Figure 4.4

The Data Adapter
Configuration
Wizard.

Stored Procedures

Stored procedures are a precompiled collection of SQL statements and control-flow statements that are given a name and processed as a unit. Stored procedures are stored within a database; can be executed with one call from an application; and allow user-declared variables, conditional execution, and other programming features.

Stored procedures can contain program flow, logic, and queries against the database. They can accept parameters, output parameters, return single or multiple result sets, and return values.

You can use stored procedures for any purpose for which you would use SQL statements, with these advantages:

➤ You can execute a series of SQL statements in a single stored procedure.

➤ You can execute other stored procedures from within your stored procedure to simplify a series of complex statements.

➤ Stored procedures are compiled on the server when they are created, so they execute faster than individual SQL statements.

Each database offers different functionality for stored procedures. For more details about what a stored procedure can accomplish for you, see your database documentation.

10. Enter the following text to select the data you want to load:

    ```
    SELECT au_id, au_lname, au_fname, city, state FROM authors
    ```

    This step of the wizard is pictured in Figure 4.5.

TIP

■■■
If you aren't sure of what tables and fields are available, you should click on Query Builder. The Query Builder lets you choose from a list of tables and fields to include in your query. It builds the SQL statement as you select the fields and adds it back into the wizard when you are finished.
■■■

11. Click Next. The wizard shows the results of the tasks it performs. Figure 4.6 shows the result pane of the wizard.

12. Select Finish to complete the wizard.

You should now see two items added to a pane below your form: OleDb-DataAdapter1 and OleDbConnection1. OleDbConnection1 is the connection to your database. OleDbDataAdapter1 is the intermediary for passing information back and forth from your database to your application. Now you can have Visual Studio generate a dataset for you based on the query you supplied to the wizard.

1. Select Generate Dataset from the Data menu.

Figure 4.5

Selecting your data.

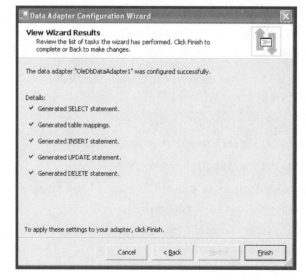

Figure 4.6

Finishing up the
Data Adapter
Configuration
Wizard.

2. Select New in the Generate Dataset dialog box and name the dataset
   dsAuthors.

3. Make sure the Authors table and Add This Dataset to the Designer are
   selected.

4. Click OK when the Generate Dataset dialog box looks like Figure 4.7.

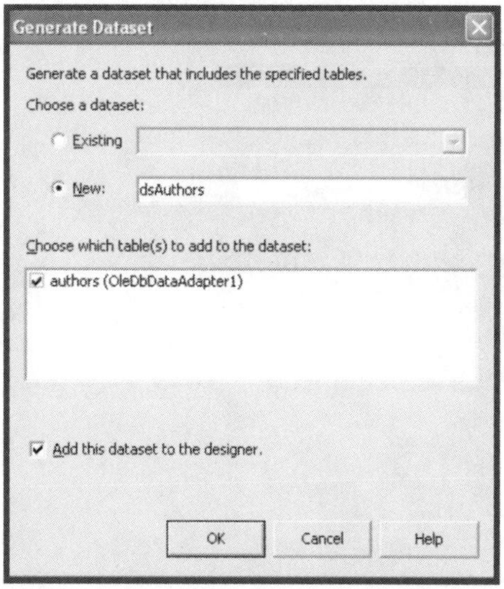

Figure 4.7

Filling in the
Generate Dataset
dialog box.

You should now see DsAuthors1 in the bottom pane along with OleDb-DataAdapter1 and OleDbConnection1. Now that you have the means to get to your data, why don't you do something with it? Let's display it in a grid.

1. Drag a DataGrid to your form from the Windows Forms tab of the Toolbox.

2. Set its (Name) property to dgAuthors.

3. Set its DataSource property to DsAuthors1.

4. Set its DataMember property to authors.

5. Resize dgAuthors so that it fills most of the form. You can see my completed form in Figure 4.8.

6. Finally, create an event handler for the Load event of the form and add these two lines of code to it:

```
DsAuthors1.Clear()
OleDbDataAdapter1.Fill(DsAuthors1)
```

The last step clears dsAuthors1 and fills it with data from OldDb-DataAdapter1. You can now build your application and browse through the

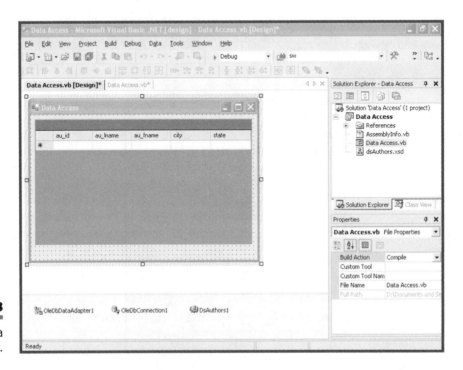

Figure 4.8

Adding data to a datagrid.

list of authors. This is great for viewing authors, but what if you want to update an author's information? The datagrid allows you to make changes to the data and add new rows of data. The changes are stored in the dataset that is associated with the datagrid. The problem is that these changes are *only* stored in the dataset; they are not written back to the database. You can fix that, though.

I'll show you how to save your changes to the database. In a few short steps, you can add a button to the form and have it update the database when the user clicks the button.

1. Add a button from the Toolbox to the form.
2. Set its (Name) property to btnUpdateDatabase.
3. Set its Text property to Update Database.
4. Create an event handler for the Click event of btnUpdateDatabase and add these two lines of code to it:

```
OleDbDataAdapter1.Update(DsAuthors1)
MessageBox.Show("Database updated!")
```

Run your application and try your hand at modifying some of the data. When you are finished with your changes, click on Update Database. Your application saves the changes to the database and displays a message to the user. If you aren't convinced that your changes were saved, exit the application and run it again. The data still shows the changes you made.

Take a Break

Take a few minutes to stretch and load up on some caffeine. I still have some more I want to show you about data access and reports before you call it a night. Come on back when you have munchies and drink in hand.

Making Changes to Your Data Components

You can also add new rows of data to the Authors table. Scroll to the bottom of the list and you will find an empty row. Fill in each of the fields and click on Update Database. Oh no! What did you do now? You should see an error message indicating that the Contract column cannot have a NULL value. The problem is that I didn't have you include the Contract column when you set up the data adapter. Let me walk you through the process of updating the data adapter and grid to include the Contract column from the Authors table.

1. Select DsAuthors1 from the pane at the bottom of the document window and delete it.

NOTE Notice that as soon as you delete DsAuthors1, the columns disappear from dgAuthors. The `DataSource` property of dgAuthors was bound to DsAuthors1. With DsAuthors gone, dgAuthors has no way to know what columns of data are available.

2. Select OleDbDataAdapter1.

3. Choose Configure Data Adapter from the Data menu to display the Data Adapter Configuration Wizard again.

4. Click Next to move through the first three panes of the wizard.

5. On the Generate the SQL Statements pane, add Contract to the list of columns. The wizard should now look like Figure 4.9.

6. Select Finish.

Figure 4.9

Adding a column to OleDbDataAdapter1.

That takes care of adding the column to OleDbDataAdapter. Now you need to regenerate the dataset that can be bound to dgAuthors.

1. Select Generate Dataset from the Data menu.
2. Select Existing in the Generate Dataset dialog box.
3. Choose Data_Access.dsAuthors from the drop-down list.
4. Make sure the Authors table and Add This Dataset to the Designer are selected.
5. Click on OK when the Generate Dataset dialog box looks like Figure 4.10.

Now that OleDbDataAdapter1 and DsAuthors1 are updated, all that you have left to do is bind dgAuthors to the Authors table again.

1. Set the DataSource property of dgAuthors to DsAuthors1.
2. Set the DataMember property of dgAuthors to authors.
3. Resize dgAuthors and the form, if necessary, so that all of the columns are visible.

Run your application again. Add a new row, filling in each of the columns. This time when you save your data, you won't get an error.

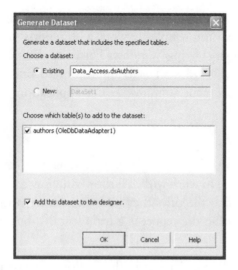

Figure 4.10

Re-creating the dataset.

Data adapters are not the only way to access data, but they are definitely one of the easiest. They allow you to easily create the connection to your database as well as to the dataset to bind to your form controls. If you prefer, you can create your connection and dataset manually.

I have only scratched the surface of what ADO.NET has to offer you. Again, I suggest you take advantage of the excellent help that Visual Studio supplies to dig deeper into alternative methods for accessing your data. There is more to data adapters than I can present here. I think you will find data adapters an invaluable resource as you continue exploring Visual Basic .NET.

Working with Reports

Okay, now you can display and update data in a Windows application. The problem is that your boss wants something he can carry with him into a meeting. Maybe when everyone has a PDA connected to your company's wireless network, your boss can just have everyone run your new .NET application and be dazzled by what they see. Unfortunately, that isn't reality today. I'll show you how to create reports that will give your boss what he wants.

Overview

Visual Studio includes support for reports through Crystal Reports for .NET by Crystal Decisions. You seamlessly work with reports inside Visual Studio just like you do when creating Windows Forms applications. As a matter of fact, you start with a Windows Forms application, define a report, and then add a report viewer to your Windows Forms application.

Creating Reports

To start, create a new Windows application and name it `Report Viewer`. This gives you a clean slate to work with. I'll show you how to create a report that shows the authors and the titles they have written from the Pubs database. The process of creating the report is a little lengthy, but it's fairly straightforward.

1. Right-click on Report Viewer in the Solution Explorer window.
2. Select Add New Item from the Add menu.

3. In the Add New Item dialog box, find and select Crystal Report.

4. Name the report AuthorTitles, and then click on Open. Figure 4.11 shows the completed Add New Item dialog box.

5. From the Crystal Report Gallery dialog box, choose Using the Report Expert and select the Standard Expert, as shown in Figure 4.12.

NOTE Take a quick look at the Report Experts that are available. The Experts take you step by step through the creation of some impressive reports.

6. Click on OK. Figure 4.13 shows the Standard Report Expert.

7. On the Data tab, double-click on OLE DB (ADO).

8. From the OLE DB Provider dialog box, choose Microsoft OLE DB Provider for SQL Server (or the provider for your database). You can see the OLE DB Provider dialog box in Figure 4.14.

9. Click on Next.

10. Enter the name of your server.

11. Enter the user ID and password for your database server. If your Windows login allows you to access your database, you can check Integrated Security instead.

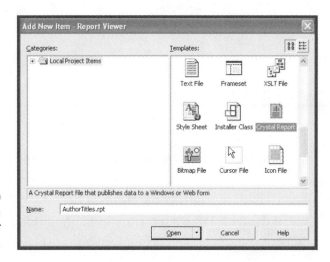

Figure 4.11

Adding a report to the Report Viewer project.

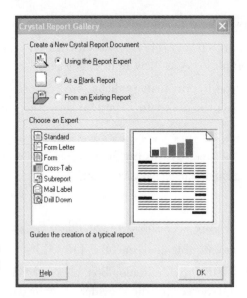

Figure 4.12

Choosing an Expert to guide you.

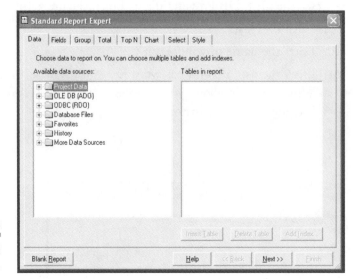

Figure 4.13

The Standard Report Expert.

12. Enter pubs for the database name. Figure 4.15 shows the completed dialog box.

13. Choose Finish to return to the Standard Report Expert dialog box.

14. Expand the OLE DB (ADO) entry in the Available Data Sources section until you can see Tables in the Pubs database.

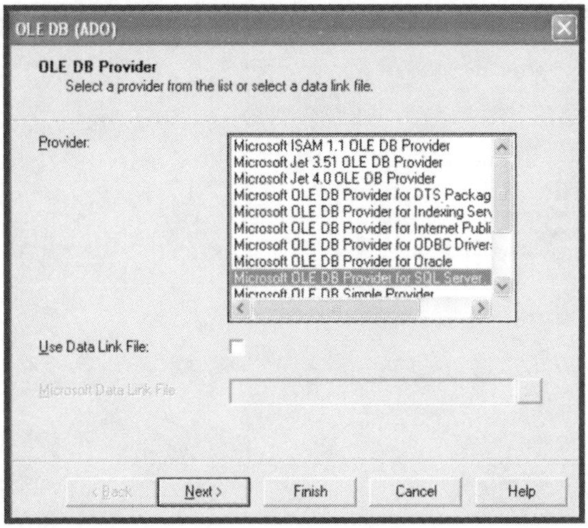

Figure 4.14

Selecting an OLE DB Provider.

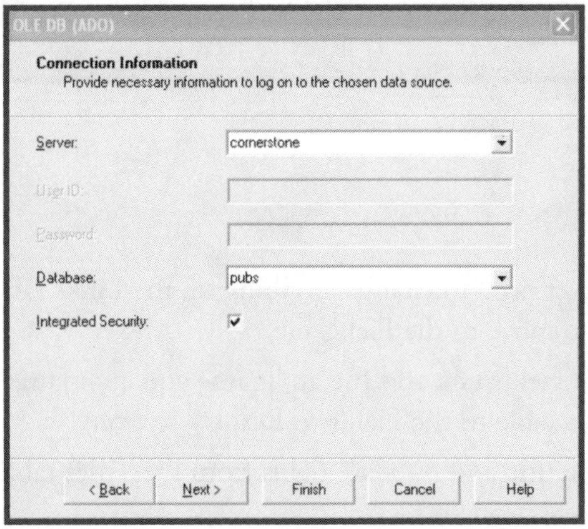

Figure 4.15

Setting database connection parameters.

15. Select Authors; then click on Insert Table to add the Authors table to the report.

16. Select Titleauthor; then click on Insert Table to add the Titleauthor table to the report.

17. Select Titles; then click on Insert Table to add the Titles table to the report. The Standard Report Expert should now look like Figure 4.16.

18. Click on Next to move to the Links tab.

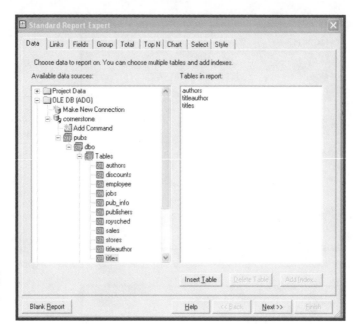

Figure 4.16

Selecting tables to
use in your report.

19. You don't need to change anything on the Links tab, so click Next again to move to the Fields tab.

20. On the Fields tab, add the au_lname and au_fname fields from the Authors table to the Fields to Display section.

21. Add the title and pubdate fields from the Titles table to the Fields to Display section.

22. One at a time, select each field in the Fields to Display section and change the Column Heading at the bottom of the dialog box to something more appropriate for each field. Figure 4.17 shows the completed Fields tab of the Standard Report Export dialog box.

23. Click on Next to move to the Group tab.

24. Add the Report Fields authors.au_lname and authors.au_fname to the Group By section. See Figure 4.18 for the Group By fields.

25. You don't need to do anything on the Total, Top N, Chart, or Select tabs, so click on the Style tab to go to the last step of the Standard Report Expert.

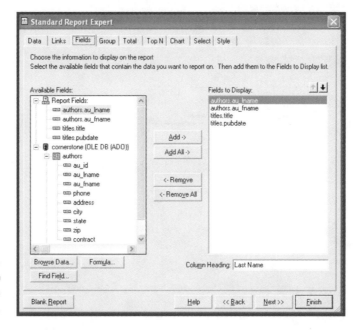

Figure 4.17

Adding fields to
your report.

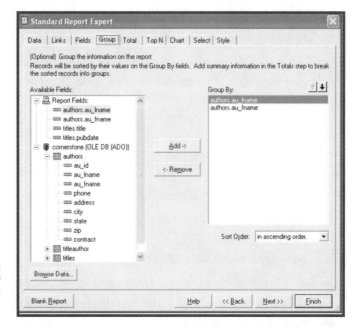

Figure 4.18

Picking the fields to
group by.

26. Set the title of the report to Authors and Titles.

27. Select Leading Break for the report style, as shown in Figure 4.19.

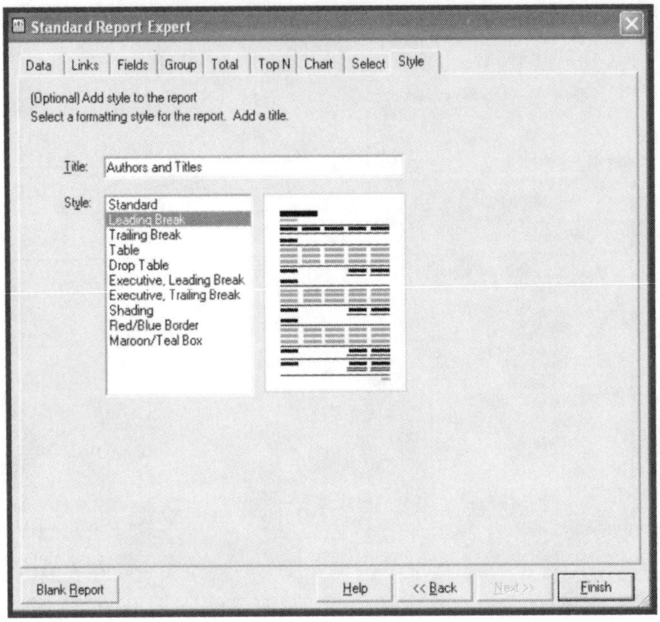

Figure 4.19

Adding the finishing touches to your report.

28. Click Finish to complete the Standard Report Expert.

That's it! You now have the AuthorTitles report available in the Solution Explorer window. And to think—it only took 28 steps!

Viewing Reports

Now that you have a report, let me show you how you can display it to your users. This isn't nearly as involved as creating the report, so don't worry. In just a few more minutes, you'll see the report onscreen.

1. Right-click on Form1.vb in the Solution Explorer and select View Designer.
2. Change the forms WindowState property to Maximized.
3. Add a CrystalReportViewer from the Toolbox to your form.
4. Change the Dock property of CrystalReportViewer1 to Fill.
5. Click on AuthorTitles.rpt in the Solution Explorer to display the Reports properties.

6. Double-click on the value of the Full Path property to select the path to the report.

7. Press Ctrl+C to copy the report path to the Clipboard.

8. Click on CrystalReportViewer1 on the form to display the Report viewer properties again.

9. Select Browse from the drop-down list of the ReportSource property.

10. Click in the File Name area, and then press Ctrl+V to paste the report path from the Clipboard.

11. Select Open.

Your Visual Studio IDE should now look similar to Figure 4.20. Run your application to view the fruit of all your hard work. The result should look remarkably like Figure 4.21. From your application, you can zoom, print, and even export your report thanks to the CrystalReportViewer control. I suggest you try to create some of the other types of reports using the available Experts.

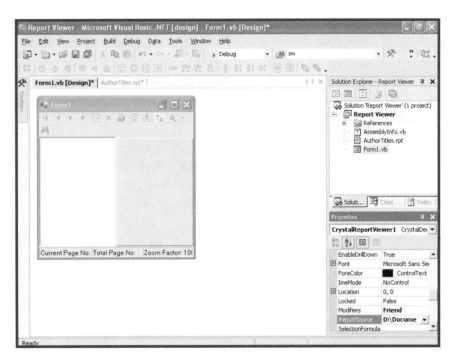

Figure 4.20

Finishing up Report Viewer.

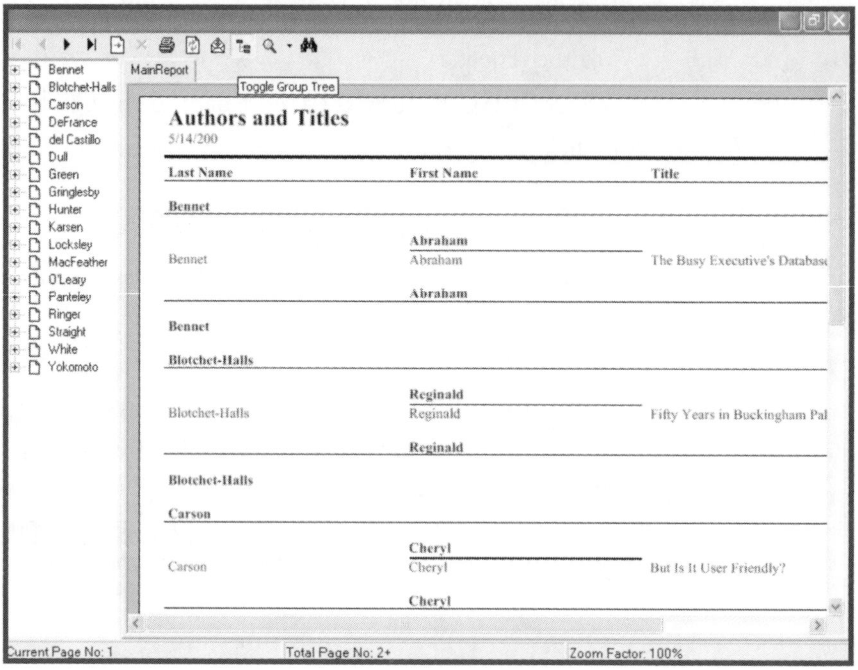

Figure 4.21

Viewing your report.

I hope your boss is happy now!

What's Next

Finally, it's time to sleep. You had better rest well, because tomorrow you will be tackling developing for the Web. You will learn about creating applications for the Web as well as Web services. You will also see how to apply some professional techniques and best practices that have stood the test of time.

Creating Web Applications

- ➤ A brief history of the Internet and Internet programming
- ➤ Introducing ASP.NET
- ➤ Web forms and controls
- ➤ Configuration and state management

I t's Sunday morning, and hopefully you've enjoyed a well-deserved night of rest. I trust that you put your head on the pillow late last night and pondered the possibilities of all things .NET and the wonderful uses for the technology. This is your third and last day of the .NET boot camp—tomorrow you will be able to proudly re-enter the work force with a new arsenal under your arm.

On Friday evening, I showed you what .NET was and how VB.NET fit into the picture. You learned the basics of the .NET platform and what was new in VB.NET. You learned how the .NET Framework helped out the development process and how it compared to other available platforms. Hopefully, your head did not blow up as in *Scanners*.

Yesterday, you learned how to build Windows applications using VB.NET's Windows Forms technology. You learned some basics of the VB.NET language and some object-oriented concepts. Last night, you learned how to use VB.NET to access files, databases, and reports. With all that, you might find your head spinning like Linda Blair's in *The Exorcist*. Hang on—there's more. . . .

Most of today will focus on building Web applications (this session) and Web services (the next session). You will be amazed at how easy Visual Studio .NET makes it to create great Web applications. So hang on—here we go!

Overview

In this session, you'll be learning about Microsoft's new flavor of Active Server Pages (ASP)—ASP.NET. There are many powerful features of this technology, and this session will only serve as an introduction to the core features. Whether you come from a "classic" ASP background or this is your first introduction to Web development, there is something in this session for you.

Before we dig too deeply into ASP.NET, I need to give those of you who are new to all of this a short background on the history of the Internet and ASP technology. If you have been doing Web development for a while and are familiar with classic ASP development with Visual InterDev, then you can skip this next section and move on to the "Enter ASP.NET" section.

A Brief History of the Internet

For those of you who are new to all of this, pay close attention and please don't skip this section: It will help you understand how ASP.NET fits in with the "big picture" of the Internet. So that you can better understand all these new technologies and concepts I will be presenting, I'm going to give you a little background on just how we arrived to this point. To give a detailed account of the entire history of the Internet would be beyond the scope of this book (and we only have a weekend—not a year to complete it!). So, in this section, you'll get the "Cliff Notes" version of how we arrived at this point. Thankfully, I've been in touch with Al Gore recently and he's been kind enough to sum things up for me quite nicely. So, here goes. . . .

Way back when flower children were abundant on street corners and the Beatles were still together (the 1960s, for those of you who missed that generation), the beginnings of the Internet were conceived. It all began back with the Department of Defense. Yep, you can blame them for just about everything. You see, they had a division called the Advanced Research Project Agency (ARPA) that had a need to share information among their advanced "supercomputers" (which, by the way, were almost as powerful as the computers embedded in today's advanced child's wristwatch). To share this information, a small network called ARPANET was created. Initially, four universities were connected to ARPANET, but it quickly grew, and by the early 1970s, there were more than 20 computers connected. Whew, talk about your bandwidth problems. . . .

Obviously, with the plethora of new computers being attached to this mega-network, standards needed to be created. Fortunately, a gentleman by the name of Vinton Cerf came along and helped form the InterNetworking Working Group (INWG). Vinton has since commonly become known as the "Father of the Internet." For those of you who are just now finding this out and are quite surprised that the "Father of the Internet" is not in fact Al Gore, please take a moment to browse your local Yellow Pages to find a suitable surgeon to perform an emergency lobotomy.

By the late 1970s and early 1980s, ARPANET had gone commercial (talk about your sell-outs!), and it had a whopping 200+ host computers connected to it. A team of programmers and scientists created TCP/IP in the early 1980s, and it soon became the de facto standard for communication. Somewhere early in the decade, the term *Internet* was coined and it soon caught on. Then, thanks to the PC revolution and the explosion of popularity during the 1980s, more and more corporations connected themselves to this new "Internet Superhighway." By the late 1980s, more than 100,000 host computers were connected to this new Internet, and e-mail and newsgroup (USENET) access was becoming more commonplace.

In the early 1990s, hypertext evolved rapidly and the World Wide Web (WWW) was born. A team of programmers from the National Center for Supercomputing Applications (NCSA) created the world's first browser—Mosaic. By the mid-1990s, more than 10 million computers were connected to the Internet, and the floodgates had swung wide open. It was at this time that companies soon discovered what the Internet was and how it could be used. Large computer companies started to take a serious look at the Internet, and the Web tool revolution had begun. Sun Microsystems, seeing a deficiency in the plain old static Hypertext Markup Language (HTML), invented Java to help beef up Web sites and provide a one-stop shop for development.

By the late 1990s, hundreds of millions of computers were hooked up to the Internet. Virtually every company had a Web site (under construction, of course!), and almost everyone from every nation worldwide was able to communicate with each other via e-mail, chatting, and instant messaging programs. The advent of the Internet had changed the way that we all work—in many ways, improving our productivity and communication.

Today, the effects of the Internet on global life in general cannot be underestimated. In most ways, it has proved a positive catalyst in many success stories. Yes, there are ways that the Internet is currently being exploited for bad things, but most of the Internet is positive, especially for corporations, schools, and people who demand information at their fingertips.

Now that you have had a little history lesson on the Internet, you might be wondering what all this mayhem looked like from a programmer's perspective. The next section will talk about just that and how it relates to how we arrived at ASP.NET.

A Brief History of Internet Programming

In the beginning of the WWW revolution, programmers were limited to static HTML as the only option for the display of information via the Internet. Almost every Web page created during the beginnings of the Internet contained very simple static Web pages that were a "one-way" street: They only provided simple informational content, and they certainly were not very interactive. About the only interaction a typical user got was being able to click on a hyperlink and have it go to another page or possibly e-mail someone. Whoa, be still my beating heart! I'm sure most of us who were around then remember the day that we received the inevitable call from our best friend, asking if we could please type in the Uniform Resource Locator (URL) of her newly created cool home page. After you browsed to the location, I'm sure you all lied (like I did) by saying that you *liked* her new page and it was indeed the coolest thing you'd ever seen. Let's face it: At this point in Internet history, although being able to read content from anywhere via your computer was somewhat cool, its usefulness was limited.

During the 1990s, as browsers matured and the Internet technologies (Java, JavaScript, and so on) grew more powerful, people found ways to exploit certain technologies to make their Web sites more interactive and useful. Instead of just browsing to sites with static content, we were greeted with new streams of coolness due to the plethora of comment forms, guest books, and cool new applets. New technologies such as Common Gateway Interface (CGI) were introduced that brought an entirely new set of functionality to the browser interface. CGI applications and scripts could be written in a number of different languages and allowed the client application that was running in a Web browser to communicate with the Web server. Now, the text input from a form within the browser could be interpreted and rendered by the Web server in an intelligent way.

With the advent of these technologies, new uses for the Internet and the World Wide Web were conceived, and a new set of Web sites was born that supported increased levels of interaction. Some sites even introduced the idea of electronic commerce (e-commerce), allowing financial transactions to take place over the Internet. Trust me—it was a big step for many individuals to begin to use the Internet in this manner. It seemed that everyone was a bit leery (with good reason) about giving out credit card information over the Internet. Nevertheless, some true pioneers shined in this arena, taking the Internet to the next level and raising the bar. In some cases, companies dared to offer dynamic content—that is, Web sites that went beyond interaction and delved into exciting new realms, such as creating customized user content based on the user's preferences or past purchasing history.

With all the great things that CGI brought to the table, serious issues still existed. First, performance was an issue. The technology didn't scale well because it required new instances of applications for each session. This tended to bog down Web servers quickly. Second, it wasn't very flexible and didn't allow Web administrators to configure their Web servers for better performance. In addition, many of the CGI solutions created were based on scripting languages (such as Perl); therefore, they were interpreted in nature. This tended to slow things down even more. There was definitely a need for change.

Microsoft saw the need for this and came up with the Internet Server Application Programming Interface (ISAPI). This new technology offered some great improvements over CGI. First, there was the scalability: ISAPI allowed a program to be loaded once (as a DLL) and used simultaneously over and over again, thereby relieving the Web server of the load-management issues that had previously existed with CGI. Second, ISAPI applications were created with a compiled language, such as C, C++, or Delphi, and performed better than their scripted CGI counterparts. Third, there were more configuration options with ISAPI over CGI.

With all of these improvements, one would think that almost everyone would have jumped the CGI bandwagon in favor of the greener pastures that ISAPI offered. Well, this is certainly what Microsoft was hoping, but it obviously didn't happen for many reasons. First, ISAPI was supported only on Microsoft platforms. Many Web developers did not like (or trust) Microsoft as a Web server solution and were instead quite content using a Unix- or Linux-based Web server. Second, ISAPI applications were harder to create and introduced much more complexity than CGI programmers were used to having to deal with.

This is where Active Server Pages (ASP) entered the picture. In 1996, Microsoft introduced ASP technology to leverage current Internet technologies and provide a better, easier way to create dynamic interactive Web sites. The basic idea was this: By augmenting the IIS Web server with a "smart" interpreter, the Web server could interpret and process HTML pages in an intelligent way instead of just serving up plain old HTML files. ASP files were simple HTML files with embedded tags, directives, and scripts that the extensions that were running on the Web server interpreted. To best illustrate this, let's look at an example of Classic ASP. For example, consider the following ASP source code:

```
<HTML>
<TITLE>
Classic ASP Example
</TITLE>
<BODY>
<H1>
The current date is <%=Date%>
</H1>
</BODY>
</HTML>
```

For those of you who are familiar with HTML, you'll recognize most of the preceding code. Take a look at the line that says this:

```
The current date is <%=Date%>
```

You might have noticed the strange presence of the <%=Date%> statement. This is where the ASP rendering engine enters the picture. When the Web server processes this Web page, it replaces the <%=Date%> with the current system date on the Web server's machine. Figure 5.1 shows what the output looks like from a typical Web browser viewpoint.

Looking at the source code that is presented in the browser, we see this:

```
<HTML>
<TITLE>
Classic ASP Example
</TITLE>
<BODY>
<H1>
The current date is 5/23/2002
</H1>
</BODY>
</HTML>
```

The Web server processed the original ASP page, and only the resultant HTML code was presented to the Web browser. This is part of the magic of

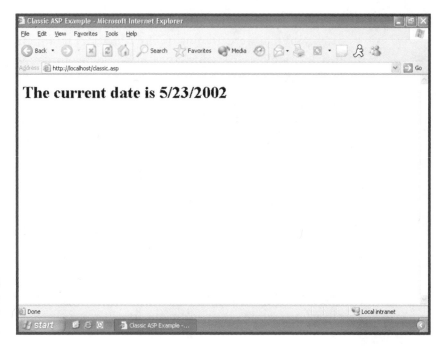

Figure 5.1

Output from a classic ASP application.

ASP: It allows you to easily create dynamic HTML code and leverage powerful server-side technologies to create truly interactive and powerful Web sites. Although this example shows only a simplistic view of the classic ASP technology, the rest of the ASP world operates in roughly the same fashion.

So, with ASP being the hottest thing in Web development since ARPANET (big grin), why didn't everyone jump on board and create ASP pages? Well, to answer this question simply, many people actually did, and that eventually led to problems. You see, many corporate development shops seized the day and the opportunity to implement ASP in their enterprise applications and Web sites. Because these sites lent themselves to a lot of code and complexity, ASP was tasked tremendously to keep up with the needs and demands of the typical corporate developer.

There were two primary problems with the original "classic" ASP approach. First, almost all of the HTML, scripting, and business logic was done in one file per Web page—and some Web pages were quite complex and needed a ton of code. One problem with this all-in-one approach was that the code contained within the page tended to be *spaghetti code*—that is, it was almost impossible to implement large portions of HTML, scripting, and business code all within one file in a neatly organized way. Because these files tended to become huge, this led to a second problem: performance. Traditional ASP code was interpreted and not compiled; therefore, the larger the ASP page, the longer it took the Web server to process.

ASP technology, because it was built directly upon the traditional HTML model, was not object oriented. It followed a top-down programming model instead of the OOP model. You could not access objects in a Web page in an object-oriented fashion. The scripts within a page, while structured in nature, were far from object oriented. Because of this and partly to increase performance and enhance functionality, developers soon started to place most of their business logic and code in server-side COM components. ASP pages could readily utilize these components without requiring fancy client-side configuration (as was the case with client-side COM controls). This, however, had two big drawbacks. First, upgrading and repairing COM components on the server side was a nasty process. It often required the developer to restart the Web server or MTS service. Of course, if you had several servers, this got old real quick. Second, only late binding was supported for COM components. This led to erroneous errors on many programmers' part (not mine, of course—big, big grin).

In addition, the development and debugging tools that were available for traditional ASP were much less than desirable. Microsoft shipped Visual InterDev, the "native" development tool for ASP, which loosely resembled the Visual Basic development environment way back in 1996. Although this environment was fairly capable with regard to coding ASP applications, it left a lot to be desired with regard to HTML and page layout issues. Debugging an ASP application was tough and was only made more complex if you had the fortune (or misfortune, as some of you might recall it) of having COM components intermingled with all your HTML, JavaScript, VBScript, and various code elements.

Don't get me wrong—I'm not complaining. ASP was great in its day, and it was cool for a lot of things. I'm merely pointing out some of the shortcomings of the traditional ASP model so that you can get an idea of where ASP is coming from and what ASP.NET brings to the table. Yes, I wound up bruising my head while banging it on my desk numerous times, and I threw quite a few neighborhood computer book burning parties, but because of ASP.NET, it's all okay now. Speaking of ASP.NET, let's take a look at what's new. . . .

Enter ASP.NET

Now that you have an idea of what the Internet is and where we have come from (both from a user's standpoint and a developer's standpoint), let's take a look at what ASP.NET offers. ASP.NET excels over previous implementations in several areas:

➤ **Easier to build.** ASP.NET is built on the .NET Framework, and it's 100 percent object oriented from the ground up. Because of the high level of code reuse and other advanced features, the amount of code required to build enterprise-scale applications is dramatically lower than in previous versions. No longer are you forced into a single-page spaghetti-infested solution; now there is *code behind*, a new technology that allows you to separate your user interface code from your business process code. Code behind also implements a clean event-driven interface model. Database integration is easier, too, as is user validation.

➤ **Easier to debug.** Because all of your code is readily accessible from within the Visual Studio .NET environment (Web pages, server components, Web services, and so on), debugging is *much* easier. You can now code, test, and deploy an entire application from within one environment.

➤ **Easier to deploy and maintain.** New deployment and configuration options exist that make it easy to put your debugged application into a production environment. No longer do you have to stop and restart crucial server-side processes.

➤ **Faster.** Gone are the days of interpreted scripts. Because ASP.NET is built on the .NET Framework, your server-side code is compiled and not interpreted. This results in dramatic increases in performance.

➤ **More reliable and scalable.** The new ASP.NET server extensions are smarter, keeping a watchful eye on your applications. If one of them "misbehaves" or starts to exhibit unwanted behavior, it is restarted automatically. In addition, ASP.NET applications are more scalable with support for *Web farms* (multiple machines working together as one Web server) and *Web gardens* (multiple CPUs in one machine).

For those of you who are just getting a start on Web development, consider yourselves lucky to have entered at just the right time. Those of us who have been doing Web development for years using ASP or other technologies have paved a path of suffering and frustration, and it is because of the development community's feedback that all these advances have been made. For those of you who have been using ASP for Web development, you will surely welcome all these changes and want to seriously consider upgrading to ASP.NET.

Web Forms

It has been said that one quick way to teach a person how to swim is to throw him into the water and make him tread water for a little while. Rest assured—people who learn to swim this way will be up to speed quickly and, although their skills might not be perfect, they'll know the basics. That being said, I'm giving you fair warning that what we are embarking on next is just that: We're going to jump into the water and learn to swim. Of course, your life will not be at stake in this scenario, but if you're not careful, you might find your career at stake. You see, ASP.NET makes Web development so easy that you might find yourself running out the door of your current employer and never turning back. You might find yourself discontent with the old way of creating Web applications. You might find yourself feeling all tingly inside, ready to take on any new challenge that awaits you. Don't say I didn't warn you. . . .

NOTE Before we dive headfirst into all things ASP.NET, make sure you have the bare minimum software installed. You'll need at least the .NET Framework runtime, the .NET Framework SDK, and Internet Information Server (IIS) 5.0 installed on your machine. If you have Windows 2000 or XP, you should already have IIS installed. Although Visual Studio .NET is theoretically not required to do .NET development, we are using it for our examples in this chapter, so you should also have Visual Studio .NET installed. If you have this installed, you automatically have all the .NET Framework requirements met.

Also note that the Visual Studio .NET environment includes a lot of useful tools that are visible by default. To save screen space and to make figures fit into the required 800 × 600 size for this book, I have purposely hidden some tools, such as the Toolbox, the Server Explorer, and other various tools. If your screen doesn't look exactly like mine, don't worry—nothing's wrong. I've simply hidden some tools in the environment to enhance and accentuate the important visual aspects of the items being addressed.

The Ubiquitous HelloWorld Example

Let's begin by starting up Visual Studio .NET. From the Start page, click on the New Project button (see Figure 5.2).

After you have clicked on the New Project button, you are presented with the New Project dialog box. Select Visual Basic Projects as the Project Type and ASP.NET Web Application as the Project Template. Type in the location as `http://localhost/LearnVB/HelloWorld`. Your completed dialog box should look like the one in Figure 5.3.

Clicking on the OK button causes Visual Studio .NET to do several things. First, it creates both a physical directory under your Web server's root directory (typically \Inetpub\wwwroot) and a virtual Web server directory called HelloWorld. For the purposes of all the examples in this chapter, each example is being created under a LearnVB "home" directory. This helps you distinguish which projects belong to this book versus other projects you might have from other sources.

After a few seconds, you will be presented with a new Web Form designer page. Visual Studio .NET will have created a new Solution and Project

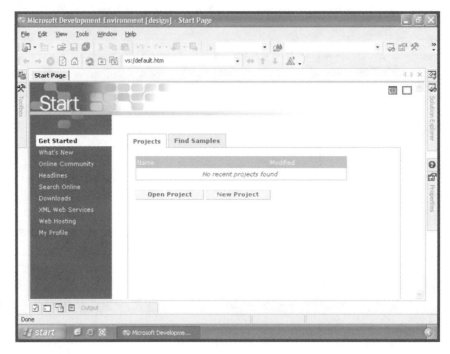

Figure 5.2

The Visual Studio .NET Start page.

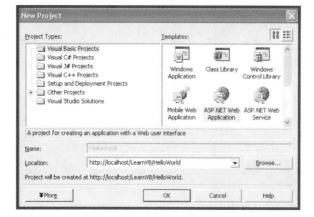

Figure 5.3

The New Project
dialog box.

named HelloWorld. Visual Studio .NET also will have created several other files with your new project, including AssemblyInfo.vb, Global.asax, HelloWorld.vsdisco, Styles.css, Web.config, and WebForm1.aspx. For now, don't worry about what each of these files is—I will explain them later in this chapter.

On the left side of the Visual Studio .NET environment, you'll notice a window titled Toolbox. Note that if you have the "Auto Hide" feature turned on, this window might be hidden. To show it, simply hover the mouse over the far left side of the main Environment window. The Toolbox contains several labeled tabs in it. Each of these tabs represents a different group of controls that we can use within our Web applications. For now, we're going to look at the Web Forms tab. If it is not already selected, click on it with the mouse. You'll see several controls on this tab, as shown in Figure 5.4.

Next, double-click on the first three controls in the Toolbox: a Label control, a TextBox control, and a Button control. Your Web Form designer page should now have three controls added to it: Label1, TextBox1, and Button1. Now, double-click on the Label control in the Toolbox once more to create yet another label: Label2. Your Web Form should now have four controls added to it.

Now we will do some rearranging. First, point the mouse to each control and click on it. Then spread them out on the page toward the bottom. Doing so frees up the space at the top of the page so that we can build our form. Next, put Label1 in the upper-left corner of the Web Form. Do this by clicking on and dragging it to the upper-left side. Next, put the TextBox1 control

Figure 5.4

The Toolbox
window with the
Web Forms tab
shown.

directly to the right of Label1. Put the Button1 control directly to the right
of TextBox1. Put the Label2 control directly below TextBox1. Finally, click
on Label2 and resize it to make the right side flush with the Button1 control. You resize the control by hovering the mouse over the side of the control you want to resize (in this case the right side) until the cursor turns into
a double-pointed arrow. Then click the left mouse button and drag the
selected control to the right until it is sized properly. Your newly created Web
Form should now look similar to Figure 5.5.

Next, we will change some properties of the controls on your new Web
Form. Controls are objects, so they have properties and methods just like any
other object in Visual Basic .NET. Notice on the lower-right side of your
environment that you have a Properties window. (Once again, this window
might be auto-hidden. If it is, unhide it by scrolling the mouse over to the
right side of the environment.) Click on the Label1 control. The Properties
window will list all the properties of Label1, as in Figure 5.6.

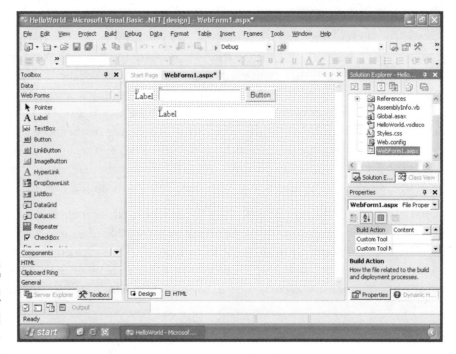

Figure 5.5

The beginnings of a new ASP.NET HelloWorld application.

Figure 5.6

The Properties window with the properties of Label1 shown.

Changing a control's properties is easy: You simply click the mouse on the control and select the property you want to change. In this case, let's click on Label1 and change its Text property to say Name:. You might have to scroll down slightly in the Properties window to see the Text property. Next, click on the Web Form and change its Title property to say Hello, world! Then click on Button1 and set its Text property to Say Hello. Last, right-click on the WebForm1.aspx file in the Solution Explorer and select Rename from the pop-up menu. Rename the file to default.aspx. Now save your work by selecting the Save All menu item from the File menu. This will save all the files in the project. Your new Web Form should now look like Figure 5.7.

Now, get ready for a big step: Double-click on the Button1 control. This will put you in the code editor, ready to edit the code behind your new Web Form. By default, Visual Studio .NET has created a new Sub for you named Button1_Click. Those of you who are familiar with other similar environments, such as Visual Basic 6 and Delphi, will be comfortable with what

Start button

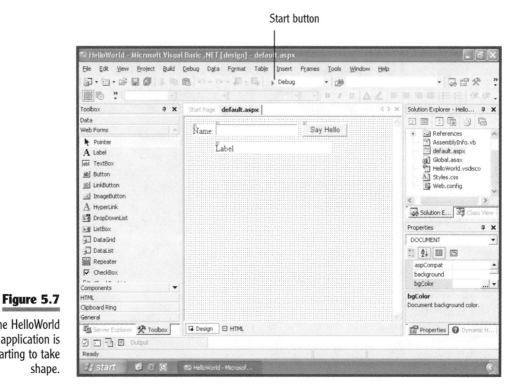

Figure 5.7

The HelloWorld Web application is starting to take shape.

you're seeing right now. For now, don't worry about all the other strange code that you see surrounding your new `Button1_Click` subroutine. Instead, type the following into the code editor:

```
Label2.Text = "Hello, " & TextBox1.Text & "!"
```

Next, select Save All again from the File menu and get ready to rumble! Your last step for this introductory lesson is to run the application. You do this by selecting the Start menu item from the Debug menu or pressing the Start button on the toolbar. (See the blue button in the top middle of Figure 5.7.) Pressing the Start button causes Visual Studio .NET to build your new project and launch Internet Explorer to run it. At startup, your new browser session should look like Figure 5.8.

Next, give your new Web application a run for its money: Enter your name into the text box and click the Say Hello button. Go ahead; try it again with a different name. Try it 100 more times (okay, maybe not 100—just a few). Close the browser window to return to the development environment.

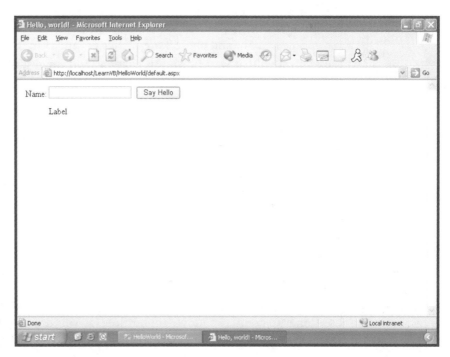

Figure 5.8

The HelloWorld Web application running in the Internet Explorer Web browser.

NOTE You do not have to run Internet Explorer to see your Web page. A simple way to do it from within the environment is to right-click the main Web page (in this case, default.aspx) and select View in Browser from the pop-up menu. This opens an instance of Internet Explorer within the Visual Studio .NET environment and allows you to run and test your code without having to leave the IDE.

Next, run Internet Explorer again (from Windows this time) and type the following URL: `http://localhost/LearnVB/HelloWorld/default.aspx`. Press Enter or click on the Go button in the browser and you will see that your application runs outside of the Visual Studio .NET environment as well. As one last "experiment," select the Source menu item from the View menu in Internet Explorer. (Alternatively, right-click on the page and select View Source from the pop-up menu.) This will show you the HTML that the Web server generated. Go ahead and look at it.

Don't worry about the details of the HTML source right now—we'll take that apart and examine it later. For now, just sit back and marvel at what you have just accomplished: You have just succeeded in creating your first ASP.NET Web application. Now all that's left to do is to call your boss and let him know that you won't be showing up to work on Monday because you have seen the light and are seeking higher ground. On second thought, perhaps you should at least finish this chapter (and the rest of the book!) before embarking on such aggressive behavior.

You have just witnessed how easy it is to create Web applications utilizing Visual Studio .NET, Visual Basic .NET, and ASP.NET technologies. If you are coming from an older legacy Web application development environment, you are now appreciating just what this new exciting development alternative brings to the table. With older technologies, creating Web applications often tended to be a tedious, complex ordeal. ASP.NET protects you, the developer, from all the mundane details behind the scenes and makes your life easier by allowing you to exploit all the benefits of Rapid Application Development (RAD) for the Web. Yes, this technology is truly revolutionary and will change the way Web applications are created now and for the future.

You might have noticed that creating a Web application is just as easy as creating a standard Windows application (as you did yesterday morning in the Saturday Morning session). Visual Studio .NET has made it easy by allowing you to use the same basic principles of Windows development (using controls from the Toolbox, using a form designer and code editor, changing object properties and methods, and so on). The basic steps are similar in concept and implementation.

Before we go too much further, however, you might be wondering what just happened and what's really going on behind all this technology. So, let's take a look at the example "under the hood" and see what makes it tick. First of all, you'll notice that the main form is named WebForm1.aspx. ASP.NET uses the aspx extension for all Web Forms. Those of you who are coming from a classic ASP background will notice that the extension for ASP applications has changed from asp to aspx.

Under the Hood of the HelloWorld Example

Go back to the development environment and click on the WebForm1.aspx file. You'll notice at the bottom that two additional tabs are available: Design and HTML. For the example, we used the Design tab to take advantage of the visual drag-and-drop interface and GUI ease of use. Now, click on the HTML tab to see the code behind the form, as in Figure 5.9.

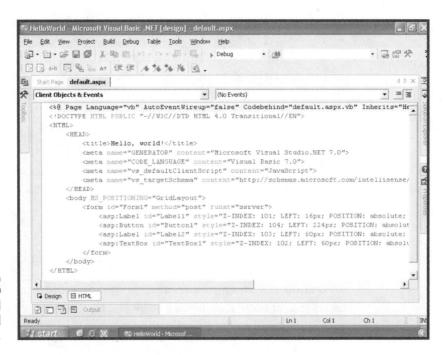

Figure 5.9

The HTML behind the HelloWorld Web Form.

The code you see should look similar to this (although some of it might appear to be formatted differently):

```
<%@ Page Language="vb" AutoEventWireup="false"
Codebehind="default.aspx.vb" Inherits="HelloWorld.WebForm1"%>
<!DOCTYPE HTML PUBLIC "-//W3C//DTD HTML 4.0 Transitional//EN">
<HTML>
    <HEAD>
        <title>Hello, world!</title>
        <meta name="GENERATOR"
        content="Microsoft Visual Studio.NET 7.0">
        <meta name="CODE_LANGUAGE" content="Visual Basic 7.0">
        <meta name="vs_defaultClientScript" content="JavaScript">
        <meta name="vs_targetSchema"
        content="http://schemas.microsoft.com/intellisense/ie5">
    </HEAD>
    <body MS_POSITIONING="GridLayout">
        <form id="Form1" method="post" runat="server">
            <asp:Label id="Label1" style="Z-INDEX: 101; LEFT: 16px;
            POSITION: absolute; TOP: 16px"
            runat="server">Name:</asp:Label>
            <asp:Button id="Button1" style="Z-INDEX: 104; LEFT: 224px;
            POSITION: absolute; TOP: 12px" runat="server"
            Text="Say Hello"></asp:Button>
            <asp:Label id="Label2" style="Z-INDEX: 103; LEFT: 60px;
            POSITION: absolute; TOP: 48px" runat="server"
            Width="216px">Label</asp:Label>
            <asp:TextBox id="TextBox1" style="Z-INDEX: 102;
            LEFT: 60px; POSITION: absolute; TOP: 12px"
            runat="server"></asp:TextBox>
        </form>
    </body>
</HTML>
```

For those of you who have coded HTML documents before, some of this will look familiar. What you see is basic HTML, marked up with some key tags, directives, and attributes that are meaningful to the Web server. Let's take a look at these statements line by line to see what they mean. First, there is the line at the top of the HTML document:

```
<%@ Page Language="vb" AutoEventWireup="false"
Codebehind="default.aspx.vb" Inherits="HelloWorld.WebForm1"%>
```

Statements that appear between the <% and %> delimiters are statements that ASP.NET processes on the Web server. On this first line, we encounter one directive and several attributes. A directive defines special behavior that is meaningful to certain sections of an ASP.NET Web page. The directive used on this first line is the Page directive, which defines attributes that are specific only to this Web page. The first attribute is the Language attribute, which is set to "vb". This tells the Web server what language is to be used when compiling server-side code. The next attribute is AutoEventWireup, which is used to automatically enable or disable events on the page. The CodeBehind attribute is next, and it is used to specify the file name that contains the code behind the Web Form. Finally, the Inherits attribute tells what class this Web page inherits from. Note that because you didn't change the default class name, it is still using the default class name that it created for you (WebForm1).

The next line in the HTML document specifies the HTML document type and version information:

```
<!DOCTYPE HTML PUBLIC "-//W3C//DTD HTML 4.0 Transitional//EN">
```

For now, we'll skip expounding on this because it is beyond the scope of this book. (It lends itself more to an HTML book explanation than to an ASP.NET book explanation.) Next, we see the HTML header and metadata elements:

```
<HTML>
    <HEAD>
        <title>Hello, world!</title>
        <meta name="GENERATOR"
        content="Microsoft Visual Studio.NET 7.0">
        <meta name="CODE_LANGUAGE" content="Visual Basic 7.0">
        <meta name="vs_defaultClientScript" content="JavaScript">
        <meta name="vs_targetSchema"
        content="http://schemas.microsoft.com/intellisense/ie5">
    </HEAD>
```

The title of our Web page is "Hello, world!", as shown above. The GENERATOR metadata tag gives the name of the creator of the document. In this case, it's Visual Studio .NET version 7.0. The next metadata tag is CODE_LANGUAGE, which tells the language used behind this Web page (Visual Basic 7.0—and you thought it was Visual Basic .NET! Big grin). The next metadata tag is named vs_defaultClientScript and is used to signify the default client scripting language used in the Web page.

NOTE By default, Visual Studio .NET creates documents that use JavaScript on the client side. This is because both Internet Explorer and Netscape support JavaScript. You can change the tag's attribute to "VBScript" to code Visual Basic Script on the client side, but your applications will only be able to run in Internet Explorer because Netscape does not natively support Visual Basic scripting. I recommend leaving the default as JavaScript unless you are sure your application will only be used with Internet Explorer or you are much more comfortable with a VBScript solution over a JavaScript solution.

The final metadata tag that is present in the HTML page header is the vs_targetSchema tag, which is used to signify the target browser for this page. In this case, Internet Explorer 5 is the default target. You can change this setting by altering the targetSchema property of the Web page.

Next, let's examine the body section of the Web page:

```
<body MS_POSITIONING="GridLayout">
   <form id="Form1" method="post" runat="server">
      <asp:Label id="Label1" style="Z-INDEX: 101; LEFT: 12px;
      POSITION: absolute; TOP: 16px"
      runat="server">Name:</asp:Label>
      <asp:Label id="Label2" style="Z-INDEX: 104; LEFT: 60px;
      POSITION: absolute; TOP: 44px"
      runat="server" Width="220px">Label</asp:Label>
      <asp:Button id="Button1" style="Z-INDEX: 103; LEFT: 224px;
      POSITION: absolute; TOP: 12px" runat="server"
      Text="Say Hello"></asp:Button>
      <asp:TextBox id="TextBox1" style="Z-INDEX: 102; LEFT: 60px;
      POSITION: absolute; TOP: 12px" runat="server"></asp:TextBox>
   </form>
</body>
```

The MS_POSITIONING attribute signifies the element positioning preferences for the Web page. The possible values are GridLayout (the default for Web

Forms created by Visual Studio .NET) and FlowLayout. I recommend sticking with the GridLayout setting.

Finally, the four controls that were created appear with their own asp prefixes. Each of these controls has its own attributes assigned to it. I won't expound on each and every attribute at this point—most of the properties are self-explanatory. The one attribute that is worth explaining is the runat attribute, which is set to "server." This attribute signifies that this control is a Web Server control; that is, it is a rich control with many more properties and more robust functionality than standard HTML control equivalents.

With ASP.NET, you have your choice of using Web Server controls or standard HTML controls. You'll recall that in Figure 5.4, I showed you the Toolbox with the Web Forms tab shown. This tab shows the Web Server controls that are available for you to use on your ASP.NET Web Forms. If you do not need the full functionality or all the properties of the Web Server controls, ASP.NET gives you a choice. Instead of using the Web Server controls, you can use the HTML Server controls, as shown on the HTML tab of the Toolbox window in Figure 5.10.

Figure 5.10

The HTML tab of the Toolbox window.

NOTE
Use HTML Server controls when advanced functionality is not needed. That is, when you are merely displaying static text or performing trivial tasks, HTML controls might do; however, when you need advanced functionality, such as event-driven programming support and data binding support, you need to use the Web Server controls instead. In general, when you need programmatic support, use Web Server controls. Otherwise, you might be able to use standard HTML Server controls.

To convert a control from an HTML Server control to a Web Server control, simply select that control and right-click the mouse. Then, choose the Run as Server Control pop-up menu item to convert the control to a Web Server control.

Next, let's take a look at the code behind the Web Form. Go back to the Visual Studio .NET environment and select the default.aspx.vb tab. You should now see the code behind your Web Form, as shown in Figure 5.11.

Notice the strange outlining that Visual Studio .NET has provided. It actually gives you the option to hide regions of code that you're not working on, allowing you to collapse and expand portions of code on demand. Okay, so

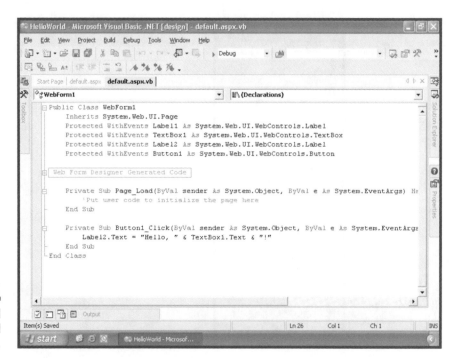

Figure 5.11

The code behind
the HelloWorld
Web Form.

when I first saw this, I was blown away, but now I'm totally addicted to it—it's very cool. The environment automatically hides regions of code that Visual Studio .NET auto-generates. To see this code, simply click on the plus sign on the left side of the code editor where the code outlining is shown. Doing so provides a full view of the complete source code behind the Web Form, as shown here:

```
Public Class WebForm1
    Inherits System.Web.UI.Page
    Protected WithEvents Label1 As System.Web.UI.WebControls.Label
    Protected WithEvents TextBox1 As _
                            System.Web.UI.WebControls.TextBox
    Protected WithEvents Button1 As _
                                System.Web.UI.WebControls.Button
    Protected WithEvents Label2 As System.Web.UI.WebControls.Label

#Region " Web Form Designer Generated Code "

    'This call is required by the Web Form Designer.
    <System.Diagnostics.DebuggerStepThrough()> _
    Private Sub InitializeComponent()

    End Sub

    Private Sub Page_Init(ByVal sender As System.Object, _
                        ByVal e As System.EventArgs) _
                        Handles MyBase.Init
        'CODEGEN: This method call is required by
        'the Web Form Designer
        'Do not modify it using the code editor.
        InitializeComponent()
    End Sub

#End Region

    Private Sub Page_Load(ByVal sender As System.Object, _
                        ByVal e As System.EventArgs) _
                        Handles MyBase.Load
```

```
            'Put user code to initialize the page here
        End Sub

        Private Sub Button1_Click(ByVal sender As System.Object, _
                                ByVal e As System.EventArgs) _
                                Handles Button1.Click
            Label2.Text = "Hello, " & TextBox1.Text & "!"
        End Sub
End Class
```

The first thing you should notice when looking at the preceding code listing is that WebForm1 is actually a class. That's right, a *class*. For those of you who have been doing regular ASP for a while, not only do you have the separation of the HTML and the code in ASP.NET, but you get to do object-oriented programming as well! This long-awaited feature will certainly enhance the technology's popularity for the implementation of enterprise-scale applications.

The next line is this:

```
Inherits System.Web.UI.Page
```

Notice the keyword `Inherits`. This Web Form is inherited from the base Page class in the System.Web.UI namespace. Next are the declarations for the four controls:

```
Protected WithEvents Label1 As System.Web.UI.WebControls.Label
Protected WithEvents TextBox1 As System.Web.UI.WebControls.TextBox
Protected WithEvents Button1 As System.Web.UI.WebControls.Button
Protected WithEvents Label2 As System.Web.UI.WebControls.Label
```

Notice that each of these controls is an instance of a base class (Label, TextBox, and Button). Visual Studio .NET automatically generated the next section between the #Region and #End Region lines. You should not change the code between these regions because it might have adverse effects on your application. Finally, two subroutines are present:

```
Private Sub Page_Load(ByVal sender As System.Object, _
                        ByVal e As System.EventArgs) _
                        Handles MyBase.Load
    'Put user code to initialize the page here
```

```
End Sub

Private Sub Button1_Click(ByVal sender As System.Object, _
                         ByVal e As System.EventArgs) _
                         Handles Button1.Click
     Label2.Text = "Hello, " & TextBox1.Text & "!"
End Sub
```

These subroutines exemplify ASP.NET's native support for event-driven programming. This style of programming was commonplace in the Windows development arena, but it's relatively new to the world of Web development. We have already looked at the Button1_Click subroutine that handles the Click event of the Button1 object. You'll also notice that another subroutine is included by default: Page_Load. This is where you find code that is to be run each time the page is rendered for the client (the Web browser).

Take a Break

It's that time again. Get up, stretch, and fill your cup (or IV!) with your *poison du jour*—we've got a lot of work left to do. I'm sure you're somewhat intrigued by what you've seen so far, and perhaps you're chomping at the bit to get some more experience in with all that ASP.NET has to offer. For now, take 5 or 10 minutes to get that rigor mortis out of your system and start to ponder the possibilities of writing Web applications the .NET way—the *right* way. Next, we'll be taking a closer look at some of the controls that ASP.NET includes, and we'll see how you can use those controls to build great Web applications.

Taking a Closer Look at Controls

Now that you've been introduced to some controls (Label, TextBox, and Button), it's time to take a closer look at the different types of controls that ASP.NET supports and how you can use them in your application. ASP.NET provides you with built-in server controls, HTML controls, and controls that help with client-side validation of your Web Forms. In addition, you can create your own "user" controls to use and reuse in many applications.

Web Server Controls

Web Server controls are similar to the controls you use to create Windows Forms applications. They are rich controls with a lot of properties, methods, and events. They support advanced functionality, such as data binding, browser detection, and advanced look and feel options, among other things. Web Server controls can be identified by an asp tag in your source code, as follows:

```
<asp:control runat="server"/>
```

Table 5.1 presents the Web Server controls and their purpose.

TABLE 5.1 WEB SERVER CONTROLS	
Control	**Description**
Label	Displays text in a set location
TextBox	Input control for inputting text
Button	A push button control
LinkButton	A button with an embedded hyperlink
ImageButton	An image that responds to mouse clicks
HyperLink	A link to another Web page
DropDownList	Single-selection drop-down list
ListBox	Single- or multiple-selection list box
DataGrid	Displays a table of data from a data source
DataList	Displays a template-defined data-bound list
Repeater	A data-bound list that is based on a template
CheckBox	Allows selection of a True or False state

Control	Description
CheckBoxList	Multi-selection check box group
RadioButtonList	Single-selection radio button group
RadioButton	Single-selection radio button
Image	Displays an image
Panel	Used as a container for other controls
PlaceHolder	Used as a placeholder for dynamically added server controls
Calendar	Displays a single month of a year
AdRotator	Displays ad banners randomly from a fixed set
Table	Displays an HTML table
XML	Displays an XML document
Literal	Reserves a location on the page to display text
CrystalReportViewer	Displays a Crystal report

As usual, the best way for you to get a handle on Web Server controls is to dive in with some concrete examples. Although there is not enough room in this book to cover all the controls in depth, you can get a good head start by trying out a few controls and working your way through the rest. I suggest trying the examples given in this chapter and then doing some of your own experimenting with the different controls.

To start, make sure you have closed any open solutions. Then start a new ASP.NET project and name it `WebServerControls`. Like the previous example, put it under the http://localhost/LearnVB root. After you have created the project, rename the WebForm1.aspx file to `default.aspx`. Next, add the following controls to the newly created Web Form:

➤ Label   ➤ DropDownList

➤ TextBox   ➤ ListBox

➤ Button   ➤ CheckBoxList

➤ LinkButton   ➤ RadioButtonList

➤ HyperLink   ➤ Calendar

This example uses all of the preceding 10 controls. Make sure you space out the controls on the page so they don't overlap one another. Next, you'll set a lot of properties of the controls. Start by setting the Button control's `Text` property to `Test`. Set the LinkButton control's `Text` property to `Click Me`. Set the HyperLink control's `NavigateUrl` property to `http://localhost/LearnVB/HelloWorld/default.aspx`. Does that last one look familiar? Yes, you're linking your current project to your previous one.

Your new Web Form should look like Figure 5.12.

Next, you need to set up the properties for the DropDownList and the List-Box. First, do the DropDownList. Select it and look at the property list. Notice that it has an `Items` collection with an ellipsis next to it. Click on the ellipsis, and you'll see a ListItem Collection Editor Dialog Box, as shown in Figure 5.13.

This is the dialog box used to edit items in many controls, such as the DropDownList, ListBox, CheckBoxList, RadioButtonList, and more. Each member in the `Items` collection has its own properties, as shown in the previous figure. For now, use the dialog box to add the following four values: North, South, East, and West. Close the dialog box and, using the same technique, add the following values to the ListBox control: Visual Basic, C#, C++, J#, Delphi, COBOL, and FORTRAN. Select the first member of the collection (Visual Basic) and set its `Selected` property to `True`.

After having done the DropDownList and ListBox controls, the following two controls should be a piece of cake. Add the following items to the CheckBoxList control: Windows 98, Windows ME, and Windows XP. Add the following items to the RadioButtonList control: TextBox, CheckBoxList, and ListBox. Make sure that the `Selected` property for the TextBox item is set to `True`.

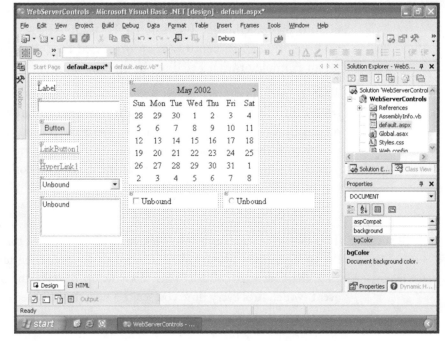

Figure 5.12

The WebServerControls Web Form (original format).

Figure 5.13

The ListItem Collection Editor dialog box.

Finally, right-click on the Calendar control and choose AutoFormat from the pop-up menu. Choose "Professional 1" as the selected style. Now you're ready to arrange the controls in an organized fashion. Look at Figure 5.14 for an example of what I've done in the way of layout.

There's only one more step left before you can test out all these server controls: Add a few lines of code to make it interesting. Start by double-clicking on the LinkButton control. Doing so opens the Visual Basic .NET editor, puts you in the code-behind source for your Web Form, and automatically generates a Click event handler for your LinkButton control. Enter the following code:

```
Label1.Text = "The link button was clicked."
```

This should be easy enough to understand. The code for this event simply sets the Text property of the Label1 control to the preceding text. Next, double-click the Calendar control. This sets you up to code the SelectionChanged event (which fires every time you select a new date). Enter the following code:

```
Label1.Text = Calendar1.SelectedDate
```

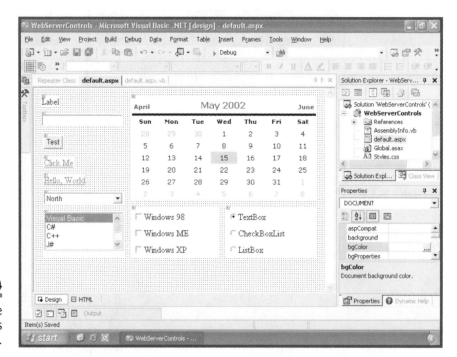

Figure 5.14

The layout of the WebServerControls Web Form.

This event simply sets the Text property for the Label1 control to the date selected on the calendar. Finally, double-click on the Button control and enter the following code:

```
Select Case RadioButtonList1.SelectedIndex
    Case 0
        Label1.Text = TextBox1.Text
    Case 1
        Dim OS As String
        Dim Ctr As Integer
        For Ctr = 0 To 2
            If CheckBoxList1.Items(Ctr).Selected = True Then
                If OS <> "" Then
                    OS = OS & ", "
                End If
                OS = OS & Right(CheckBoxList1.Items(Ctr).Text, 2)
            End If
        Next
        Label1.Text = OS
    Case 2
        Label1.Text = ListBox1.SelectedItem.Text
End Select
```

This code snippet deserves some explaining! First, the action that the code takes depends on the currently selected item of the RadioButtonList control. If the selected item is TextBox (item 0), then the Label1 Text property is simply set to the Text property of the TextBox control. That's easy enough so far. If the selected item is ListBox (item 2), then the Label1 Text property is set to the selected item in the ListBox control. If the selected item is CheckListBox (item 1), then things are a bit more tricky. The idea behind this code is to set the Label1 Text property to a comma-separated list of the operating systems that are chosen with the check boxes. Therefore, all this code is doing under this item is putting together a string (OS) that will list the operating systems, with the prefixed Windows text removed.

Now that you have all the code entered, run the program by pressing F5 to see what you have! Go ahead and try out all the features. Enter some text into the TextBox control and then click the Test button. Select a few dates from the calendar. Select a couple of operating systems and then click the Test button again. What happened? The label's text didn't change, did it? You need to select CheckBoxList from the radio buttons. Select a language from the list box, select ListBox from the radio buttons, and click the Test button a third time. See how this works? You should see a running example much like the one shown in Figure 5.15.

Next, it's time to dig into one of the most powerful (and complex) Web Server controls: the DataGrid control. The DataGrid control displays and edits data in a table format—that is, in row-column format like a spreadsheet. This next example shows you first how to display the data, and then how to allow the user to edit and update the data.

As always, close the current solution. Then, start a new ASP.NET Web application project and name it `DataGridControl`. Make sure you create it under the same http://localhost/LearnVB path as before. Next, rename the Web-Form1.aspx to `default.aspx` and give the Web Form a title of `Testing the DataGrid control`. Next, drop a Panel control on the Web Form and make sure it is aligned in the top-left corner of the page. Give it a light blue color as I have done in Figure 5.15. Make the `Height` of the Panel 16 pixels and

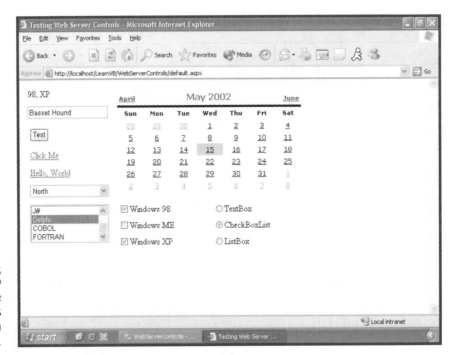

Figure 5.15

The WebServerControls application running.

the Width 100%. Then, drop a Label control inside the Panel control and give it a Text value of EMPLOYEES. You might want to make the font size extra large, like I have done in Figure 5.15. Then, add a DataGrid control and place it below the Panel control. Right-click on the DataGrid control and select AutoFormat from the pop-up menu. Select the Professional 1 scheme. Name the DataGrid control EmployeeGr. Your Web Form should look similar to mine, shown in Figure 5.16.

Next, double-click on the Web Form to bring up the Page_Load event code. In this event, you will add code to "bind" the data from a data source (in this case, the Employees table in the Northwind database) to the grid. While in the code editor, add the following two lines to the top of the source file:

```
Imports System.Data
Imports System.Data.SqlClient
```

These two lines are necessary because you'll be using the classes contained in these namespaces to access data in the database. Next, you need to create some code to get the data from the database.

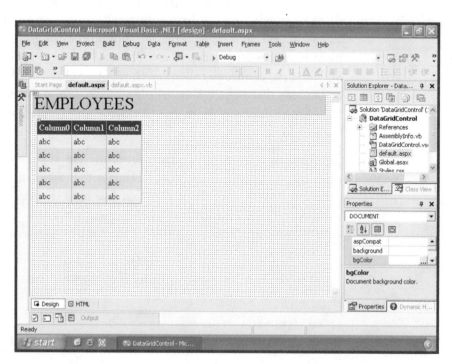

Figure 5.16

The DataGridControl Web Form in design mode.

Add the following subroutine below the `Page_Load` subroutine:

```
Private Sub BindGrid()
    Dim ConStr As String
    ConStr = "server=localhost;uid=sa;pwd=;database=northwind"
    Dim Con As New SqlConnection(ConStr)
    Dim Sql As String
    Sql = "SELECT EmployeeID, LastName, FirstName " & _
            "FROM Employees"
    Dim Da As New SqlDataAdapter(Sql, Con)
    Dim Ds As New DataSet()
    Da.Fill(Ds, "Employees")
    EmployeeGrd.DataSource = Ds
    EmployeeGrd.DataBind()
End Sub
```

Much of this code should be familiar to you from the previous session on ADO.NET and database access. However, just in case you need a reminder, I'll go through the code so you can understand it better. First, a connection string is constructed. Note that you might have to change the connection string slightly in case you have a different server, password, and so on. Then a new connection is made using the connection string. Next, the SQL statement is constructed and a new SQLDataAdapter is constructed using the SQL and the connection. You can think of a SQLDataAdapter object as the go-between that helps a DataSet object send data back and forth between a SQL Server database. Next, the DataSet object is filled with the data from the Employees table.

The last two statements in the subroutine are key. First, the `DataSource` property of the grid is set to the DataSet that was just created. Then the `DataBind()` method of the grid is called to bind the data from the DataSet to the DataGrid. This is where all the magic happens—populating the grid with the rows and columns retrieved from the SQL statement.

Now all that is left to do is to call this new `BindGrid()` method. This will be called in the `Page_Load` event. Enter the following code into the `Page_Load` subroutine:

```
If Not IsPostBack Then
    BindGrid()
End If
```

NOTE

The IsPostBack property of the Web Form is used to check whether the page is being loaded due to a client "postback." That is, the IsPostBack property is set to True when the page is loaded due to a client request coming from the browser. This is the case, for example, when the user presses a button on the Web Form that has code behind it. The client request is sent back to the server, and then a Page_Load event is triggered. The IsPostBack property is set to False the first time a page is loaded. That is why you will see "If Not IsPostBack Then" in your code a lot. In effect, what this is saying is "if this is the first time you're loading the page."

Next, build the project, right-click the default.aspx file, and select View in Browser. This is a shortcut to view your application (run your application) in a browser. You should see the grid populated as in Figure 5.17.

Pretty easy, eh? Next, let's add some code to perform editing and updating of the data behind the grid. This gets a little more tricky, so pay close attention. First, right-click on the previewed Web page tab and select Hide to go back into design mode. Right-click on the EmployeeGrd control and select Property Builder from the pop-up menu. This brings up a dialog box that

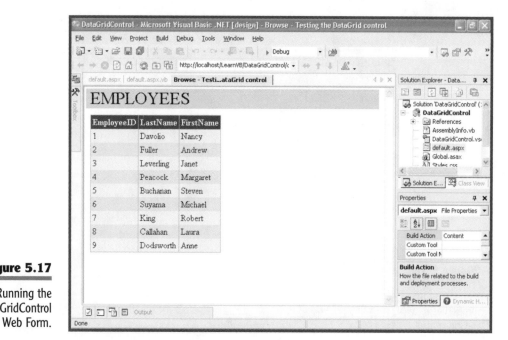

Figure 5.17

Running the DataGridControl Web Form.

allows you to edit many of the properties of the DataGrid control. When the dialog box is up, click on the Columns tab on the left side. You should now see something like what is in Figure 5.18.

Now, click on the Button Column tree node in the middle of the dialog box, and you'll see the tree list expand to include three choices. Choose the Edit, Update, Cancel option and click on the > button. This is where you add buttons for selecting, editing, updating, canceling, and deleting rows in the DataGrid control. Things are a lot different in the Web Forms world than they are in the Windows Forms world. With Web Forms, you don't have all the luxuries of the Windows Forms, and almost everything has to be generated to the client via DHTML or other scripting options available in the client browser. Sometimes, as in this case, you have to go an extra mile when creating Web applications versus Windows applications.

Before you press the OK button in the dialog box, type `Option` in the Header Text text box. You should now see the grid with a new column on it. The heading of the new column should read `Option`. You'll see a lot of LinkButton controls on the left side that read `Edit`. Go ahead and run the application again. Click on the Edit button for any row. What happened? Nothing. Hmmm. . . .

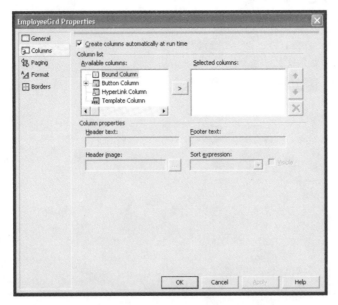

Figure 5.18

Changing the properties of a DataGrid control.

Go ahead and get back into design mode. You need to add code behind the grid to handle the edit, update, and cancel events from the grid. For the DataGrid control, these events are named EditCommand, UpdateCommand, and CancelCommand, respectively. Following is the code that is necessary to handle the three commands for the EmployeeGrd control. The code should be put before the End Class statement at the bottom of the code window. Here is the code:

```
Private Sub EmployeeGrd_EditCommand(ByVal source As Object, _
ByVal e As System.Web.UI.WebControls.DataGridCommandEventArgs) _
Handles EmployeeGrd.EditCommand
    EmployeeGrd.EditItemIndex = e.Item.ItemIndex
    BindGrid()
End Sub


Private Sub EmployeeGrd_CancelCommand(ByVal source As Object, _
ByVal e As System.Web.UI.WebControls.DataGridCommandEventArgs) _
Handles EmployeeGrd.CancelCommand
    EmployeeGrd.EditItemIndex = -1
    BindGrid()
End Sub


Private Sub EmployeeGrd_UpdateCommand(ByVal source As Object, _
ByVal e As System.Web.UI.WebControls.DataGridCommandEventArgs) _
Handles EmployeeGrd.UpdateCommand
    Dim ConStr As String
    ConStr = "server=localhost;uid=sa;pwd=;database=northwind"
    Dim Con As New SqlConnection(ConStr)
    Dim Sql As String
    Sql = "UPDATE Employees SET LastName = @LastName, " & _
        "FirstName = @FirstName WHERE " & _
        "EmployeeID = @EmployeeID"
    Dim Cmd As New SqlCommand(Sql, Con)
    Cmd.Parameters.Add(New SqlParameter("@LastName", _
                    SqlDbType.NVarChar, 20))
    Cmd.Parameters.Add(New SqlParameter("FirstName", _
                    SqlDbType.NVarChar, 20))
    Cmd.Parameters.Add(New SqlParameter("@EmployeeID", _
                    SqlDbType.Int))
```

```
        Dim EmployeeID, LastName, FirstName As String
        EmployeeID = CType(e.Item.Cells(1).Controls(0), TextBox).Text
        LastName = CType(e.Item.Cells(2).Controls(0), TextBox).Text
        FirstName = CType(e.Item.Cells(3).Controls(0), TextBox).Text
        Cmd.Parameters(0).Value = LastName
        Cmd.Parameters(1).Value = FirstName
        Cmd.Parameters(2).Value = EmployeeID
        Con.Open()
        Cmd.ExecuteNonQuery()
        Con.Close()
        EmployeeGrd.EditItemIndex = -1
        BindGrid()
End Sub
```

Whew! There's a lot to digest in this sample! First, take a look at the EmployeeGrd_EditCommand subroutine, which handles the EditCommand event on the DataGrid control. The first line of this subroutine simply sets the EditItemIndex property of the EmployeeGrd control to the ItemIndex property of the item that is passed back to the event. In this case, the event is handed a DataGridCommandEventArgs object, from which is extracted the exact item that the user selected. In effect, this is pointing the DataGrid control to the row that is being edited. Next, the BindGrid() subroutine is called to rebind the data to the grid control.

Next, take a look at the EmployeeGrd_CancelCommand subroutine. This is called when the user selects Cancel from the Option column of the grid. This code sets the EditItemIndex property of the grid back to −1. This has the effect of putting the grid back in its original, non-editing state.

Finally, look at the EmployeeGrd_UpdateCommand subroutine. It contains some pretty complex stuff, but it's my hope that you've retained some of the knowledge you learned from the ADO.NET session to help you. As was done in the BindGrid() subroutine, the first order of business is to actually connect to the database. Next, a SQLCommand object is created that uses the UPDATE SQL statement. This object updates the data from the database. Three parameters are then added to the Cmd object. These correspond to the last name, first name, and ID values for the row that is being edited.

Then the three values are extracted from the TextBox controls in the DataGrid control by using the CType function, which typecasts the control in the grid to a TextBox control. After these three values are retrieved, the parameters for the Cmd object are set up with the values. Finally, the connection is opened and the SQLCommand object is run by executing the ExecuteNonQuery method. At the bottom of the subroutine, the connection is closed, the EditItemIndex property of the grid is reset, and the data is rebound to the grid.

Now you're ready to run the project! First, build the whole solution to make sure all the code is compiling correctly. This time, press F5 to run the application in a separate browser window. Go ahead and try out the Edit, Update, and Cancel functionality. Your running application should look like mine in Figure 5.19.

If you want, you can take the time now to experiment more with the Data-Grid control. Many more properties and methods are available to you—too many to be detailed in this book. However, you have much to learn about this control and the DataList control, so the more you can devote to experimenting with them, the better. Next, we'll move on from looking at Web Server controls and take a brief overview of HTML Server controls.

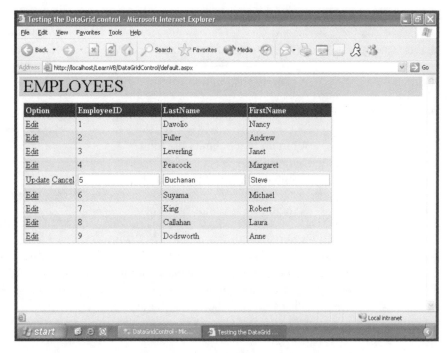

Figure 5.19

Editing and updating data in the DataGridControl application.

HTML Server Controls

HTML Server controls are standard HTML controls that are visible to and programmable on the server. Standard HTML controls can be used in ASP.NET Web pages, and this is perfectly fine as long as you don't need to access the HTML controls in your code anywhere. What delineates a standard HTML control from a HTML Server control is the following attribute:

```
runat="server"
```

If you have a standard HTML control and you want to convert it to an HTML Server control, all you need to do is add the attribute to the HTML and you will have converted it to an HTML Server control. Alternatively, in the Web Form designer, you can right-click the control and select Run As Server Control from the pop-up menu.

Table 5.2 presents the HTML Server Controls and a description of their purpose.

TABLE 5.2 HTML SERVER CONTROLS

Control	Description
Label	Displays text in a set location
Button	A generic push button control
Reset Button	A button that resets the form's controls to their initial values
Submit Button	A button that submits the form
Text Field	A single-line text input control
Text Area	A multi-line text input control
File Field	A file upload control that has a text box and a browse button
Password Field	Same as a Text Field control, but the input text is not displayed
Checkbox	Allows the selection of a True or False state
Radio Button	A single-state selection button

Control	Description
Hidden	Used to transmit state information back and forth to the server
Table	Used to format content into rows and columns
Flow Layout Panel	A panel that supports the flow layout model
Grid Layout Panel	A panel that supports the grid layout model
Image	Displays an image
Listbox	Used for list boxes or drop-down lists
Dropdown	Used for list boxes or drop-down lists
Horizontal Rule	Draws a horizontal rule (line)

Validation Controls

Validation controls serve a special purpose: They provide an easy way to validate input on the client side without requiring any information be sent back to the server. (This only works for browsers that support DHTML). This is crucial because anytime information has to be sent back to the server and then back to the client, performance is impacted. Validation controls are used to test for valid ranges, dates, phone numbers, zip codes, and more. Validation controls can be customized to suit your own validation needs.

Validation controls are added to Web Forms just like any other control. Each Validation control is assigned to an associated Server control on the same Web Form. As the user's input is put into the Server control, the validation controls test the input against the validation rules. If the validation rules are broken, the entire page is set to an invalid state, which keeps it from being submitted back to the server.

Validation controls have a property called `ErrorMessage` that is used to give a user-friendly message to the client application. Error messages can be displayed in-place (next to the control that violated the validation rule), in a summary message box (by using the ValidationSummary Server control), or in a mix of both.

The five kinds of Validation controls are described in Table 5.3.

TABLE 5.3 VALIDATION CONTROLS

Control	Description
RequiredFieldValidator	Signifies that the input control is a required field
CompareValidator	Compares the input value to another input value or constant
RangeValidator	Ensures that the input falls within a specified range of values
RegularExpressionValidator	Ensures that the input matches the pattern of a regular expression
CustomValidator	Performs user-defined validation rules against the input control

In addition to the controls in Table 5.3, a ValidationSummary Server control is used to display a summary of all validation errors in one concise area of the Web Form. It is often a good idea to use this control instead of putting error messages all over your Web Forms.

As always, the best way for you to learn about Validation controls is for you to construct an application. To start, close any solutions you might have open. Then create a new ASP.NET application and name it ValidationControls. Once again, make sure you create it in the http://localhost/LearnVB location. After you have created the application, rename the WebForm1.aspx file to default.aspx. Title the page Testing Validation Controls.

Next, add five Label controls to the Web Form and give them the following Text values: Name:, What's 1 + 1?, Salary:, Email Address:, and Prime Number:. Lay these out along the left side of the Web Form, evenly spaced. Next, add five TextBox controls to the Web Form and place them next to each Label control. Name these NameTxt, MathTxt, SalaryTxt, EmailTxt, and PrimeTxt. Add a Button control and place it at the bottom of the Web Form. Give its Text property a value of Submit. Add a ValidationSummary control to the Web Form and place it below the Submit button.

Next comes the fun part: adding the validation controls to the Web Form. First, add a RequiredFieldValidator control and place it next to the NameTxt text control. Each Validator control has many properties that you can set to customize the validation rules. For the RequiredFieldValidator, change its `ControlToValidate` property to `NameTxt`. Set its `ErrorMessage` property to `The name field is required`. Set its `Text` property to * (the asterisk character). The `ControlToValidate` property associates a Validation control with an input control (in this case, a TextBox control). The `ErrorMessage` property holds the error message that you want to present to the client application when the validation rules are violated. The `Text` property shows the text that will appear on the Validation control when an invalid state is encountered.

In this example, you are using a ValidationSummary control. This control is used to "batch up" all the messages into one cohesive area at the bottom of the Web Form. When a Validation control has no `Text` property, the Validation control displays the same text as the `ErrorMessage` property when the validation rules are broken. In this case, you are giving the `Text` property an asterisk to display next to the offending control. This is a more user-friendly approach in most cases, and it causes less clutter on the Web Form.

Let's continue adding other Validation controls. Next, add a CompareValidator control and place it next to the MathTxt control. Once again, set its `ControlToValidate` property to point to the appropriate control (MathTxt) and set its `Text` property to an asterisk. Set its `ErrorMessage` property to `You need a basic math course`. You are using this Validator control to compare two values, so set the `Type` property to `Integer` and the `ValueToCompare` property to 2 (the number 2).

Now that you're getting the hang of it, let's zip through the last three Validator controls. Add a RangeValidator and put it next to the SalaryTxt control. Set up the `ControlToValidate` and `Text` properties. (You *are* getting the hang of this, aren't you?) Set the `Type` property to `Currency`, the `MinimumValue` property to `1000`, and the `MaximumValue` property to `1000000` (one million). Set the `ErrorMessage` property to `Get real`. You're having some fun now! Add a RegularExpressionValidator control (try saying that 10 times real fast!) to the Web Form and put it next to—you guessed it—the EmailTxt control. Once again, point the Validator control to the appropriate control and give it the regular `Text` property setting. See how I'm getting more and more vague here? Hint: I'm trying to get you to learn this stuff—it's for your own good! Go ahead and enter `Nice Try`. `How's about entering your REAL e-mail address?` into the `ErrorMessage` property. This control has a

ValidationExpression property that is used to validate the input control. Go ahead and click on the ellipsis of this property. You will see a Regular Expression Editor dialog box pop up. This is where you can enter (or in this case, choose) your regular expression. Fortunately for you, Microsoft has given you several predefined regular expressions to work with. Because the input control is supposed to have a valid e-mail address in it, go ahead and choose Internet E-mail Address from the list box, as shown in Figure 5.20.

Finally, you've arrived at the last Validator control for this example. Doesn't that make you want to jump up and down? Well, if it doesn't, you certainly will want to when you see what all this Validator stuff is about. Add a CustomValidator control next to the PrimeTxt control. Of course, as you've done what seems like countless times before, point it to the appropriate input control and set up its Text property. Then enter Please enter a PRIME number, Einstein. into the ErrorMessage property. Nice error messages, eh? Hey, one can't be *too* serious, right? After all, this is an example program, not one that will be used in production at NASA (well, not yet, anyway). The CustomValidator control, as its name so aptly alludes to, is used to add your custom validation rules to an input control. This control can have its validation occur on the client side or the server side. Because all the other controls are using client-side validation, I'll let you code this one as a server-side validation rule just to keep you on your toes.

To add the server-side validation rule, double-click on the CustomValidator control on the Web Form. This brings up the code editor with a ServerValidate event ready to handle your server-side validation. Type the following code into this subroutine:

```
Dim Arg As Integer
Arg = Integer.Parse(args.Value)
args.IsValid = IsPrime(Arg)
```

Figure 5.20

The Regular Expression Editor dialog box.

Look at the source code for this event. The first line should be obvious to you by now; if it's not, GOTO page 1 of this book and start over. Okay, I couldn't resist putting a little BASIC humor in there. Look at the second line. The `ServerValidate` event procedure takes two arguments: one is the source object that called the event, and the other is a variable named `args` that allows you to examine the value of the input control you are validating. Neat, huh? So, all this line does is parse the value of the input control into an `Integer` value and store it in a variable named `Arg`. Next, take a look at the last line. The `args` variable contains a property called `IsValid`. Using this property, you can tell the CustomValidator control whether the input is valid based on your custom criteria. In this case, it simply returns the result of the `IsPrime` function to determine whether the number contained within the input control is a prime number. There's just one small thing—there is no such function named `IsPrime` yet. I guess you'll just have to write one. If you're the type of person who likes a challenge, go ahead and try to write one on your own. Make it a `Private Function` of the current Web Form.

Okay, for the other 4.3 billion of you who chose *not* to write your own `IsPrime` function, I have included the source code for my own version, which I'm sure is in use somewhere at NASA:

```
Private Function IsPrime(ByVal Arg As Integer) As Boolean
    Dim Ctr As Integer
    For Ctr = 2 To (Arg / 2)
        If (Arg Mod Ctr) = 0 Then
            Return False
        End If
    Next
    Return True
End Function
```

This function should go directly above the `ServerValidate` event handler code. I won't go into all the details or the theory of prime numbers; instead, I'll just let you get to the next step. Are you ready? That's right—it's time to run the application! Before you run the application, however, look at my example form in Figure 5.21. Yours should look somewhat similar to this.

The moment of truth has come. Ladies and gentlemen, start your application! (I couldn't help throwing in a little Indy 500 humor there; after all, I am writing this book in the month of May, and I happen to be only a few

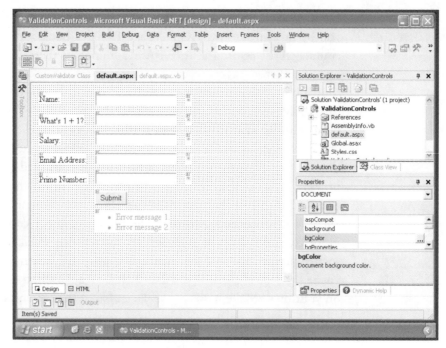

Figure 5.21

The
ValidationControls
Project at design
time.

miles from the Indianapolis Motor Speedway.) Anyway, press F5 to run the application. Go ahead and click the Submit button. This causes the Validation controls to evaluate the page. You'll see that one validation rule has already been broken—the name field is required. Go ahead and try breaking more rules. Look at my example in Figure 5.22; I've broken just about every rule! (Some things never change, right mom?)

Look closely at Figure 5.22. The Validator controls caught everything except for the obvious non-prime number of 1,000. Why didn't that Validator control work? Can I call NASA and get my money back? Before you start scratching your head too much and causing a dandruff blizzard, consider this: The first four Validator controls are client-side Validation controls. This means that their validation rules are being evaluated before the page is sent to the server. Is the light bulb going on over your head yet? The prime number validation code is server-side, so it is only executed after all the client-side validation is complete. In other words, the first four Validators must pass inspection before the prime number validation code is called. So, go ahead and satisfy the first four Validators and enter some valid text. Then click the

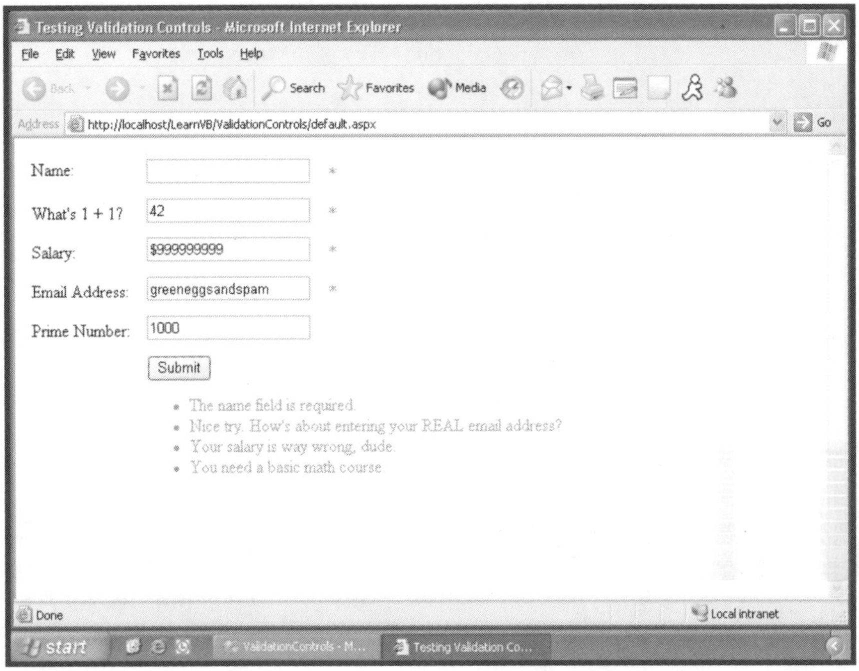

Figure 5.22

The
ValidationControls
application in
action.

Submit button again with a non-prime number (like 1,000 perhaps). By golly, it works! As you can see in my example from Figure 5.23, the prime number validation has done its job and caught my meager attempt at entering a non-prime number.

"That's all fine and dandy, but I want my prime number validation to occur on the client side!" Okay, you can do that; it's really quite easy. To convert your CustomValidator control to do client-side validation, a few things are necessary. First, comment out the ServerValidate event in the VB code behind the Web Form. Next, go back to the page designer and click on the page. Change the DefaultClientScript property to VBScript instead of JScript. Then click on the HTML tab to edit the raw HTML for your Web Form. Insert the following VBScript code just below the <HEAD> tag in the HTML:

```
<script language="vbscript">
  <!--
  Function IsPrime(Arg)
    Dim Ctr
```

```
      For Ctr = 2 To (Arg / 2)
          If (Arg Mod Ctr) = 0 Then
              IsPrime = False
              Exit Function
          End If
      Next
      IsPrime = True
  End Function
  Sub ValidatePrime(source, args)
      args.IsValid = IsPrime(args.Value)
  End Sub
  ' -->
</script>
```

Finally, click on the CustomValidator control on your Web Form and change the `ClientValidationFunction` property to ValidatePrime. This is the name of the function that will be called to validate your input control on the client side. Now you can validate the prime number input control on the client side

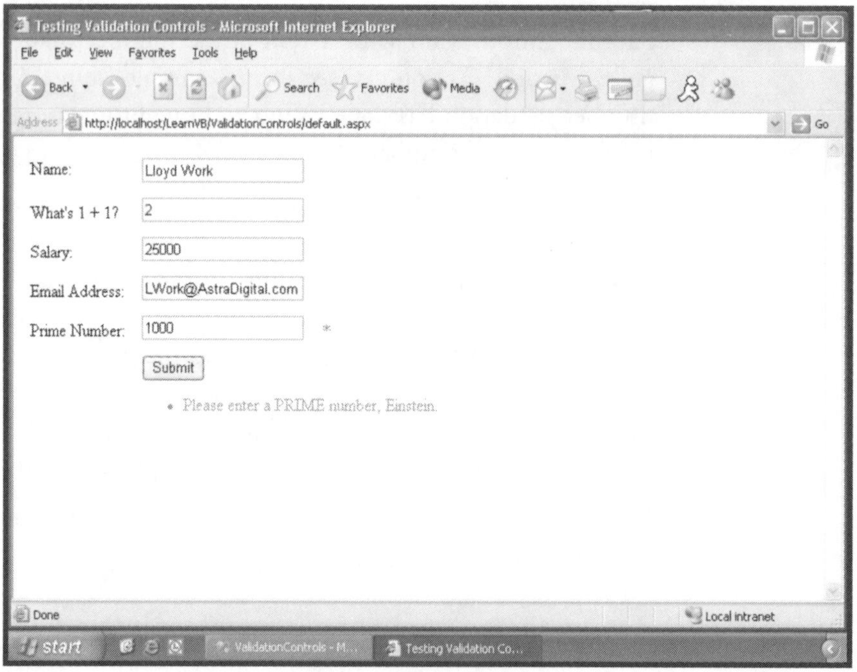

Figure 5.23

Testing the prime number validation code.

without a trip to the server! I call it "Prime Number Validator XP". Hold
on—NASA's on the phone, ordering an upgrade to the new version. . . .

Configuration and State Management

You've gotten your feet wet; you've seen some of what ASP.NET is all about,
and you're probably foaming at the mouth right now, ready for more, more,
more. But, before you go "Cujo" on me, I need to take you down an important side trail. Before you can go delivering your Web applications to everyone on every planet in the universe, you might want to think about some
other issues related to Web development in ASP.NET. One of the major topics that hasn't been discussed yet is that of state management and general
configuration issues.

Configuration

One of the most important configuration files at the heart of any ASP.NET
Web application is the Global.asax file. This file is automatically generated
with each new Web application you create. It contains a class named Global
that inherits from the HttpApplication class. The Global class has many
application and session-oriented events that you will find useful. Here is a
listing of a bare Global.asax file:

```
Imports System.Web
Imports System.Web.SessionState

Public Class Global
    Inherits System.Web.HttpApplication

' (Component Designer Generated Code Skipped)

    Sub Application_Start(ByVal sender As Object, _
                        ByVal e As EventArgs)
        ' Fires when the application is started
    End Sub

    Sub Session_Start(ByVal sender As Object, _
                    ByVal e As EventArgs)
```

```vb
      ' Fires when the session is started
   End Sub


   Sub Application_BeginRequest(ByVal sender As Object, _
                          ByVal e As EventArgs)
      ' Fires at the beginning of each request
   End Sub


   Sub Application_AuthenticateRequest(ByVal sender As Object, _
                          ByVal e As EventArgs)
      ' Fires upon attempting to authenticate the user
   End Sub


   Sub Application_Error(ByVal sender As Object, _
                    ByVal e As EventArgs)
      ' Fires when an error occurs
   End Sub


   Sub Session_End(ByVal sender As Object, ByVal e As EventArgs)
      ' Fires when the session ends
   End Sub


   Sub Application_End(ByVal sender As Object, _
                    ByVal e As EventArgs)
      ' Fires when the application ends
   End Sub


End Class
```

As you can see, this file contains many event handlers. Look at the preceding code listing. Each of the event handlers has a comment in it giving an overview of what the event handler's purpose is. Generally, you'll want to use the Session_Start event to initialize variables and perform certain operations when a new user session starts. In the same manner, you'll want to use the Session_End event to clean up any resources used in the Session_Start event. Similarly, Application_Start and Application_End events are useful for handling operations at the start or end of an application. You will have the chance in a moment to get your feet wet by coding an example application that uses some of these events as well as some session management.

Another configuration file you might become familiar with is the Web. config file. This is created for you when you start a new Web application project. The Web.config file is an XML-based file that has numerous XML tags in it for purposes such as session and execution timeout values, session state parameters, SQL connection parameters, cookie usage flags, and much more. Go ahead and open the Web.config file to view it. Do this by double-clicking the file in the Solution Explorer window.

Diving into each of the Web.config file tags and their purpose would be beyond the scope of this book. The help that is provided on MSDN and included with Visual Studio .NET should be sufficient for you to grasp the concepts as you get closer to doing production ASP.NET development.

Another file that you should be aware of is the Machine.config file. This file, unlike the previously mentioned two configuration files, is not added to a new Web project automatically. Instead, it is installed in the core .NET Framework directories. Like the Web.config file, the Machine.config file is a long XML file, containing configuration tags on hundreds of .NET-related items. This file, along with other similar configuration files, such as Security.config and other enterprise configuration files, is too technical and way beyond the scope of this book. Once again, the help that Visual Studio .NET provides should get you rolling on these configuration files if you need them.

State Management

You should know about two primary state management-related objects: Application and Session. The Application object stores information that is used throughout your application, from the moment the application is first accessed until the last person has closed the application or the Web server is shut down. The Session object stores information that is used throughout a user session; that is, a user can have several browser windows open at the same time and have multiple sessions, but he might, in fact, be using only one application. In this case, the Session object stores information that is related to each browser window (session), whereas the Application object stores information that is related to the entire application.

I can't think of a better way to illustrate this than—you guessed it—yet another example program. Get your gloves on and strap on those goggles. You're in for another round of ASP.NET on wheels.

To prepare, as always, close out any current solution you have running. Then start a new ASP.NET Web Application project under the http://localhost/ LearnVB path and name the project AlteredStates. Okay, I'm probably dating myself here, but I couldn't resist the temptation to allude to the old sci-fi thriller, *Altered States*. After you've created the application, go ahead and do the inevitable change from WebForm1.aspx to default.aspx. Next, add a Label control, a TextBox control, and a Button control to the form. The Label control should have the Text property set to Hello... we're taking a quick poll: what's your favorite movie? Name the TextBox control MovieTxt. Name the Button control SubmitBtn and set its Text property to Submit Vote. Set the Title property for the Web Form to Testing State Management.

This project has two Web Forms in it, so it's time to add the second Web Form. Right-click on the AlteredStates project and select Add, Add Web Form from the pop-up menu. Add a new Web Form with the name thanks.aspx. For Title, type Thank you! Add two Label controls to the form. For the first one, give it a Text property of Thanks for your vote., and name the second Label control StatsLbl. Clear its Text property and make sure it's at least 500 pixels wide.

Next, it's time to add some code. First, you need to do something you've never done before: Add a line of code to the Global.asax file. To do this, double-click on the Global.asax file in the Solution Explorer window. Then add the following line under the Session_Start event handler:

```
Session("Voted") = False
```

Using the Application and Session objects, you can add and query arbitrary named parameters. In this case, you've just set the Voted parameter to False. Think of the Voted parameter as a session variable. It will be set to False every time a new session is created.

Now go back to the default.aspx page and double-click on the SubmitBtn control. Add the following code to the event handler:

```
If MovieTxt.Text <> "" Then
    If Session("Voted") = False Then
        Application(UCase(MovieTxt.Text)) += 1
        Session("MovieName") = MovieTxt.Text
        Session("Voted") = True
    End If
```

```
        Response.Redirect("thanks.aspx")
End If
```

Let's examine this code. First, the MovieTxt.Text property is checked to see if the user put data into it. If you like, you can enhance this example by adding your own RequiredFieldValidator to the Web Form. (Remember how to do that? Just checking.) Next, the Voted session variable is checked to see whether the person has submitted his vote in this session. If he hasn't, it is valid to accept the vote and move on. Moving on entails using the Request object's Redirect method to go to the thanks.aspx page.

If the user has not submitted his vote yet, a new Application variable is created with the name of the movie as the parameter (variable) name. This variable name needs to be converted to uppercase so that you don't get into case sensitivity issues. Therefore, this variable will keep track of how many times people have voted for a particular movie. The variable stores a counter to keep track of the votes for the movie. Next, a Session variable is created with the name of the movie. Finally, the Voted session variable is set to True.

The last coding task on this project is on the second Web Form, thanks.aspx. Go ahead and bring that Web Form up in the designer and double-click on the form. This takes you to the Page_Load event for the thanks.aspx Web Form. Add the following code to this event handler:

```
If Session("MovieName") = "" Then
    Response.Redirect("default.aspx")
End If
Dim Cnt As Integer
Dim Str As String
Cnt = CInt(Application(UCase(Session("MovieName")))) - 1
Select Case Cnt
    Case 0
        Str = "are no other people"
    Case 1
        Str = "is one other person"
    Case Else
        Str = "are " & Cnt & " other people"
End Select
StatsLbl.Text = "By the way, there " _
            & Str _
```

```
              & " who share your love for '" _
              & Session("MovieName") & "'."
```

First, take a look at the top three lines of code. If the user hasn't voted yet, he needs to be redirected to the default.aspx page so that he can vote. How can the user get here, you ask? Well, if he typed the direct URL to the thanks.aspx page into his browser, the browser would normally take him to that page. However, it makes no sense to take the user there if he hasn't voted; therefore, he is redirected to the default.aspx page.

Next, a count of how many other people have voted for the same movie is obtained. Note that because this value was just incremented by the person voting, the value needs to be decremented by one to exclude the current user's vote. Based on the vote count, a string is constructed with a nice message for the user, telling him how many other people have voted for the same movie. Finally, the StatsLbl.Text property is populated with the Str String variable.

Your default.aspx Web Form should look similar to the one shown here in Figure 5.24.

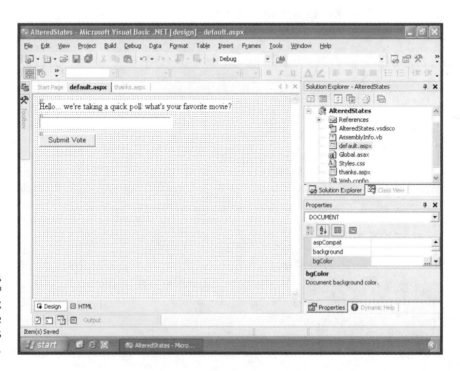

Figure 5.24

The default.aspx Web Form of the AlteredStates project.

Your thanks.aspx Web Form should look similar to the one shown here in Figure 5.25.

Now comes the moment you've been waiting for: It's time to run the project and see what all this state management fuss is all about. But wait! Before you press the handy F5 button, please choose Build Solution from the Build menu to ensure that all source files are compiling and ready for prime time. After the project is built, *don't* run it from within the environment. I want you to open a new browser window and point to the following location: http://localhost/LearnVB/AlteredStates. This should bring up the initial default Web Form, as shown in Figure 5.26.

Go ahead and enter your favorite movie into the TextBox control. (You can see by the figure what my favorite movie is!) Then, click the Submit Vote button. You should see a thank you Web Form similar to Figure 5.27.

Because this is your first time running the application, you'll have accumulated 0 votes so far, so you should receive a message showing you that no other people share your love for your favorite movie. Go ahead and click the

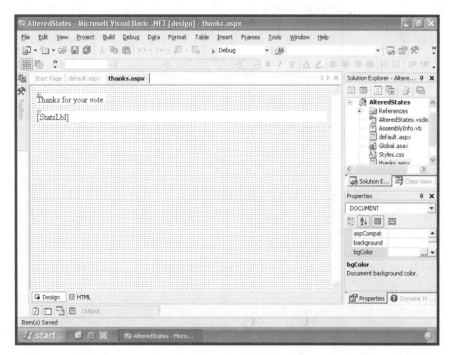

Figure 5.25

The thanks.aspx Web Form of the AlteredStates project.

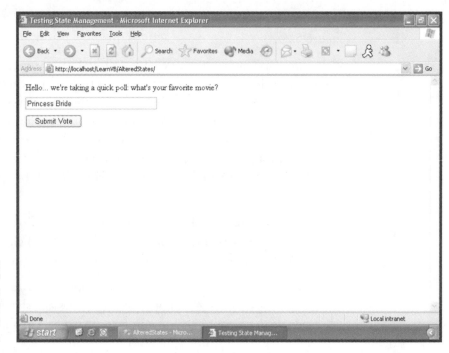

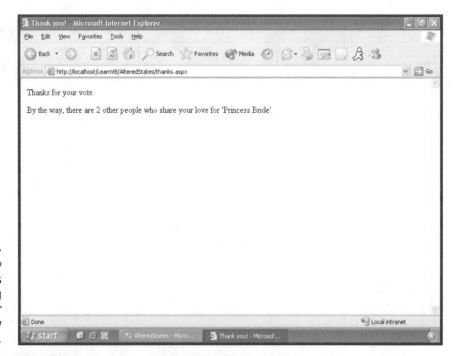

Figure 5.27

The AlteredStates
application showing
how many other
people like my
favorite movie.

browser's Back button and try resubmitting your vote. Notice that the vote counter did not go up. Instead, it skipped counting your vote twice.

Now open a second browser window while keeping the first one open. Type the URL for the application, just as you did before. Try entering the same movie again. When you click the Submit Vote application, you should see that one other person also has that favorite movie. (Okay, so you're the same person, perhaps with multiple personalities. Sybil? Is that you?) Now go back to the first browser window and return to the default page. Click the Submit Vote button again. You'll see that the counter in your first browser window has been updated to show that another person has voted for your favorite movie.

Finally, open yet another (a third) browser window and point the URL to http://localhost/LearnVB/AlteredStates/thanks.aspx. Notice that the application took you immediately to the default page instead of the thanks page. This is because of the code you added to ensure that no one got to the thanks page without voting. Neat, huh? Perhaps you could enhance this by adding more validation pieces, such as requiring the movie to be entered on the first page and throwing an exception if anyone enters `Ishtar`. Just a thought. . . .

The Mobile Internet Toolkit

Microsoft has a free downloadable add-on to ASP.NET that allows you to create mobile Web applications quickly and easily. This download is named `Mobile Internet Toolkit`, and it's available from Microsoft at http://www.microsoft.com. This toolkit contains server-side technology that enables ASP.NET applications to render themselves in a markup-friendly format to a number of mobile devices, including cell phones, pagers, and Pocket PCs.

The next session on XML Web Services shows you how to create a mobile application using the Mobile Internet Toolkit. In addition, the next session shows how the Mobile Internet Toolkit can be used to consume an XML Web service. Before you embark upon the next session, you might want to take the time now to download the Mobile Internet Toolkit from the Microsoft Web site. In addition, although it's not required, you can download a mobile browser, such as the OpenWave Mobile Browser available in the OpenWave SDK from http://www.openwave.com.

What's Next

Now that you've had an introduction to developing Web applications with ASP.NET, we're going to move further down into one of the most promising and exciting technologies to come about in recent years: XML Web Services. I'm sure by now you've heard some chatter or hype about what Web Services are and what they can do. You're about to find out for yourself what possibilities exist when you combine all that you've learned about Web applications, mobile applications, and other .NET capabilities with the power and flexibility of Web Services. I think you'll agree that not only are Web Services a revolutionary step in modern Internet computing, but they also have the potential to fundamentally change the way applications are developed in the future.

Creating and Consuming Web Services

- ➤ Introducing Web services
- ➤ Building Web services
- ➤ Consuming Web services asynchronously
- ➤ Consuming other Web services
- ➤ Consuming Web services from Office XP

225

N ow that you have an idea of what ASP.NET is and how to build Web applications, you're ready to be introduced to the new revolutionary technology at the core of the .NET platform: XML Web services. Microsoft has put Web services at the forefront of its .NET marketing campaign. Microsoft sees Web services as the cornerstone of .NET—it's that important.

NOTE This chapter uses the terms XML Web services and Web services interchangeably.

Introducing Web Services

When companies such as Microsoft make such high stakes on technology like Web services, the entire development community stands up and takes notice. One can hardly go to a technical Web page today or read a recent technical publication without observing how much attention is being given to Web services. It's not just Microsoft touting Web services' capabilities, either; virtually every front-running development tool vendor has either implemented or announced support for some sort of Web service architecture.

This next section will introduce you to the world of Web services and show you how you can build and consume them using Visual Basic .NET and Visual Studio .NET. As you have seen, creating Web applications with ASP.NET is easy and has brought RAD to the Web development initiative. You will see in the next hour or so just how easy it is to create Web services using these new technologies from Microsoft and just what it means to you and your business.

Rapid Application Development, or RAD as it is commonly known, describes a process by which applications are developed in a rapid fashion. For Windows development, RAD has been a reality for many years. However, in the world of Web development and Web service development, RAD is only just now becoming a true reality.

What Are They?

Before we can dive too deep into the world of Web services, you might find yourself wondering what in the world they are. As is with the .NET Framework, if you ask five people, you're bound to get five different answers. However, at the most basic level, a Web service is a non-visual component that you can access via standard Internet protocols. You've already studied Windows Forms and Web Forms, and by now you're familiar with what a component is and how it can be programmed to perform certain functions and expose public interfaces for clients to consume that functionality. The components you've seen so far are visual in nature, as you have seen with the Visual Studio designers—a component's properties and methods can be explored via the Properties window in the Visual Studio .NET environment. In a way, Web services are parallel to this architecture and related with regard to how they are used. The one huge difference is that Web services have no visual interface as the standard Windows and Web components have that you've already seen. Instead, a standard set of protocols expose the interfaces to Web services, and many different kinds of applications can consume them. Windows applications, Web applications, and even mobile applications can easily use Web services to augment intrinsic functionality and exploit a truly powerful distributed architecture.

Web services allow applications to use functionality and capabilities from other applications in a platform-independent way. Because Web services are standardized, it does not matter what platform they run on or what kind of device uses the Web service—standard protocols exist so that applications and Web services can talk to each other without being tied to a particular platform or implementation. Web services are by nature independent "islands of code." That is, they exist without dependency or assumption of other implementation details. Applications use Web services in a collaborative way to exploit pre-built functionality and save a tremendous amount of development time.

Think of Web services as a new standardized way of integrating systems and applications, with the Internet being the transport for the communication between the applications and the services they use. Because Web services are built on XML and other standardized technologies, they do not suffer from the drawbacks of older technologies such as DCOM, CORBA, DCE, RMI, and other Remote Procedure Call (RPC) mechanisms. If you've dabbled in any of these legacy technologies, you know what I'm talking about—they all had their benefits and drawbacks. By far, the most serious drawback to all

---

WEB SERVICES = INTERNET + SERVICE-BASED COMPUTING

Web services are essentially the result of a convergence between two technologies: the Internet and service-based computing. Of course, as you have seen, the Internet has been around for a while now (although its usefulness has only become apparent in recent years), and service-based architectures have been around for a longer time than that. However, never have two technologies converged into something so great. I'm not saying it's better than what Reece's did with the Peanut Butter Cups (Hershey's chocolate + peanut butter)—but it's pretty darn close. The Internet brings to the table the widespread universal communication piece and well-proven technologies such as HTML and XML. The service-based architecture model has been around in older legacy systems for many decades and is commonplace among many enterprise applications. Web services bring these two together, creating a plethora of new opportunities to exploit the two technologies to gain tremendous benefits.

---

these legacy technologies was that they were hard to implement and totally incompatible with one another. This meant that an application that used DCOM as its method of communication was incompatible with Java's RMI, which was incompatible with CORBA, and so on.

NOTE Don't worry if some of the acronyms used in the preceding paragraph scare you; if you've used some legacy technologies before, you might recognize some of these and know what they are. If you haven't, you're entering into computing at the right time and certainly aren't missing anything!

For many enterprises, it was commonplace to have many technologies in use even under the same roof. Getting applications to "talk" to one another and share data or reuse functionality was pretty much impossible unless you had a technical wizard on staff who could code some sort of middleware interapplication communication interface. Even worse, companies could not easily share each other's data without having to go through a lot of coding nightmares and jumping through hoops. If two companies wanted to share data, there inevitably had to be a lot of upfront work and agreement of API mechanisms for the handshaking to work.

What Do They Offer?

Because Web services are being promoted as being so great, you might be wondering what exactly they can do for you and your business. First, they allow companies to streamline their middleware communication layers and integrate all the pieces together much more cleanly. Second, they allow applications to share data easily without regard to how each application is implemented or what platform it is run on. No longer do you need to spend months doing custom communication-brokering coding to get two applications to communicate; now, as you will soon see, it's as easy as writing a few lines of code. No longer will your code be locked up in islands of automation, never to be reused again. Now you can program your Web services and use them over and over.

Businesses have many more opportunities to create and use open solutions using Web services. New revenue stream potentials exist, allowing companies to broker valuable information to sell to consumers. Web services can be utilized to connect companies with their suppliers, customers, and partners, improving communication and streamlining supply-chain relationships.

Examples of Web Services

As you might have guessed, companies have already jumped headfirst into the world of Web services, and many high-profile companies currently have both free and fee-based Web services available. Some of these include the following:

➤ A package tracking service from Federal Express

➤ A mobile phone messaging service

➤ Numerous data lookup services (countries, zip codes, stocks, and so on)

➤ Email and fax services

➤ Weather and GPS services

➤ Conversion and calculation services

➤ And many, many more!

Many public sites are available for you to view and see for yourself what services are already published on the Internet. I will expound on this in the section titled "Consuming Other Web Services" later in this chapter.

How Can Web Services Be Used?

Web services have many potential uses. Here are just a few of them:

➤ **Robust, interactive, intelligent Web pages.** Web services can be used to enhance the functionality of plain, static Web pages, allowing a new level of dynamic content and data delivery with greater ease than ever.

➤ **Mobile applications.** These applications are small and limited in nature, so exploiting external functionality such as Web services greatly increases the opportunity to create more powerful mobile applications.

➤ **Rich Windows-based client applications.** Consumers of Web services are not limited to just Web applications; traditional Windows-based applications can use Web services to enhance their functionality and power as well.

➤ **Multiplatform and multilanguage applications.** Because Web services are platform independent, you can easily write a Web service in one language on one platform and consume the service using an entirely different language on a different platform.

➤ **Other Web services.** Yes, even Web services can call other Web services!

The New World of Application Development

Because of Web services, the future of application development might be drastically different from what it has been in the past. Let me give you an example. In the traditional application development world, developers would work in teams to create applications. From these teams of programmers would come many reusable portions of code, which were often put into shared code libraries. These libraries were then put on the network somewhere so that everyone could use them. Of course, to use them, developers would need to know what shared code was available, where it was located, and how to use it. In addition, only developers who were using the same technologies could reuse shared code; if two teams used disparate tools and technologies, the chances of code reuse between them were small.

Now, with Web services as an option, any team within an enterprise can reuse the code within its own corporation regardless of what platform or technology is being used. In addition, developers can now use the thousands of publicly and privately available Web services at their fingertips.

What happens, therefore, is that the new model of application development is becoming more of a plug-and-run model than the old build-it-from-scratch model. Therefore, application development is much more of a collaborative process, utilizing not only the resources of the team but also the shared resources and prebuilt code behind Web services. The amount of code reuse in this new model is drastically increased, leading to new heights of productivity and significantly lowering the cost of the entire application development process. Code snippets and islands of functionality can be coded, tested, and exposed as a Web service to be used over and over again.

Some Technical Terms

Before I get into some examples of how to create and use Web services, you should know some basic terminology and concepts so that you can better understand the baseline architecture behind Web services in general.

◄◄◄

Extensible Markup Language (XML) is a universal format for structured documents. This is not a binary format, so documents can be freely sent back and forth over the Web via a standard HTTP port. This will become important later in this session when we talk about sending datasets back and forth across the Web.

XML Schema Definition (XSD) is a standard of built-in types that Web services support. Because Web services can be created on a variety of platforms with a variety of languages, XSD provides a standard so that disparate technologies can converse.

Simple Object Access Protocol (SOAP) invokes remote procedures in Web services. It is a highly advanced standardized object messaging protocol, allowing remote method invocation and responses to be marshaled properly across the Internet.

Web Services Description Language (WSDL) is an XML schema used to describe Web services. WSDL depicts the data types used in the Web service, the messages that can be exchanged, the methods that can be invoked, the ports that can be used, and a description of the service. WSDL acts as a contract mechanism between the client (consumer) and the server (the Web service).

Universal Description, Discovery, and Integration (UDDI) lists the services that are available and the companies that offer them.

◄◄◄

Although the preceding acronyms might seem unfamiliar to you now, you'll soon be seeing them as you dig deeper into Web services. Their meaning will become clearer to you as you work through some of the examples in this chapter.

Building and Consuming XML Web Services

Now that you have had an introduction to Web services and all they entail, I'm sure you're ready to get going and see for yourself just how easy and powerful Web service creation and consumption can be with Visual Basic .NET.

This section shows you how to build and consume three basic Web services. The first is a calculator Web service that does some simple math calculations. The second is the converter Web service that does some temperature conversions. The third is a data service that shows how to retrieve datasets and other complex types via a Web service.

In addition, this section shows you how to consume Web services that are not necessarily created with .NET technologies—Web services that exist somewhere on the Internet and are publicly available. You'll also see how to consume a Web service in Microsoft Office XP.

So hang on—you're about to become savvy with Web service development and consumption!

 TIP As you read this chapter, you'll be presented with many examples. I'll walk you through each example step-by-step. It is important to go through each example and not skip through the chapter because some examples build on previous ones. Also, you'll have the chance to work through some examples on your own after you have had a sufficient introduction to the technical material.

The Calculator Web Service

To start building your first Web service, make sure you are in the Visual Studio .NET environment and that you've closed all other active projects. Next, click on the New Project button from the Start page. This time, instead of creating an ASP.NET Web application, we'll create an ASP.NET Web service. So, make sure that you've selected the Visual Basic project type and ASP.NET Web Service as the project template. After you've selected those, type in the location of the Web service as `http://localhost/LearnVB/Calculator`. Your New Project dialog box should look like Figure 6.1.

Next, click on the OK button. Visual Studio .NET will create the Calculator Web service and display a screen that looks like Figure 6.2.

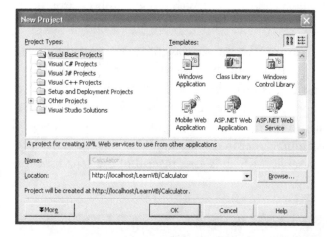

Figure 6.1

Creating the Calculator Web service.

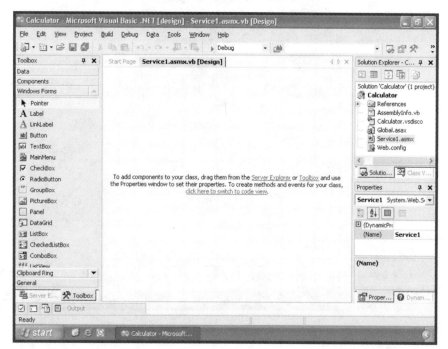

Figure 6.2

The blank Calculator Web service.

Before you start coding, rename the Service1.asmx file in the Solution Explorer to `Calculator.asmx`. (Do this by right-clicking the file in the Solution Explorer and choosing Rename from the pop-up menu.) Next, you need to add code to your Web service to perform some calculations. Click on the hyperlink that says `Click here to switch to code view`. This puts you in the Visual Studio .NET editor. If you hide some of your tool windows (as I have done in Figure 6.3), you will be able to see more of the underlying code for your Web service. Your environment should now resemble Figure 6.3.

Notice that a Web service class has been created for us (`Service1`), and that it is inherited from the base `WebService` class in the `System.Web.Services` namespace. Notice also that on the right side of the environment in the Solution Explorer, several files have been created for you. Many of these are similar to the ones created for you when you built your first ASP.NET Web application earlier in this session. One notable difference is the extension of a Web service, which is `asmx` instead of the `aspx` used for a Web page.

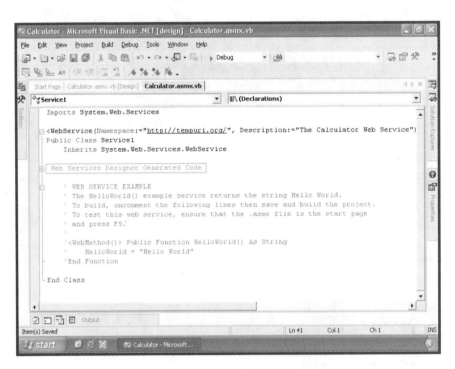

Figure 6.3

The code behind the Calculator Web service.

Next, look at the sample code that Visual Studio .NET has provided for you:

```
' WEB SERVICE EXAMPLE
' The HelloWorld() example service returns the string Hello World.
' To build, uncomment the following lines then save and build the
' project.
' To test this web service, ensure that the .asmx file is the
' start page
' and press F5.
'
'<WebMethod()> Public Function HelloWorld() As String
'      HelloWorld = "Hello World"
' End Function
```

This code is provided as a template for creating new Web services. Microsoft has been nice enough to include this here so that when you create your own Web services, you'll have something to work from. Let's go ahead and do an experiment. Uncomment the last three lines of code, starting with `'<WebMethod()>` and ending with `'End Function`. Next, save your project and run it by pressing F5. A new instance of Internet Explorer is created, resulting in a screen similar to Figure 6.4.

Visual Studio .NET has created a test page for your Web service. Isn't that nice? Why don't you take a moment right now to call your friends and tell them how wonderful you think it is that Microsoft is doing all this for you. Perhaps you can add Bill Gates to your holiday postcard list. Or, you can read the next paragraph and learn more about Web services.

TIP

You do not have to run Internet Explorer to see your Web service. A simple way to do it from within the environment is to right-click the main Web service (in this case, `Calculator.asmx`) and select View in Browser from the pop-up menu. This opens an instance of Internet Explorer within the Visual Studio .NET environment and allows you to run and test your Web service without having to leave the IDE.

This page is automatically created every time you create or update your Web service. Go ahead and click on the `HelloWorld` link near the top of the Web page. You should see the Web page change to something similar to Figure 6.5.

Figure 6.4

The Calculator Web service information page.

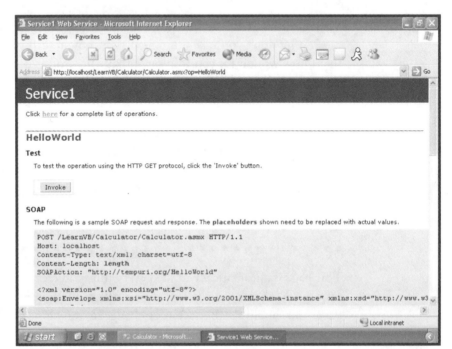

Figure 6.5

The Calculator Web service test page.

This Web page allows you to test the methods of your new Web service and to see the SOAP, HTTP GET, and HTTP POST sections. These sections of the page show you sample requests and responses for each type.

Next, click on the Invoke button on the page to invoke the Web service. The browser sends a request to the Web server, and the HelloWorld method invokes the Web service. After this method executes, you should see the results shown in Figure 6.6.

What you're looking at in Figure 6.6 is the XML result of executing the HelloWorld method of your new Web service. Simply put, it is returning an XML document consisting of one header plus one string ("Hello World").

Now, close the browser window and return to Visual Studio .NET. It's time to add some real functionality to our Web service. After you're back in the environment, comment out the HelloWorld function and type the following lines of code into the code editor:

```
<WebMethod()> Public Function Add(ByVal a As Integer, _
ByVal b As Integer) As Integer
    Return (a + b)
End Function


<WebMethod()> Public Function Subtract(ByVal a As Integer, _
ByVal b As Integer) As Integer
    Return (a - b)
End Function


<WebMethod()> Public Function Multiply(ByVal a As Integer, _
ByVal b As Integer) As Integer
    Return (a * b)
End Function


<WebMethod()> Public Function Divide(ByVal a As Integer, _
ByVal b As Integer) As Double
    Return (a / b)
End Function
```

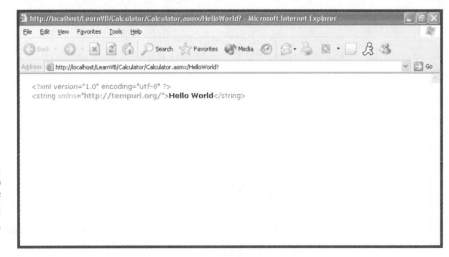

Figure 6.6

The results of running the Calculator Web service.

Most of this code should look familiar to you. You have just created four basic calculation functions. The one statement that needs explaining is the `<WebMethod()>` code that prefixes all the functions. This is called the `WebMethod` attribute, and it is used to describe the method, give session management and transaction directives, give caching directives, and more. This attribute allows the functions within your Web service class to be called externally. Without this attribute, the functions would not be accessible externally via the Web service.

For now, add a small description to the `Add` method, as shown here:

```
<WebMethod(Description:="Adds two integers together")> _
Public Function Add(ByVal a As Integer, ByVal b As Integer) _
As Integer
    Return (a + b)
End Function
```

Next, add your own descriptions to the other three methods. If you scroll up to the top of the code editor, you'll notice that the `Service1` class has a `WebService` attribute. The purpose of this attribute is similar in purpose to the WebMethod attribute. Go ahead and add a description to the WebService attribute, as shown here:

```
<WebService(Namespace:="http://tempuri.org/", _
Description:="The Calculator Web Service")>
```

Finally, run the Web service by pressing F5. You should see a new instance of Internet Explorer running, along with a new Web service information page, as shown in Figure 6.7.

Notice that the Web service now has a description, and each of the methods is listed with its own descriptions. (Your descriptions might vary from mine, so don't worry if your screen doesn't look exactly like mine.) Go ahead and click on the Multiply hyperlink (the first method in the list). This will take you to the Multiply method test page. You should now have a screen that looks like Figure 6.8.

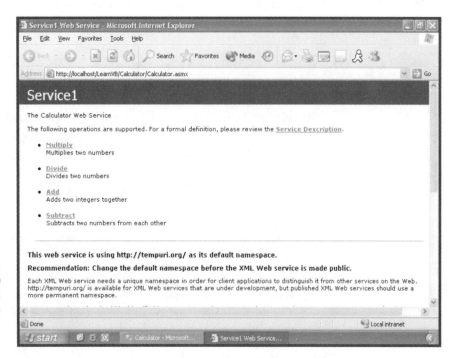

Figure 6.7

The complete Calculator Web service information page.

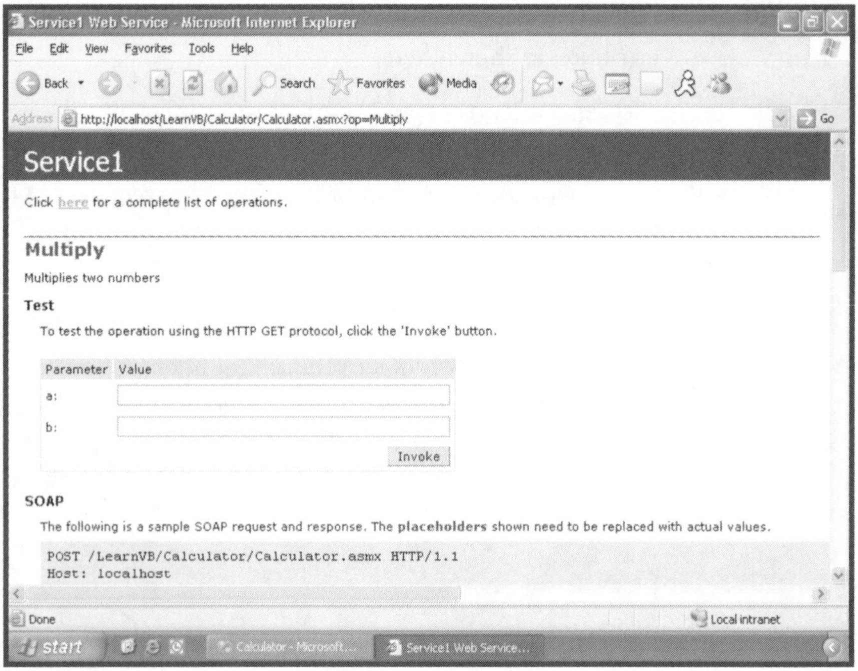

Figure 6.8

The `Multiply` method test page.

Notice that once again, Visual Studio .NET has created a nice test page for you to test your new Web service methods (in this case, the `Multiply` method). The environment has even provided text boxes for you to type in the possible values for the `a` and `b` parameters. Go ahead and put in any number you want and click the Invoke button. This runs the `Multiply` method of the Calculator Web service, passing it the values for the `a` and `b` method parameters. A new instance of Internet Explorer will be created, showing you the XML result of running the Web service.

See how easy it is to create Web services in Visual Studio .NET? Other than adding a couple of simple statements to your class, it took next to no effort to get your Web service up and running. Before we build a client for the Web service you just created, activate the Web browser and return to the Calculator Web service information page. Click on the hyperlink that says `Service Description` on the upper right-hand corner of the Web page. You should see something that resembles Figure 6.9.

What you are looking at is the WSDL for the Calculator Web service. Aren't you glad you didn't have to write this on your own? Once again, Visual Studio

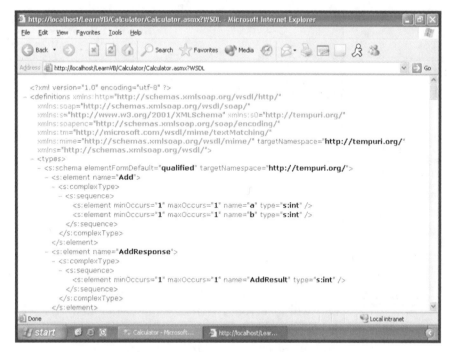

Figure 6.9

The Calculator Web service WSDL.

.NET has done all the work for you, making your job easy. Go ahead and add Bill Gates to your holiday postcard list now.

NOTE

The WSDL, as you learned earlier in this section, describes the Web service so that it can be called from an external client. The WSDL forms a contract between the client and the Web service.

Go ahead and shut down your browser session now.

Next, let's create a Web-based client to test the new Calculator Web service. To do this, right-click your solution name (Calculator) and select Add, New Project from the pop-up menu. This time, you will add a new ASP.NET Web application to the solution. Go ahead and name it `CalculatorClient`. Your Add New Project dialog box should look like Figure 6.10.

Click the OK button to bring up a blank ASP.NET Web application to test your Calculator Web service with. Because you created a Web application using ASP.NET earlier in the chapter, I'll just give you a quick list of the

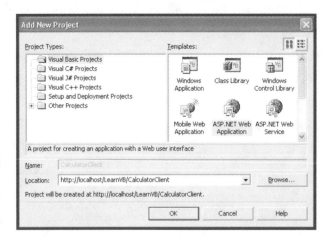

Figure 6.10

Creating a Web-
based client for the
Calculator Web
service.

steps required to build the client application. Note that for this client application, you will use Web Server controls and not HTML Server controls. This will give you a chance to test your new ASP.NET Web application development skills! Before you get started adding controls to the Web Form, rename the WebForm1.aspx file to default.aspx.

1. Add two Label controls to the Web Form. Give them Text properties of First Value: and Second Value:.

2. Add two TextBox controls to the Web Form. Name them TextBoxA and TextBoxB. Put them to the right of the first two labels.

3. Add a third Label control and give it a Text value of Operation:.

4. Add a RadioButtonList control to the form. Name it OpButtonList. Add the values Add, Subtract, Multiply, Divide to its Items collection. Set the Selected property of the Add value to True.

5. Add two more Label controls to the form. Give the first one a Text value of Answer:. Name the second label AnswerLabel and clear its Text property. Set its ForeColor property to a bright red color.

6. Finally, add a Button control to the form and give it a Text value of Calculate.

Your newly created Web Form should look similar to the one shown in Figure 6.11.

Next, you need to add the code necessary to call the Calculator Web service to give it the answers you need. First, you need to add a reference to

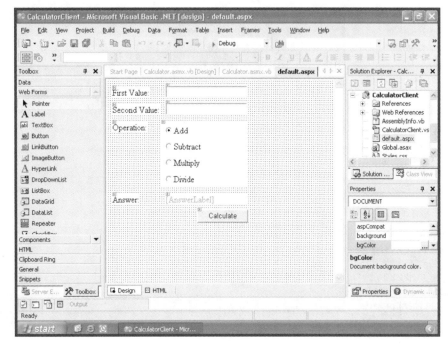

Figure 6.11

The completed
Web-based client
for the Calculator
Web service.

the Web service to your current project so that your Web page will know how to call the Web service. To do this, right-click the `Calculator.asmx` file in the Solution Explorer. Select View in Browser from the pop-up menu. This shows you the Web service information page again. Now, copy the text from the URL combo box on the Web toolbar from within the environment. The URL should be pointing to http://localhost/LearnVB/Calculator/Calculator.asmx. You will need this URL to add a reference to the client project.

Now you need to add the reference to the `CalculatorClient` project. Right-click on the project in the Solution Explorer and select Add Web Reference from the pop-up menu. You are now presented with the Add Web Reference dialog box. In the Address combo box, paste in the URL you copied previously (http://localhost/LearnVB/Calculator/Calculator.asmx). Click on the green arrow (the Go button), and you will see that the Web reference information is loaded into the dialog box for you (see Figure 6.12). All right, if you haven't added Bill Gates to your holiday postcard list yet, what the heck is holding you up? Can't you see what the man is doing for you here?

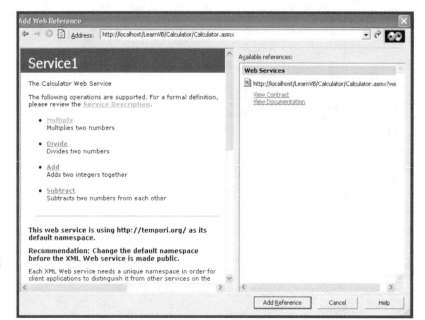

Figure 6.12

Adding a Web
service reference to
the client project.

Clicking on the Add Reference button in this dialog box adds a reference to the Calculator Web service into your `CalculatorClient` project. After the dialog box closes, you will see a new node in the tree view of the Solution Explorer for your project. It is named Web References, and it has conveniently added your new Web service to the `CalculatorClient` project. But wait—what's that "localhost" thing doing there? Fear not: It is simply a "temporary" namespace given to your Web service. Right-click on the `localhost` entry and select Rename from the pop-up menu. Rename it to `CalcSvc`. Now you're ready to add code to the client application!

Double-click on the Calculate button in the Web Form designer and add the following code:

```
Dim ws As New CalcSvc.Service1()
Select Case OpButtonList.SelectedIndex
    Case 0
        AnswerLabel.Text = ws.Add(TextBoxA.Text, TextBoxB.Text)
    Case 1
        AnswerLabel.Text = ws.Subtract(TextBoxA.Text, _
        TextBoxB.Text)
```

```
    Case 2
        AnswerLabel.Text = ws.Multiply(TextBoxA.Text, _
        TextBoxB.Text)
    Case Else
        AnswerLabel.Text = ws.Divide(TextBoxA.Text, TextBoxB.Text)
End Select
```

Here's what's happening in the preceding code. First, the ws variable is declared as a new instance of CalcSvc.Service1. Note that because the name of the Calculator service was never changed from Calculator.asmx, the service name shows up as Service1. If you want, you can go back and change it to Calculator. If you did that, it would show up as CalcSvc.Calculator instead of CalcSvc.Service1.

TIP

I don't have many complaints about Visual Studio .NET; it is nearly flawless in many ways. However, there is one caveat that drives me crazy: The environment creates "default" names for Web pages and services, assuming you'll change them later. Thus, it creates such unfriendly names as Service1.asmx, the Service1 class, and localhost. Until Microsoft corrects this (by adding a helpful dialog box to ask you what you want them named instead of assuming names for you), here is a tip: Whenever you create a new Web service, immediately delete the WebService1.asmx file and add a new Web service by selecting Add, Add Web Service from the pop-up context menu that is presented when you right-click on the project. Using the dialog box that is presented, you will get to choose the name for your Web service and underlying class instead of having it created for you.

After the Web service is instantiated, it is ready to use. The next several lines are used to examine the selected index of the OpButtonList control. Depending on what is selected (Add, Subtract, Multiply, or Divide), the AnswerLabel.Text is changed to the result of the Calculator Web services' associated method. Note that because we have Option Strict turned off at the moment, we don't have to do any fancy conversions from Integer to String and vice versa.

Finally, all that's left is to set the startup project as the CalculatorClient instead of the Calculator Web service. To do this, right-click the CalculatorClient project and select Set as Startup Project from the pop-up menu. Finally, save all your files and choose Build Solution from the Build menu. This ensures that everything is built and ready to go. All that's left is to run the client application! Press F5 to run it and see what you get. Hopefully, you'll have a running Web client application that uses your new Calculator Web service. Go ahead and put a few numbers in and try out each of the operations. Figure 6.13 shows a sample of what my screen looks like when I run the client application.

Pat yourself on the back—you did it! You built your first ASP.NET Web service and your first consumer of your Web service. Now you know just how easy it is to create these in Visual Studio .NET. From a programming perspective, a lot is going on under the hood, but the environment and language have sheltered you from having to deal with such low-level tasks as working with the raw WSDL and XML, leaving instead just a few steps necessary to create XML Web services.

Having done the previous example, you should have an understanding now of what Web services are. Of course, the example is simple in concept and implementation, but you should start to see the big picture and how Web services can be used. In yesterday's world, you might have created a shared

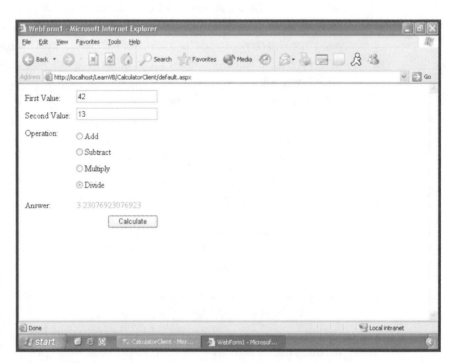

Figure 6.13

Running the Web-based client for the Calculator Web service.

library with a bunch of functions and procedures in it to encapsulate and reuse some business functionality. Now, with Web services, you can put all that functionality into the Web service model instead and have that functionality exposed over your intranet, extranet, or the Internet. Any client application in any language on almost any platform would be able to consume the Web service. The possibilities are virtually limitless, and this represents a revolutionary step in application development.

Take a Break

You might find that your head is spinning rapidly at this point, so please do yourself a favor and take a break before you turn into the headless horseman .NET. Get up, walk around, grab a fresh cup of <beverage/>, and take a few minutes to ponder what Web services are and how they will impact you where you are. Next, you'll be creating more examples of .NET Web services and learn how to consume some Web services that were created outside the .NET platform.

The Converter Web Service

Now that you have gotten your feet wet, as the saying goes, why don't you try an experiment on your own? Using the previous section as a guide, create a Converter Web service. The purpose of this Web service will be to convert Fahrenheit to Celsius and Celsius to Fahrenheit. I'm not giving you the exact steps this time, either—it's up to you. Of course, you'll need to close the current solution and start a new one and take it from there. Just like in the previous example, build your Web service first and your client application after you've built and tested the Converter Web service. Just for fun, try making a Windows Forms client this time. To make things a little easier for you, I'm going to give you the prebuilt Visual Basic .NET code necessary to do the conversion:

```
' Converts Fahrenheit to Celsius
Return ((Fahrenheit - 32) * 5) / 9
' Converts Celsius to Fahrenheit
Return ((Celsius * 9) / 5) + 32
```

Use the preceding code snippets when creating your new Converter Web service. When you're done, you should have a Windows client application that uses your Web service. Figure 6.14 shows what mine looks like as a completed application.

Figure 6.14

A sample Windows-based client that uses the Converter Web service.

Notice in my example that I have entered −40 for the Fahrenheit value and clicked the Convert to Celsius button, which converts it to −40 Celsius. I'd be willing to bet that you never knew that −40 Fahrenheit was −40 Celsius, did you? See—you never know what you might learn while reading a book!

Hopefully, you were able to successfully create your own Converter service and Windows client. If you need help, please download the source code for this book. It includes my example so you can see what the finished product looks like.

The DataServer Web Service

Web services are not just limited to intrinsic data types, such as the String, Integer and Double data types. You can use your own data types and even datasets within Web services. This section will show you how to do just that. You will build a new Web service named DataServer and will pass a structure, array, and dataset from the Web service to your client application.

If you have a solution open in the Visual Studio .NET environment, please close it and start a new project. Like you've done before, you will need to create a new ASP.NET Web Service project. This time, name it DataServer. After you have created the project, rename the Service1.asmx file to DataServer.asmx. Next, switch to code view and paste the following import statements and structure definition into the code just below the Imports clause (at the top of the source file):

```
Imports System.Data
Imports System.Data.SqlClient
```

```
Public Structure Point
    Dim x As Integer
    Dim y As Integer
End Structure
```

The Imports statement will include helpful namespaces in our source code that will be used in the GetEmployees method of the Web service. The Point structure will be used in the GetPoint method.

Next, you need to add three new functions to your Web service. Paste the following code into the end of the source file (just before the End Class statement):

```
<WebMethod(Description:="Returns a list of employees")> _
Public Function GetEmployees() As DataSet
    Dim cn As New _
    SqlConnection("Server=localhost;Database=Pubs;User Id=sa")
    Dim da As New SqlDataAdapter("SELECT * FROM Employee", cn)
    Dim ds As New DataSet()
    da.Fill(ds)
    Return ds
End Function


<WebMethod(Description:="Sample structure passing")> _
Public Function GetPoint() As Point
    Dim pt As Point
    Randomize()
    pt.x = CInt(Int((100 * Rnd()) + 1))
    pt.y = CInt(Int((100 * Rnd()) + 1))
    Return pt
End Function


<WebMethod(Description:="Returns array of 10 integers")> _
Public Function GetIntArray(ByVal inc As Integer) As Integer()
    Dim ctr As Integer
    Dim arr(9) As Integer
    For ctr = 0 To 9
        arr(ctr) = (ctr + 1) * inc
```

```
        Next
          Return arr
End Function
```

Let's examine each of the methods in the previous code listing:

➤ **GetEmployees.** This method returns a populated dataset to the consumer of the Web service. The dataset is returned as XML, thereby making it Internet firewall friendly. For this example, the pubs database is used. (Note that you might have to change your user ID and password options if they are different from this example). A simple SELECT statement retrieves all the records from the Employee table.

➤ **GetPoint.** This method returns a populated Point structure to the client application.

➤ **GetIntArray.** This method returns a populated array of 10 integers that are incremented by a value passed from the client.

Now that you have built the DataServer Web service, it's time to build the client application. As you did before, right-click on the solution name (DataServer) and choose Add, New Project. Choose to create a new Visual Basic ASP.NET application. Name it DataServerClient. Next, rename WebForm1.aspx to default.aspx.

Before you begin using your new Web service and its three methods, you need to add a Web reference to the client application. To do this, you'll need the WSDL, just as you have seen in previous examples. Right-click on DataServer.asmx and view it in the browser. Copy the URL with the WSDL location on it. Finally, right-click on the DataServerClient project and select Add Web Reference from the pop-up menu. This brings up the Add Web Reference dialog box again. Paste your WSDL URL into the Address combo box and click the Green Go button. You should see the dialog box populate with all the operations that your DataServer service supports (see Figure 6.15).

Now that you've added the DataServer Web service to the DataServer client project, rename the localhost namespace in the Solution Explorer to DataSvc. While you're there, go ahead and set DataServerClient as the startup project.

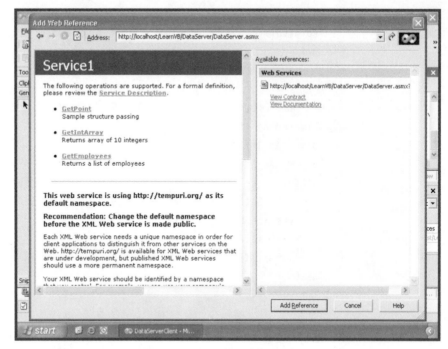

Figure 6.15

Adding the
DataServer Web
service to the
DataServer client
project.

The final task is to set up your client application to get the data from the DataServer Web service. To do this, add three new buttons to your Web Form. Name them GetPointBtn, GetArrayBtn, and GetDataSetBtn, and give them text of Get Point, Get Array, and Get DataSet, respectively. Next, add a label next to the GetPointBtn. Name it PointLbl. Add a ListBox control next to the GetArrayBtn and name it ArrayLstBox. Finally, add a DataGrid next to the GetDataSetBtn and name it EmployeesGrd. Right-click on the grid and choose the Professional 1 AutoFormat option.

Finally, you'll need to add code to your client application to call the Web service. For this, I'll help you by providing my source code:

```
Private Sub GetPointBtn_Click(ByVal sender As System.Object, _
ByVal e As System.EventArgs) Handles GetPointBtn.Click
    Dim pt As New DataSvc.Point()
    Dim ws As New DataSvc.Service1()
```

```
        pt = ws.GetPoint()
        PointLbl.Text = "The point is (" & pt.x & ", " & pt.y & ")"
End Sub


Private Sub GetArrayBtn_Click(ByVal sender As System.Object, _
ByVal e As System.EventArgs) Handles GetArrayBtn.Click
    Dim arr As Integer()
    Dim i As Integer
    Dim ws As New DataSvc.Service1()
    Randomize()
    arr = ws.GetIntArray(CInt(Int((100 * Rnd()) + 1)))
    ArrayLstBox.Items.Clear()
    For Each i In arr
        ArrayLstBox.Items.Add(i)
    Next
End Sub


Private Sub GetDataSetBtn_Click(ByVal sender As System.Object, _
ByVal e As System.EventArgs) Handles GetDataSetBtn.Click
    Dim ws As New DataSvc.Service1()
    Dim ds As New DataSet()
    ds = ws.GetEmployees()
    EmployeesGrd.DataSource = ds
    EmployeesGrd.DataBind()
End Sub
```

Next, arrange the controls on your Web Form so that they look like Figure 6.16.

Pressing the F5 key will run your completed project. You should see a Web Form running in your browser. Go ahead and click on all three buttons. You should see something similar to Figure 6.17.

That's it! You've just created a Web Form client that obtains complex data from a Web service. Next, you'll create a mobile client application that obtains data from a Web service listed on http://www.xmethods.com.

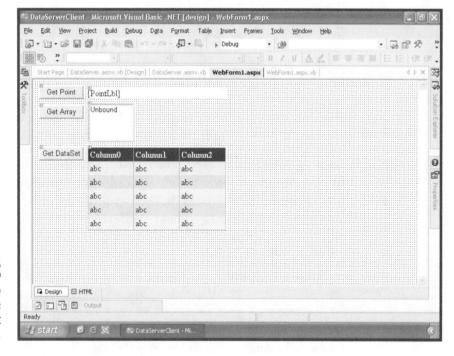

Figure 6.16

The completed Web
Form for the
DataServerClient
project.

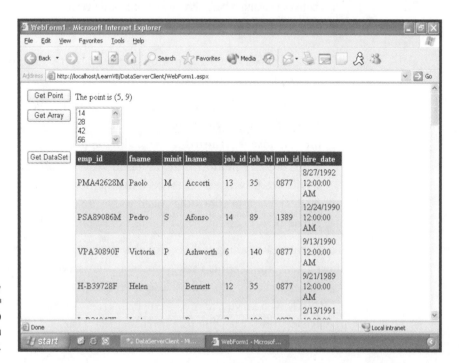

Figure 6.17

The completed Web
Form running in a
browser.

Consuming Web Services Asynchronously

By default, Web services are called synchronously. That is, your application is put in an indefinite wait state while it waits for the result of the Web service. For some applications, this behavior might be okay, whereas for others, it is unacceptable. In some cases, you might want to call a Web service asynchronously—that is, call the Web service and have your application continue while waiting for the result of the Web service.

As usual, Visual Basic .NET and Visual Studio .NET make this process easy for you. You might have already noticed while digging into the WSDL for some previous Web services that you created that other methods were created for you with the Begin and End prefix. For example, in the previous `DataServer` Web service example, the WSDL contains additional methods for `BeginGetPoint` and `EndGetPoint`. These methods are created for you automatically to support asynchronous consumption of Web services.

NOTE There is no such thing as an "asynchronous" Web service—all Web services are created the same. The difference lies in how they are called. This section shows you the difference between calling a Web service synchronously versus asynchronously.

To call a Web service asynchronously, you have two options: callbacks and wait handles. These are explained as follows:

➤ **CallBack function.** This function waits for the Web service to produce a response; when the response is ready, the End method is called and the response is returned to the calling application.

➤ **WaitHandle function.** This function waits for one or more Web services to produce a response. This method is commonly used in ASP.NET applications that need to ensure all Web service calls are completed before sending the final response back to the caller's browser.

To demonstrate calling a Web service asynchronously, you will create a Windows client application that accesses a Web service you will create named `AsynchService`. To do this, close any active solutions and create a new ASP.NET Web service named `AsynchService`. After you've created it, rename the `WebService1.asmx` file to `AsynchService.asmx`.

This new Web service uses a system thread to wait a caller-defined amount of time and then return a string to the caller denoting that the Web method is finished. Therefore, before you add code, you need to add the Imports System.Threading statement under the Imports System.Web.Services statement at the top of your AsynchService.asmx.vb file. Next, add the following code to the source file:

```
<WebMethod(_
Description:="Long web method - don't fall asleep waiting!")> _
Public Function LongWebMethod(ByVal SleepPeriod As Integer) _
As String
    Thread.Sleep(SleepPeriod)
    Return "I'm back!"
End Function
```

The preceding code causes the Web service to wait for a user-defined period and then return with the I'm back! string. Next, add a new Windows Forms application to the current solution and name it AsynchClient. Of course, you need to add a reference to the AsynchService Web service, so go ahead and do that now. After you've added that, rename the Web reference to AsynchSvc. Don't you like how I'm letting you use your experience gained from earlier in this chapter to give you high-level directives instead of step-by-step directions? This will help you learn to build Web services and client applications in the real world when you're finished with this book.

Next, let's start building the user interface. First, add three Label controls to the Windows Form. Make their Text property Wait Period:, Counter:, and Response:, respectively. Line them up near the left side of the form. Next, add a TextBox control and name it WaitPeriodTxt. Put the WaitPeriodTxt control next to the Wait Period: label. Then, add two more Label controls and put them below the text box. Name them CounterLbl and ResponseLbl. Finally, add two Button controls. Name one SynchBtn with the Text property set to Call Synchronously. Name the other AsynchBtn with the Text property set to Call Asynchronously. Give the form's Text property the setting of Asynchronous Web Services. Your form should resemble Figure 6.18.

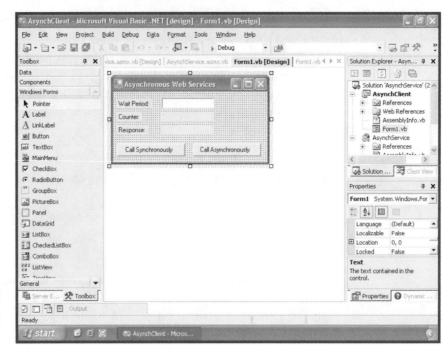

Now comes the tricky part. Double-click the SynchBtn control to go into the code behind the form. Add Imports System.Threading to the top of the source file. Then, add the following code:

```
Private Sub SynchBtn_Click(ByVal sender As System.Object, _
ByVal e As System.EventArgs) Handles SynchBtn.Click
    Dim i As Integer = 0
    Dim ws As AsynchSvc.Service1 = New AsynchSvc.Service1()
    CounterLbl.Text = i
    ResponseLbl.Text = ""
    Application.DoEvents()
    ResponseLbl.Text = ws.LongWebMethod(WaitPeriodTxt.Text * 1000)
    Application.DoEvents()
    While ResponseLbl.Text = ""
        i = i + 1
        CounterLbl.Text = i
        Application.DoEvents()
    End While
End Sub
```

```
Private Sub AsynchBtn_Click(ByVal sender As System.Object, _
ByVal e As System.EventArgs) Handles AsynchBtn.Click
    Dim i As Integer = 0
    Dim ws As AsynchSvc.Service1 = New AsynchSvc.Service1()
    Dim cb As AsyncCallback = New _
    AsyncCallback(AddressOf AsynchCallBack)
    CounterLbl.Text = i
    ResponseLbl.Text = ""
    Application.DoEvents()
    ws.BeginLongWebMethod(WaitPeriodTxt.Text * 1000, cb, ws)
    While ResponseLbl.Text = ""
        i = i + 1
        CounterLbl.Text = i
        Application.DoEvents()
    End While
End Sub


Public Sub AsynchCallBack(ByVal Result As IAsyncResult)
    Dim ws As AsynchSvc.Service1 = Result.AsyncState
    ResponseLbl.Text = ws.EndLongWebMethod(Result)
    Application.DoEvents()
End Sub
```

There's a lot to "consume" on your part here. First, look at the code behind the SynchBtn Click event. This code behaves the same as any Web service client code you have written thus far. First, the Web service is instantiated, and then the LongWebMethod is called, passing it the period it should wait. The period parameter is in milliseconds, so it is multiplied by 1,000. (The user will be putting in the number of seconds to wait.)

Next, take a look at the code behind the AsynchBtn. Now, this is different! First, the Web service is instantiated as always, but then there is this line:

```
Dim cb As AsyncCallback = New _
AsyncCallback(AddressOf AsynchCallBack)
```

The variable cb is of type AsyncCallBack. This is a special pointer to the AsynchCallBack function (in .NET terms, known as a delegate) that will be used when calling the Web service asynchronously.

◄◄◄◄◄◄◄◄◄◄◄◄◄◄◄◄◄◄◄◄◄◄◄◄◄◄◄◄◄◄◄◄◄◄◄◄◄◄◄

A *delegate* is a reference type that refers to a shared method of an object. If you have used C, C++, or Delphi before, you might be familiar with the concept of a function pointer. A .NET delegate is similar in concept to a function pointer.

◄◄◄◄◄◄◄◄◄◄◄◄◄◄◄◄◄◄◄◄◄◄◄◄◄◄◄◄◄◄◄◄◄◄◄◄◄◄◄

The next strange line you should see is this:

```
ws.BeginLongWebMethod(WaitPeriodTxt.Text * 1000, cb, ws)
```

This is where the `Begin` method is used. Remember, the "normal" method name is `LongWebMethod`. However, for asynchronous consumption, the `BeginLongWebMethod` and `EndLongWebMethod` functions have been automatically created for you. This line initiates a call to the `BeginLongWebMethod` function and passes it the wait period (multiplied by 1,000), a pointer to the callback function, and the object context variable (the Web service). The key difference between the asynchronous call and the synchronous call becomes evident with the ensuing code: A `While` loop increments a counter and updates the form. During a synchronous call, the caller is put into a wait state, waiting indefinitely (or until a timeout occurs) for the Web service to return a response. In the asynchronous example, the Web service is called and the code continues to run, allowing the program to continue. After the Web service is finished, the callback function is called (in this case, `AsynchCallBack`). In this function, the value of the `ResponseLbl.Text` property is changed, thereby breaking the `While` loop and ending the example.

NOTE

I have included the `Application.DoEvents()` statement several times in this example. This function allows the application's events to "catch up," allowing things like the labels on the forms to be updated. Without these calls in the middle of the code, the form's labels would not be updated until all of the code was completed.

Now it's your turn to give it a try. Run the program by pressing F5 and enter 5 for the wait period. First, try it synchronously. See how the counter is not running? This shows that the code is "stopped" for 5 seconds, waiting for the Web service to complete. Next, try it asynchronously. Here, you can see immediately that the counter runs while the Web service is being called. When the Web service returns, the counter stops. You should see results similar to those shown in Figure 6.19.

Figure 6.19

Running the
AsynchClient
Windows
application.

Consuming Other Web Services

Of course, Visual Basic .NET is not the only language that supports Web services. Many other languages can and have been used to create a myriad of Web services that are published in UDDI and other directories. One such directory is http://www.xmethods.com (see Figure 6.20). This example uses one such Web service published on the site. The service is called AnyWho, and it's hosted by Kazoo Software in Santa Clara, California. The service was written with Delphi, and I am showing you this example to demonstrate that a .NET-compatible language can consume a non-.NET Web service. The AnyWho service allows client applications to send in any phone number in

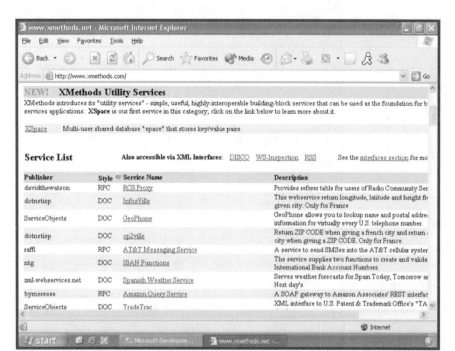

Figure 6.20

The http://www.
xmethods.com Web
service directory.

the United States and get back the name of the owner and the address associated with the phone number (if available).

Can you think of a better client application for this than a mobile one? Imagine this: You're in a meeting and someone calls your mobile phone. Unable to take the call, you let the phone call go to voice mail. However, the caller does not leave a message. Who called? Should you blindly call back and ask who it is? Imagine if you could simply retrieve the name and address of the caller just by typing in the phone number and using the AnyWho Web service.

NOTE This chapter uses the Mobile Internet Toolkit (available as a free download from Microsoft at http://www.microsoft.com) and the OpenWave Mobile Browser (available as a free download from OpenWave at http://www.openwave.com).

To begin, close any solution you might have open and then create a new mobile Web application. Name it `AnyWhoClient` (as seen in Figure 6.21).

After you've created the mobile Web application, rename `MobileWebForm1.aspx` to `default.aspx`. Next, rename `Form1` to `AnyWhoFrm`. Before you add more controls or code to your mobile application, you need to add a Web reference to the AnyWho Web service. To do this, browse to http://www.xmethods.com using your Web browser. Find the link to the AnyWho service on the main page and click on it. You should see a page displayed like in Figure 6.22.

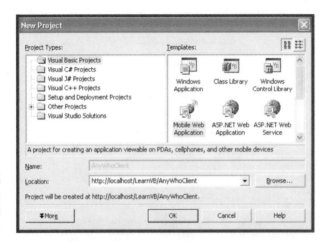

Figure 6.21

Creating the
AnyWhoClient
mobile application.

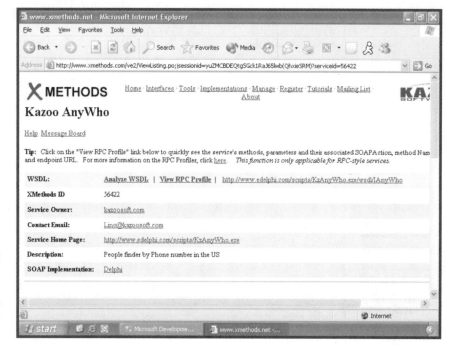

Figure 6.22

The http://www. xmethods.com information page on the AnyWho Web service.

Click on the WSDL link (the one beginning with http://www.edelphi.com). Copy the WDSL link (using the Clipboard) and return to your AnyWhoClient application in the Visual Studio .NET environment (see Figure 6.23). Then, add the Web reference to your client application using the WSDL you have copied to the Clipboard. Then rename the Web service reference to AnyWhoSvc.

Next, you need to add some controls to the Mobile Web Form. The first control you need is a Label control. Name it PhoneLbl and set its Text property to Enter 10-digit phone number:. Next, add a TextBox control and name it PhoneTxt. Next, add another Label control and name it NameLbl. Give it a Text property of Name:. Finally, add a Command control and name it GetNameCmd. Your form should now look like Figure 6.24.

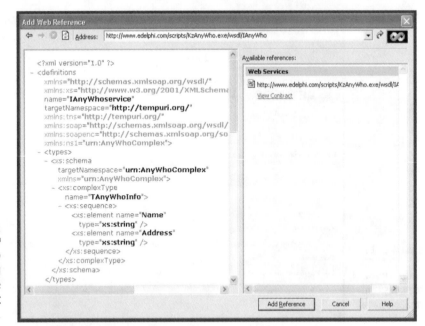

Figure 6.23

The AnyWho Web service WSDL being added to the AnyWhoClient application.

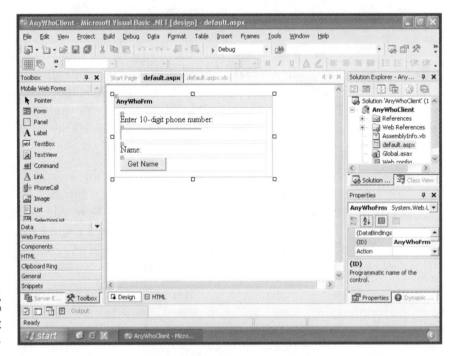

Figure 6.24

The AnyWhoClient Mobile Web Form.

The only thing left to do now is add the code to call the AnyWho Web service from your mobile client application. Add the following code under the Click event of the GetNameCmd control:

```
Dim ws As New AnyWhoSvc.IAnyWhoservice()
Dim data As New AnyWhoSvc.TAnyWhoInfo()
Dim area As Integer
Dim phone As String
area = Left(PhoneTxt.Text, 3)
phone = Right(PhoneTxt.Text, 7)
data = ws.AnyWho(area, phone)
NameLbl.Text = "Name: " & data.Name
```

Now, you're ready to run the application! You can either press F5 to run the application in a standard Web browser, or use the OpenWave Mobile Browser to view the application. As seen in Figure 6.25, I have typed in the URL of the mobile application (http://localhost/LearnVB/AnyWhoClient/default.aspx) and used the application to look up a phone number (I used my company's phone number). Go ahead and type in a 10-digit phone number to see if it returns the correct name for the phone number.

Figure 6.25

The AnyWhoClient mobile Web form in action.

There! You have now created and consumed many Web services and seen them put to use. How do you feel? Do you get the idea and the underlying concepts? The light bulb should be coming on in your head right about now, and you should be realizing the full potential of Web services and what they mean to modern computing.

NOTE Many other public Web service registries are available besides http://www. xmethods.com. Some of these include http://uddi.microsoft.com and http://www-3. ibm.com/services/uddi/. Here, you will find a wealth of interesting and useful Web services and information on the companies that provide them.

Consuming Web Services in Office XP

From a business perspective, Web services are only as good as they are practical in everyday use. Client applications need to be created that consume Web services for their full potential to be realized. One such client application that is in use all over the world that is Web-service ready is Office XP.

NOTE Although this example is designed specifically for Office XP, you might be able to use the code in previous versions, such as Office 2000.

Using Microsoft Office, you can write applications using Visual Basic for Applications (VBA) that call Web services via a special object called MSXML. This example shows you how to perform such a task using Excel. For simplicity, we will reuse the existing DataServer service to return some arbitrary numbers to Excel. Although this example might not win awards for practicality, it shows you how simple it is to call Web services from within Office XP.

To begin, start Microsoft Excel and create a new spreadsheet named WebServiceExample.xls. In cell A2, add an Increment: text value, and in cell A3, add a Sum: text value. Next, make sure the Forms toolbar is showing and add a Button control to the spreadsheet. When the pop-up dialog box asks you to assign a macro to the button, click on the New button and create a new macro named GetSumBtn_Click(), as shown in Figure 6.26.

Your spreadsheet should now look like Figure 6.27.

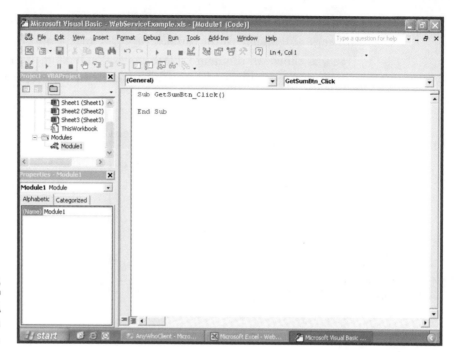

Figure 6.26

Adding a VBA macro to call a Web service.

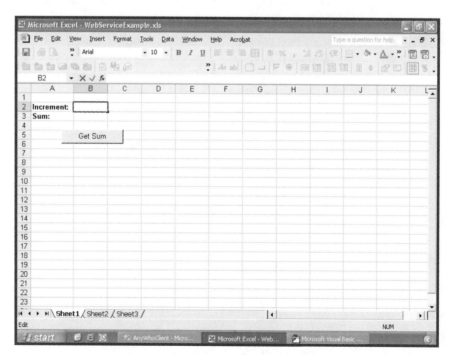

Figure 6.27

The WebServiceExample. xls spreadsheet.

You need to right-click on the button you created in Excel to change its macro assignment to the `GetSumBtn_Click` macro and its text value to `Get Sum`, as shown in the figure. Next, go to the Tools menu in the VBA editor and select the References menu item. Check the Microsoft XML v3.0 object, as shown in Figure 6.28.

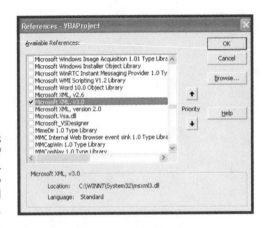

Figure 6.28

Adding the MSXML v3.0 reference to the Excel spreadsheet.

Next, enter the following code into the Excel `GetSumBtn_Click` macro:

```
Dim ws As MSXML2.DOMDocument
Dim inc As String
Dim result As String
Dim ctr As Integer
Dim num As String
Dim sum As Integer
Dim chars As Integer
inc = ActiveSheet.Range("B2").Value
Set ws = New MSXML2.DOMDocument
ws.async = False
ws.Load ("http://localhost/LearnVB/DataServer/DataServer.asmx" & _
"/GetIntArray?inc=" & inc)
result = ws.Text
sum = 0
chars = Len(result)
For ctr = 1 To chars
    If Mid(result, ctr, 1) = " " Then
        sum = sum + Val(num)
        num = ""
    ElseIf ctr = chars Then
```

SUNDAY AFTERNOON Creating and Consuming Web Services **267**

```
            num = num & Mid(result, ctr, 1)
            sum = sum + Val(num)
        Else
            num = num & Mid(result, ctr, 1)
        End If
    Next
ActiveSheet.Range("B3").Value = sum
```

Here's how the code works. First, a new instance of an MSXML2.DOMDocument is created. This is used to call the Web service. The inc variable is set to the value to increment by (as determined by the value of the B2 cell). Then the Web service is called using the URL of the DataServer service created earlier in conjunction with the inc value. The Text property of the DOMDocument object returns the result of the Web service call, and it contains a string with the "raw" results (such as 1 2 3 4 5 6 7 8 9 10). The raw results are parsed to come up with a summary value, which is populated into the B3 cell.

Go ahead and try the spreadsheet for yourself. If you've entered all the code correctly, you should get the correct sum value. For example, Figure 6.29 shows that by using an increment of 15, a sum of 825 is returned.

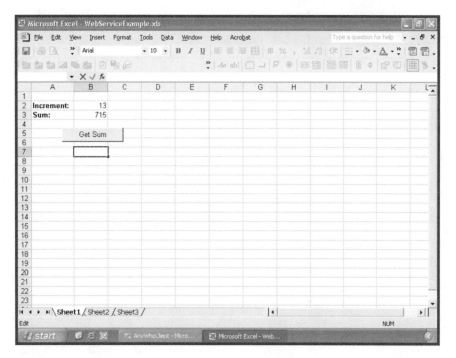

Figure 6.29

The WebServiceExample. xls spreadsheet in action.

NOTE The VBA code used in this example differs slightly from normal Visual Basic .NET code. Basically, VBA is one revision behind; however, future versions of Office should "catch up" and be compatible with Visual Basic .NET.

What's Next

In the next session, you'll learn some professional techniques to apply to your development cycle to help you create the most effective bug-free applications. You'll learn about a typical project lifecycle and how to perform proper requirements analysis to ensure you get it right the first time. You'll learn about best practices, such as implementing GUI and coding standards. Finally, you'll learn how to properly implement databases and effectively test your applications.

Best Practices

(Bonus Session)

➤ The project lifecycle
➤ Effective GUI design
➤ Implementing a help system
➤ Implementing coding standards

Now that you have been introduced to the .NET Framework and Visual Basic .NET, there is only one thing left to do. Before you head back to work tomorrow morning, you need to know how to implement all that you've learned *the right way*. That is, you shouldn't just "dive in" and start coding a project without following some proven guidelines and standards. The focus of this, the final chapter in this book, is to show you some "best practices"—that is, some key practices to follow when embarking on any software development project.

The .NET platform best practices encompass many facets of the software development process—all the way from the initial requirements analysis and design through the coding, testing, deployment, and maintenance phases. The best practices provided in this chapter help you produce the best quality software products possible. Following these guidelines and best practices does not guarantee that you'll be successful in your software development endeavors; other mitigating factors might adversely affect your projects. However, following these guidelines will make the chances of success much greater than if you had no guidelines to follow.

The Project Lifecycle

The first thing you should know with regard to best practices is how to properly implement the project lifecycle—that is, how to take a project from inception to completion and beyond. I'm sure many of you have been through several projects at some time or another in your careers; whether you're new to all this or a seasoned veteran, you should pay attention to the guidelines in this chapter; they might save you heartache in the long run.

Project Lifecycle Approaches

The project lifestyle has two standard approaches: waterfall and iterative. Each of these is defined next.

The *waterfall approach* is the approach used by "traditional" software projects (see Figure 7.1). That is, each phase (requirements analysis, design, coding, testing, and release) is completed before beginning the next phase. As Figure 7.1 shows, the approach resembles a "waterfall" because each phase "falls" into the next one.

The *iterative approach* is the approach that is now considered to be much more realistic and true to life than the waterfall approach (see Figure 7.2). This approach entails doing the requirements analysis phase up front (as in the waterfall approach), and then doing a high-level design. Then, an iterative cycle of low-level design, coding, testing, and release is commenced; this cycle repeats until the project is completed.

◀◀◀◀◀◀◀◀◀◀◀◀◀◀◀◀◀◀◀◀◀◀◀◀◀◀◀◀◀◀◀◀◀◀◀◀◀

If you have been doing software development for a long time, chances are pretty good that you have encountered the waterfall approach sometime in your career. This is the more "traditional" approach to software development, but it is by no means the best approach.

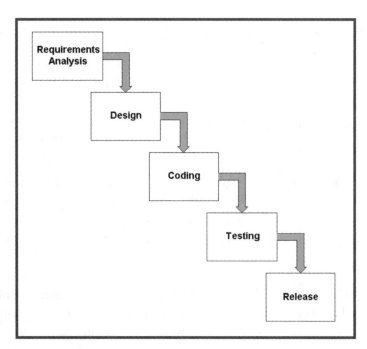

Figure 7.1

The waterfall project lifecycle approach.

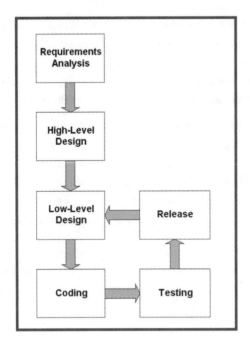

Figure 7.2

The iterative project lifecycle approach.

The Waterfall Approach

The waterfall approach consists of autonomous stages of software development that happen in succession. At the project's inception, a requirements analysis phase is completed, followed by a design phase, a coding phase, a testing phase, and finally a release. As Figure 7.1 shows, each of these phases happens in succession, with each phase being completed 100 percent before embarking on a new phase.

Although the waterfall approach might seem logical and familiar to most of you, it has many drawbacks. Having been involved in dozens of large-scale projects, I have witnessed firsthand some of these drawbacks. First, the waterfall approach assumes that each phase is 100 percent complete before the next phase begins. As many of you have probably seen, it is rare that any project has 100 percent of its analysis and design completed before coding begins. Of course, any programmer can tell you that it is unrealistic for the coding to be completed without having to revisit analysis or design issues. In addition, it's unrealistic to assume that testing can commence without further coding tasks needing to be completed—no one (not even me!) creates 100 percent bug-free code 100 percent of the time.

Thus, the waterfall approach is seen as unrealistic. However, trying to explain this to project managers is fruitless most of the time. "This is the way it has always been done!" is the cry of many project managers. Project management tools, unfortunately, often cater to the waterfall approach and make it hard to use any other approach. This has the adverse effect of frustrating both the project managers who are managing the projects and the developers who are trying to complete their projects with a doomed approach.

The Iterative Approach

The iterative approach consists of an initial requirements analysis and high-level design phases followed by a repeated cycle of low-level design, coding, testing, and release phases. In this approach, only the initial requirements analysis and high-level design phases should be completed 100 percent before moving forward.

After these first two phases are completed, the rest of the project begins to be "hashed" out. As new details are designed, they are hashed out in the form of code. After the code is tested, a "release" is produced. This release represents a portion of the final functionality that is to be delivered with the final system; it might be a prototype of some initial forms; it could include some forms, data access, and reports.

The feature set of each release depends on the type of product you are developing; there is no set guideline for each release. Instead, each release should be built around project "milestones"—that is, key points in the project lifecycle. As each milestone is reached, the next phase is planned and that plan is executed. This approach continually refines each deliverable after each milestone until the final product is complete. The result is a much more realistic approach with more attainable goals and expectations.

At first, project managers might feel somewhat uneasy about the iterative approach. After all, this is not the way their project planning software works, and it is not the way project managers were probably taught to do their projects. However, after the project managers see progress after each milestone is reached, they usually come around and see the light. This results in much less frustration for both the project managers and the developers. Needless to say, all of your development projects should follow the iterative approach and not the waterfall approach.

Requirements Analysis

Perhaps the most important phase of any software development project is the requirements analysis phase. If the requirements are not gathered properly and analyzed up front, it can have devastating effects on the rest of the project. Research has shown that it is far more costly to "discover" new requirements in the coding and testing iterations than it is to discover everything up front. Therefore, the more thorough of a job you do with the requirements analysis phase up front, the better the chance your project has of being a success.

Requirements gathering is not an easy process. Often, it is hard for a developer to put aside the technical view of things and try to see the process or problem as the user sees it. However, to perform effective requirements gathering and analysis, it is imperative that you (or someone else who is assigned the responsibility) understand the views of the user from their standpoint, not yours. Your view of the world is tainted. Most likely, because you are a programmer, you will think of things with a preconceived notion and bias toward the computer. What might seem logical to you might in fact seem illogical for a user.

Therefore, I recommend taking time up front in any project to sit down with the user (or users) of a system to talk personally. If there is an existing system, you will definitely want to take the time to walk through the system with them, having them explain the system to you and give you feedback on each function. Pay close attention to their description of the system and its advantages and drawbacks. Try to see the system as they see it—as a user and not a developer.

If there is not an existing system, take the time to meet with the potential users of the system you will be developing. Learn what their expectations are and what they are used to. Have them give examples of other existing systems that they liked and did not like. Attempt to see from their point of view what is acceptable versus what is not.

In many cases, you (the programmer) are not the person best suited for the responsibility of requirements analysis. Doing proper requirements gathering and analysis often takes a seasoned professional who is good at it and has done it time and time again on many projects. This kind of person is often referred to as a business analyst. Often, a business analyst will be provided as a representative for the user base. If this is the case on your project, don't be offended. Just because you're giving up the responsibility for requirements gathering and analysis doesn't mean that your skills are lacking in any way; it simply means that you can now focus on what you do best (programming) and let the business analysts do what they do best.

In any case, the result of any proper requirements analysis phase should be a requirements document that lists the high-level requirements of the system. Remember that this part of the iterative project lifecycle does not repeat; therefore, you should make sure that all the requirements are gathered and analyzed up front before moving on because this phase is not revisited at another time. This is primarily because changing requirements later on in the project lifecycle is far too costly. Therefore, try to make sure you gather and document all the requirements up front and have the user (or business analyst) review them and sign off on the document before moving on to the high-level design phase.

TIP

Some great third-party tools (such as Rational's RequisitePro) are available to help you keep track of your requirements. I recommend looking into these products to determine which ones best suit your needs. Using a software tool to assist you in this phase will help to streamline your analysis and design phases and ensure that no requirements are overlooked.

After you have documented the requirements, you need to put a change management system into place. In other words, any time a new requirement is encountered or an existing one is changed, you should document it on a change management form to have a permanent record of that change. This helps control "scope creep"—that is, the scope of the project creeping further and further away from its original design. As each change is introduced, maintaining a record will help you have an audit trail of when something was introduced and who asked for it. If the original schedule keeps getting changed and bumped back, you might be asked to provide reasons why it is taking longer than expected to code the project. Having these changes documented will help you account for the difference between what was planned versus what really happened.

High-Level Design

After all the requirements have been gathered, analyzed, reviewed, and approved, you can assimilate design issues. Design issues that are brought up at this phase might be where to place certain business rules (in objects on the client or server, in stored procedures, and so on), the delivery mechanism (Web Forms, Windows Forms, mobile application, Web Service, and so on), database architecture, and so forth. High-level classes might be hashed out at this point, with their implementation and other low-level classes to come later in the project. Standard components (either in-house or third-party) might also be selected at this point to ensure that everyone is using the same tools.

At this point, prototyping might be a good idea. Prototyping involves either working out an interface via a white board (with the users and system developers present) or developing a quick "shell" interface with a development tool. In either case, the purpose of the prototype will be to hash out the details with regard to the visual representation of the system. The users will then review the prototype to either approve or veto its suggested implementation. I recommend doing prototyping early in the project so that little time is wasted doing a full implementation of something that does not meet the user's expectations. See the section titled "Effective GUI Design" later in this chapter to get some tips on making your applications (and prototypes) look great.

Of course, one goal of any proper high-level design phase is to meet the requirements of the system. After all, if your design doesn't fulfill the requirements, why are you doing the system in the first place? Another goal is to figure out what the milestones of the project are going to be. In other words, what key points exist in the project timeline whereby you can gauge your progress?

NOTE The iterative approach to the project lifecycle should not be seen as a "free-for-all" approach. That is, just because you know you will be revisiting the design, coding, and testing phases does not give you a license to go about the development haphazardly or without forethought. Instead, the initial requirements analysis and design phases should be thorough and well documented. The ensuing iterative phases should be well thought out and planned.

After you have determined your milestones, the rest of the project can be planned. Remember: The remaining phases of the project are all iterative (repeating); therefore, you should plan a mini design, coding, testing, and release phase for each iteration. Each iteration of the project will help to translate some high-level details into low-level implementation details.

After a high-level design is complete, it should be documented in a design document and reviewed by the project team and the users.

Low-Level Design

The low-level design phase is used to hash out low-level implementation details relevant to each milestone planned in the high-level design document. The implementation details should be thorough enough so that the programmers on the team know how to carry out their tasks without much handholding or explaining necessary. Whereas the high-level design is somewhat ambiguous with regard to implementation, the low-level design should be anything but. Instead, details should be presented in a low-level design document that leaves no stone unturned.

Wherever possible, low-level design documentation should be created either in the form of straight narrative documents or diagrams. You should use object modeling and other process flow diagramming techniques during this phase to make the transition from the high-level design to the coding of the implementation as smooth and easy as possible for the programmers to understand. Use the requirements analysis document to "discover" the classes that need to be hashed out and implemented during this phase.

As each low-level design phase is approached, a new set of scenarios and use cases should be written. These are descriptions or graphs of processes and real-life cases of system usage. They are often created by the people who are responsible for the requirements of the system; the scenarios and use cases help ensure that the final system meets the requirements proposed at the inception of the project. I recommend reviewing these scenarios and use cases with the users of the system to ensure that you understand what the expected behavior of the final system will be. Your users might also want to come up with their own set of use cases and scenarios.

Wherever possible, you should implement your systems using object-oriented techniques. That is, instead of mixing business rules with presentation logic, try abstracting your business rules and encapsulating them within classes that model the behavior and processes of the systems you are building. Your use cases, scenarios, and diagrams should help you identify the classes in your system and how they are to interact and integrate with each other. They should be made available to everyone on the programming team so that everyone understands the model they are programming against. This helps to prevent programmers from coming up with duplicate classes with their own implementations. A number of third-party object modeling tools are available to help you and your fellow programmers hash out the system's object models. I suggest doing your own research to determine which one best suits your needs.

The scenarios, use cases, and other associated diagrams that are created during this phase are often used to create the test cases that will eventually be used to measure the degree of accuracy that your system holds with regard to the original requirements.

Coding

Ah, yes. Coding. You are a programmer, aren't you? For those of you who simply adore programming and can't get enough of it, I'm sure you can't wait to start coding on any new project you encounter. Personally, I'm with you for the most part; I've seen the good and the bad from coding too soon. Trust me—it's almost all bad! Although spending too much time on requirements analysis and design can also be bad, an adequate amount of time needs to be spent on both before coding should commence.

Therefore, resist the temptation to dive in head first on new projects by coding before you have hashed out all the details with regard to requirements and design. Jumping in like this only creates more headaches and more work for you later. Plus, when you start coding prematurely, any new requirements or design issues will most surely affect your coding adversely and either cause you to completely throw away or have to rewrite your current code. As was stated earlier, this has the effect of dramatically increasing the cost of the system that is being developed.

After coding has begun, periodic checkpoints should be planned for. Some organizations will implement micromanaging, having you check in several times a day or week as to how the coding phase is progressing. Some organizations will have you check in once a millennium (or so it seems), implementing a radical hands-off approach to the development phase. I have seen both used to an extreme, and I believe that the best practice exists somewhere between the two.

Whatever the case might be in your organization, the fact is that programmers will be left alone at some point to code their portions of the project. Because of this, standards and guidelines should be put in place to ensure that each programmer is "on the same page." All too often, I have seen programmers code their portions of projects completely differently, resulting in a mess "under the hood" of the system. To ensure consistency and quality, standards should be written, published, and agreed upon by everyone before coding is to begin. Be sure to read the section titled "Implementing Coding Standards" later in this chapter for helpful tips on writing these standards.

TIP Regardless of your team's size, it is always a good idea to use a version control system to keep track of the revisions of the source code and other related documentation. This facilitates regular checkpoints during the project lifecycle and also provides an audit trail of changes that were made, which is always a good idea if you're trying to track down where a new requirement, bug, or other system feature was introduced.

After you have completed coding for an iteration, you should do a peer review. A peer review requires that another programmer sit down with you and review your code—perhaps not line-by-line, but on more of a conceptual level with some integrated implementation details. Peer reviews help you ensure that your coding is up to the standard, and that the way you are implementing the system is the best possible way. These reviews should be approached constructively, not critically. Too often, I have seen other developers look at someone else's code only to say "What the *!$#? Why are you doing that? Are you crazy?" The approach should be more supportive, such as this: "I see what you're doing here. Let me give you a few pointers as to how I've done this type of thing before."

The end result is to produce an environment in which peer reviews are helpful and programmers can freely help one another without fear of being made fun of or rebuked for asking for help. Members of the programming team should be encouraged to seek one another's help when needed. Regular meetings between the programmers should be scheduled so that ideas can be shared in a group and issues can be tackled at the group level instead of relying on one person's opinion.

Testing

Of course, testing is crucial to any successful project. In the iterative approach to the project lifecycle, testing is done after each mini design and coding phase. The purpose of testing in this approach is to ensure that each release is as bug-free as possible.

It is always a good idea to have someone else test your code. You will most likely always follow the same pattern with regard to a testing plan, and someone else will most likely do things differently than you would. In many cases, this results in unseen bugs surfacing their ugly heads. As a programmer, don't worry about having bug reports returned to you during the testing phase of each iteration—it is much better to find them now than to have a final released product make it to the general masses with a nasty bug.

I distinctly remember many times when I would hand a project over to someone else to test only to have that person return it to me with a few hidden "anomalies." When the person explained what he did, my reaction would typically be, "You did what?" and then I would realize that this person was just doing things differently than I was. As illogical as it seemed to me, I had to plan on users not thinking the way I think (big grin).

TIP

I recommend always including either a system logging feature or system information feature in your products. When errors occur, a user-friendly message box should be displayed and an error log or information should optionally be available. This information can then be sent back to you (the programmer) for analysis. Too often, I have seen strange bugs appear, only to wonder how in the world the user got to that point. Since integrating system information and logging in my systems, the number of times I have been left in the dark has been few. Therefore, I suggest you include this type of feature with all the systems you release to help facilitate a speedy resolution to any error the user might encounter.

Before handing over a system for testing, it is always a good idea to create test cases. Test cases are small narratives or scripts that describe test scenarios. These test cases should be based on the requirements, use cases, and scenarios that come up during the analysis and design phases of the project. Make the test cases thorough, ensuring that every portion of functionality included in the system is tested. Document the results of each test case as to whether the tests passed or failed, and then make notes as to why it failed.

You will perform four basic tests to a varying degree during each iteration:

➤ **Unit testing.** You perform this during coding to ensure that your portion of the program is running correctly. You should do this regularly during the end of your coding phase to ensure you're on the right track and that no big surprises are awaiting you.

➤ **Integration testing.** You perform this after most of the coding is done to test how well your portion of the program integrates with the rest of the program. Your program might run fine, but when it's integrated with the rest of the system, it might not perform correctly. This type of testing will catch those types of bugs.

➤ **System testing.** This type of testing encompasses the entire system (hence the name). Typically, the test cases that have been written are used to measure the degree of compliance and accuracy of the final working system. Often, test cases are run through repeatedly after each release. This is known as regression testing—testing what has already been tested once.

➤ **Acceptance testing.** The users of your system typically perform this to ensure that the product you're delivering meets their requirements and expectations. Ultimately, they are the ones who will determine whether your system is acceptable.

Regardless of how you go about testing, it is always a good idea to use software solutions to streamline the process as much as possible. I recommend looking into third-party defect tracking and testing software packages to help keep track of the reported bugs and their associated resolution. After all, what good is all this testing if all the bugs are not resolved and fixed? Having a third-party package available to you will help ensure that no bugs slip through the cracks into the final system.

In most cases, your development machine is nothing like what the end-user will have. Therefore, I recommend either obtaining separate machines for testing or having a machine available with several different operating systems on it. Although you would think that your system would run the same on most systems, inevitably you will find small differences between different operating systems, even within the same OS family (such as Windows). Therefore, I strongly recommend testing in these environments on separate machines to ensure you have no surprises when delivering your systems.

Release

In the iterative software development process, releases are created periodically with each milestone to provide concrete points of review and adaptation for ongoing development. As each release is given to the users, the users can provide feedback that will help you refine the next release until it matches exactly or comes close to matching their expectations.

I recommend facilitating each release cycle by providing your users and other system testers with a simple way to provide feedback to you. Perhaps you can provide a simple e-mail address or a Web site; whatever the case, it will make your life and their life easier if the communication between the user and developer is streamlined, and their ideas, recommendations, concerns, and bug reports can be tracked.

Just as a peer review serves as a checkpoint for the coding phase, I recommend a release review after each release so that a checkpoint can be established and new tasks can be added or modified for the next iteration. Then you can modify the project schedule and refine the next iteration plan.

Effective GUI Design

One of the most important parts of any system you create is the user interface. It is the medium by which your users will interact with the system. A poorly designed user interface will inevitably lead to further problems down the road. Your users will not be able to understand how to use the system or get the results they want. They will undoubtedly voice their complaints to you and others. Your system might perform perfectly and meet all the other requirements just fine, but if the interface is poorly designed and implemented, all your efforts will be wasted. Your users will always remember the user interface to the system; more often than not, the success of the system is gauged by how well the user interface is done.

Users like clean interfaces—ones that are easily understood and used. The more user friendly and intuitive a user interface is, the better chance it has of being accepted by the users, and the better chance you have of selling your system to other users.

How do you design a system to be user friendly? Read on.

As you might have guessed, the key to designing a user-friendly system is to understand the view of the system that the user takes on. In other words, try to see the system from the user's point of view and not yours. What menu options would make sense to the user? In what order should the process flow be presented to the user? What text should be put in forms and dialog boxes to ensure that the user knows (in his own language) what is expected?

What might seem logical to you might seem foreign and unnatural to a user. Remember: You're a developer with first-hand knowledge of computers. The users of your system will probably not have this level of detail about how computers work. In fact, many users will be somewhat intimidated by computers and need a system that can "hold their hand" through the workflow processes. Although you might think that over-simplifying things is mundane and unnecessary, your users might feel quite at home with it.

One sure-fire way to get to know the users' point of view is to sit down with them and have extended design and prototyping sessions. Try to get the users to flesh out their ideas on paper or on a white board and listen to their opinions on how things should look. Of course, their ideas should be taken in context; users often do not know exactly what they need or how they should get it. They will need your help to make sure their ideas are brought to the surface. Sometimes, the user knows what he wants, but he doesn't know how to get it. In these cases, it's up to you to use your experience and know-how to help the user decide what the best user interface would be to get the desired results.

Here are some quick guidelines to keep in mind when you're developing the user interface for your systems:

➤ **Usability.** Your systems should be designed to maximize the usability of the system. That is, the key functional mechanisms in the system should be easily accessible and obvious. Users should not have to spend a long time "hunting" down the path to find the way to perform a particular task. If designed correctly, the system should follow a user-defined natural flow, and users should be able to easily find their way around it.

➤ **User friendliness.** Your systems should be user friendly. That is, they should make the user's job easy. After all, why is the user using your system versus another system or doing it manually? The answer is, of course, that your system should make the user's job easier than any other method of implementation and that your system should enable the user to do his job more quickly and more efficiently. Thus, you should design your systems to cater to your user's needs and to make the user's experience with your system as friendly as possible.

➤ **Intuitiveness.** Often, as a developer, you will have run across certain situations in which an intuitive interface can help make the user's job easier. Don't hesitate to bring up your ideas to help implement intuitive GUI design. Often, the user will be thankful if you can eliminate certain manual steps or combine mundane tasks into one simplified process. Implement one-step operations, if possible. Implement wizards where necessary. Don't forget that some users will be "power" users who want to use the system differently from others. Take the time to think about what the task at hand is and try to come up with ways to shorten or simplify the process. Your users will love you for it!

➤ **Workflow.** Make sure your systems implement a logical workflow process and that it is easy to go from one step to the next. Ensure that proper tab order is kept on forms and that the order of the fields is appropriate. Often, users of data entry applications detest having to reach for the mouse. In these cases, you might want to implement keyboard shortcuts for them to choose items without having to reach for the mouse.

➤ **Standards.** Before developing your first prototypes, a set of user interface standards should be agreed upon. These standards will vary depending on what type of system you're creating (a Windows application or a Web application, for instance). In most cases, published samples are available on the Internet (check Microsoft's site for the latest versions), and you and the other developers should quickly come to some consensus as to which standards you will adopt and adhere to.

➤ **Consistency.** One key issue with regard to many systems is consistency. Your forms, menus, and other interface elements should remain consistent throughout the entire system. This is very important! Forms should look somewhat similar and flow easily from one to the next. Colors should remain consistent across the board. Dialog boxes should be consistent, as should any integrated error-reporting mechanisms. The implementation of standards should help in this regard, as should the regular releases and reviews of the system to help catch inconsistencies.

Implementing a Help System

No matter how small your application might be, it is always important to include a help system with it. A help system gives your users a point of reference to help them understand the system. It also helps cut down on the number of support calls you will receive. Providing a help system with your application helps to enhance the user friendliness of the system and gives your users a chance to get help whenever they need it.

Often, users are intimidated by new systems, and showing them that they can get help by merely clicking a button or pressing F1 helps ease their fears. Users are comforted by the fact that they can obtain help easily and that they can possibly answer their own questions this way.

The help system you create should be well organized, and it should be easy for the user to find the information he needs quickly. A well-designed help system is context sensitive to what the user is working on at the time he needs help. That is, when invoked, a well-designed help system should take the user to the place in the help system that addresses the portion of the system he's working on. If the answer is not available on the initial help page that the user brings up, he should be able to quickly jump to either a table of contents or an index where he can find the answer he needs. If possible, provide a way for the user to search the help material to find the desired answer.

TIP

Once again, several third-party software packages can help you in this process. Rather than trying to come up with a solution on your own, I recommend researching what software packages are available and picking one to use. This saves you a lot of time and provides you with added features that might be hard to create on your own.

In addition to a comprehensive help system, you might want to think about also providing the following:

➤ **A user manual.** Sometimes, this is nothing more than a printed version of the help file, but it is often helpful to the user to be able to have something concrete to hold in his hands and read "offline." It also helps enhance the value of your system and makes it seem more professional.

➤ **A tutorial.** Often, users need a "kick-start" to help them get up to speed. A tutorial that explains the basic building blocks of the system and has short step-by-step instructions on getting started would be very helpful.

➤ **Tips.** Sometimes, users like to get helpful tips on how to invoke certain functionality in a system. Often, applications come with a "tip of the day" feature that shows the user one tip a day.

➤ **Quick reference guide.** This is a hardcopy sheet of paper—often laminated—that the user can keep on his desk to refer to as he is learning the system. Once again, things like this increase the perceived value of the entire package.

➤ **FAQ.** A Frequently Asked Question (FAQ) document can help answer some questions that are encountered often. Users can be instructed to refer to this document before calling for support on the product. It has been my personal experience that FAQ documents are crucial in cutting down the number of support calls to a minimum.

Overall, you should *never* deliver an application without an integrated help system. Delivering an application without an integrated help system is interpreted as being unprofessional and will no doubt be looked down upon by the users. Do your users a favor and develop good help systems to go along with your good applications.

Implementing Coding Standards

Previously, I mentioned the importance of having GUI standards so that the interface you present to the user is professional, easy to understand, and consistent. In the same manner, you should come up with a set of coding standards so that the applications you create are just as professional, easy to understand, and consistent "under the hood." Implementing coding standards helps ensure that all programmers who are working on a project are "on the same page" and that the result of their work is similar.

This is especially crucial for large projects in which many software developers are working on parallel tasks. Of course, it is impossible to split one programmer into many pieces to get the project done on time. However, one goal of programming standards is to make it look as if one programmer worked on the entire project. It should not be apparent who worked on which pieces of the project. In other words, if all the programmers use the same conventions, it should be nearly impossible to distinguish one programmer's work from another. Of course, sometimes you will want to have one person's work noted (as is the case with making comments, version control, and so on). However, if your standards are being implemented correctly, you should find that your source code looks very much the same regardless of who worked on it.

Statistics show that as much as 80% or more of an application's life is spent in maintenance. That is, you will be maintaining an application for a much longer period after it is developed than you spent developing it initially. This is one reason why coding standards are so important; if you are responsible for maintaining a program that you originally didn't work on, how much easier would it be to work on it if you were all using the same standards?

Implementing coding standards has the following positive effects on your software projects:

➤ **Consistency.** As was mentioned earlier, coding standards help ensure that the underlying code is implemented consistently across the entire application.

➤ **Architecture.** Having to think about your code beforehand, combined with the imminent peer review process, has the effect of encouraging better overall architecture than if there were no standards or reviews in place.

➤ **Reliability.** Standards have a way of increasing the reliability of software by enforcing certain rules upon the code that is created.

➤ **Maintenance.** You, as a developer, will appreciate the implementation of standards because it will make your job easier. Code will be easier to understand and read if standards are enforced.

Readability

It is well known that your code will perform the same whether you use comments, indentation, and so-called "white" space. However, a clear advantage exists for those programs that do have more readable code: You (or someone else who will eventually maintain your code) will have a much easier time understanding your code and finding errors that exist if your code is "readable." Many times, in haste, developers forget to comment their code, and they get lazy about indenting rules and other readability issues. What happens is that you wind up with "spaghetti code"—that is, code that is virtually unreadable and seemingly has no structure whatsoever.

I personally have had the misfortune of inheriting portions of code (and complete applications) that were a total mess under the hood. It was literally easier for me to start over than it was to try to modify or maintain the source code I was given. In one case, almost every programming convention known to mankind was broken in a single program: Virtually no white space was used, tabs were not used, there were no comments, procedures had non-descriptive names such as A1, A2, and A3, and variables named x1, y1, and z1 were all over the place. In this particular case, I "threw out" the source code the first day I received it and started over with my own requirements analysis phase. Eventually, the entire product was re-created from scratch. To have attempted to maintain the previous source code base would have been impossible.

To avoid leaving this kind of impact on your other team members and future maintainers of your code, always try to make your code as readable as possible. By "readable," I don't mean that it should be as neat and clean as a book; it simply should be easy for someone to "inherit" your code (or to look at your code in a peer review) and quickly be able to understand what's going on. Some of you will tend to lean toward the "as little as possible" camp and put some comments in here and there and possibly some proper white space here and there and relatively consistent indentation. Some of you (like me!) will lean toward the "too much" camp and put a ton of white space and comments in your programs. The goal is to find a happy medium whereby the code can be readable but not take too much of your time.

Here are some suggestions for making your code readable:

➤ **Use white space.** Don't be afraid to press the Enter key a few more times than is needed; it often helps to separate processes into code "paragraphs" to make them easier to read.

➤ **Use comments.** Always provide comments at the beginning of every file of source code and the beginning of any class, procedure, or function. Also insert comments where complex processes that might need to be documented occur in the code. Avoid commenting code that should be obvious to a programmer just by looking at it.

➤ **Indent your code.** Always try to indent blocks of code to make it more readable. Constructs such as `Case` statements, `If Then Else` statements, and other Visual Basic .NET statements should be properly indented.

Naming Conventions

Naming conventions are important when it comes to having consistency in your programs. Each programmer is different, and it is quite possible that every programmer on a project will have his own idea of how to implement a naming convention. If no naming conventions are decided upon before development begins, you can wind up with a huge mess under the hood of your application.

To prevent this mess, you and your team should meet to discuss coming up with an appropriate naming convention. Because you have so many options in this area, I am not going to make the decision for you and provide you with a long list of conventions you should use. Some developers like a prefix notation (`strLastName`, for instance); some like a postfix notation (`LastNameStr`, for instance). Some developers like *no* notation! The latter can be the toughest ones to deal with, so be sure to enforce standards strictly so that all of your developers comply.

Here are some suggestions for implementing naming conventions:

➤ **Decide on standard abbreviations.** You and your team should meet immediately to decide (by committee) whether you will be a prefix shop or a postfix shop. You will need to nail down the details and document your naming conventions so that everyone knows what names are expected for their variables, procedures, classes, forms, controls, and other items.

➤ **Avoid non-descriptive and overly descriptive names.** Avoid short, non-descriptive names, such as x and y, for both variables and procedures. In the same manner, avoid overly long names that are a bear to type. The names for these should instead contain at least a somewhat short, meaningful name that alludes to its purpose.

Variables and Data Types

Of course, your programs will undoubtedly contain many variables. To help prevent errors from happening, you should keep the following guidelines in mind:

➤ **Always use Option Explicit.** This undoubtedly will keep you from banging your head against the wall, trying to figure out why your program is exhibiting strange behavior. This option forces you to declare all variables before they are used, helping prevent erroneous usage of undeclared variables.

➤ **Group your variable and constant declarations.** When declaring variables and constants, group them together to make the code more readable. Although this is not required, it will help you find your variables and constants quickly without having to search through all the code to find them.

➤ **Use the proper type.** Try to use the data type in your code that best suits the job at hand. Generally, avoid using strings unless they are needed, and avoid using variants altogether.

Procedures and Functions

Here are some guidelines with regard to procedures and functions:

➤ **Keep them small.** Generally, you should keep procedures and functions small; I have seen monolithic versions of these procedures and functions, and by the time you get to the end of the procedure, you generally have forgotten what the procedure existed for! As a guideline, try to keep the line count per procedure/function under 1,000 lines.

➤ **Maximize reusability.** When possible, try to separate your logic into small, reusable portions of code so that the same code can be used throughout the application and beyond, possibly in other applications.

➤ **Expect the unexpected.** Always implement stringent exception handling, making sure your code does not "blow up" without having as clean an exit as possible. Providing good exception handling allows your programs to "recover" from serious errors and allows the application to have a chance to handle these errors gracefully. Remember: It is always a good idea to write errors or exceptions to a log file for error reporting and auditing purposes.

Object-Oriented Programming

If at all possible, use object-oriented programming to code your projects. When you do, keep these guidelines in mind:

➤ **Code business logic in classes, not forms.** Many times, "RAD" is taken to mean that an application should be created so quickly that to take the time to put business logic in classes would be futile. This could not be more false. In fact, you should always ensure that any business logic put into your application is put into a business class and not the code behind the form.

➤ **Maximize inheritance.** As with procedures and functions, you should always be looking for areas in your code to reuse. In this case, you can help prevent redundant coding by implementing inheritance wherever it makes sense. Remember: Visual Basic .NET now supports implementation inheritance, so you should be able to take advantage of any OOP feature.

➤ **Put data, properties, and methods in the right place.** When you're writing classes, keep in mind the user of the class and what he needs to see and shouldn't see. Decide early on the scope of what you are creating—that is, whether it should be public, private, or protected.

Conclusion

That's it! You're finished! Now all you need to do is proudly walk into work tomorrow morning and announce your resignation. Actually, check that—you might want to hold off a bit. After all, perhaps there is some chance that you, yes you, could be the one who gets to introduce the .NET Framework and Visual Basic .NET to your organization. Perhaps a tremendous change is needed, and you believe that .NET is the way to go. Perhaps there are so many compelling reasons to integrate .NET into your work environment that you feel brave enough to take a stand and voice your opinion. Perhaps you feel that the introduction of this technology into your workplace can have an immense positive effect.

Your task now is to take all that you've learned to the next level. For some of you, that might mean developing your own small prototype/test applications. For some, it might mean diving deeper into the technical side of things, learning more details from the MSDN documentation and other technical resources. For others, it might present an opportunity for you to have your chance to really make a difference.

Whatever the case, I hope this book has provided you with a jumpstart on your .NET career and that you now hold the knowledge and confidence to take what you've started to the next step. I wish you the best. Good luck!

Migrating to Visual Basic .NET

- ➤ Upgrading to VB.NET
- ➤ Changes to the language
- ➤ Tips for veterans

In this Appendix, I'll share with you some of the ups and downs of moving to VB.NET. Although there are many reasons for moving your projects to VB.NET, sometimes it just makes sense to keep things the way they are. Because VB.NET is a departure from the way previous versions of Visual Basic worked, moving your existing applications to VB.NET is not a trivial task. Microsoft has provided tools to help you, though.

Upgrading from Previous Versions of Visual Basic

The Upgrade Wizard only works with projects from Visual Basic 6.0. If you want to upgrade an application from a version of Visual Basic prior to 6.0, you need to move your application to Visual Basic 6.0. Actually, the first item on your agenda should be to weigh the pros and cons of moving an application to VB.NET. To help you with that decision, I'll give you some things to consider.

Is It Worth It?

Should you move your application to VB.NET? I'll answer that with a resounding—it depends. If your existing application is working fine, requires little maintenance, and is not scheduled to have new functionality added, then you should stick with what works. Don't migrate your application to VB.NET unless you'll gain something in the process.

Some applications are naturally easier to migrate than others. To make an informed decision, you need to know what language features your application takes advantage of. Some of those features might not be available in VB.NET. To gain many of the new features in VB.NET, some features of earlier versions had to be broken or removed.

On the other hand, your application might be begging for some of these new features. The benefits might outweigh any broken functionality. That brings to mind another thought: You also need to consider whether you should start with the existing code from an application or whether you should rewrite the application. I hope the rest of this section gives you the information you need to make that call.

One important aspect of migrating to VB.NET that I can't help much with is your developers. VB.NET is an object-oriented language that requires a little different set of programming skills than Visual Basic 6.0. Make sure that your developers can handle the switch. Although it probably won't be as big of a leap as moving a Visual Basic 6.0 developer to C# or C++, the move to VB.NET is more than an update to the syntax of the language.

Unsupported Features

Okay, it's time for the bad news. Here is a list of some of the pieces that will no longer work. If your application relies heavily on one of these technologies, you are basically looking at a redesign of your application:

➤ **OLE container control.** VB.NET has no equivalent.

➤ **Dynamic Data Control (DDE).** VB.NET no longer supports DDE.

➤ **DAO/RDO data binding.** The Data control and RemoteData control no longer exist. You can still access DAO and RDO through code. Applications that use DAO and RDO data binding have to be updated to use ADO.

➤ **Visual Basic 5 controls.** The Visual Basic 5 versions of the Windows Common controls and the Data-Bound Grid control are incompatible with VB.NET.

➤ **DHTML applications.** VB.NET has no equivalent. However, applications can interoperate with VB.NET technologies.

➤ **ActiveX documents.** VB.NET has no equivalent. ActiveX documents should be rewritten as user controls or left alone.

➤ **Property pages.** VB.NET has no equivalent.

➤ **User controls.** User controls that were created in Visual Basic 6.0 can be used in VB.NET. There isn't design-time support, however, and user controls can't be upgraded.

➤ **Web classes.** VB.NET has no equivalent. Web classes can, however, interoperate with VB.NET technologies.

How Much Work Will It Take?

Even if your application doesn't depend on features that VB.NET no longer supports, you still have some work ahead of you. Some items can't be mapped directly to VB.NET, so they will require some rework.

The easiest way to figure out how much rework it will take is to run the Upgrade Wizard. The wizard generates an Upgrade Report that includes a list of issues. Here are some additional considerations to factor into your upgrade decision:

➤ **Single-tier database applications.** Simple applications that use DAO to bind controls directly to a local database might need a significant amount of rework.

➤ **Visual Basic add-ins.** The extensibility model of the Visual Studio IDE is quite different from that of Visual Basic 6.0. Add-ins require a considerable amount of rework.

➤ **Games.** Games usually rely on specific performance characteristics of Visual Basic 6.0. VB.NET has different performance characteristics that might require rework.

➤ **Graphics.** VB.NET forms do not support graphics methods. Also, the shape and line controls no longer exist. Good luck if you have a graphics-intensive application!

➤ **Drag and drop.** The drag-and drop models between Visual Basic 6.0 and VB.NET are significantly different. Plan to rewrite all drag-and-drop code.

➤ **Variants.** The Upgrade Wizard converts Variant data types to Object. If your application relies heavily on variants, some subtle differences could be introduced.

➤ **Windows APIs.** Many Windows API calls will need to be replaced with calls to .NET Framework functions.

Language Considerations for Upgrading

You might want to make some changes to your project before you upgrade it to VB.NET. Making these changes before you upgrade can reduce or eliminate some of the rework required after you run the Upgrade Wizard.

➤ **Compile your application in Visual Basic 6.0.** If you can't compile your application in Visual Basic 6.0, then it won't upgrade successfully.

➤ **Disable Timers.** In Visual Basic 6.0, you could disable a timer by setting its `Interval` property to 0. That won't work in VB.NET. Instead, set the `Enabled` property to `False`.

➤ **Menus.** VB.NET now has two controls for menus: MainMenu and ContextMenu. All of your Visual Basic 6.0 menus will be upgraded to a MainMenu. You will need to re-create any ContextMenus.

➤ **PrintForm.** VB.NET does not support the `Form.PrintForm` method.

➤ **Clipboard.** The Clipboard in VB.NET has been greatly enhanced. As a result, Clipboard statements cannot be automatically upgraded.

➤ **Name Property.** In VB.NET, you cannot access the `Name` property of a form or control at runtime. You can no longer iterate the Controls collection looking for a control with a specific name.

Some keywords have been completely removed. You will need to remove the following keywords from your application before you upgrade:

➤ `DefBool, DefByte, DefInt, DefLng, DefCur, DefSng, DefDbl, DefDec, DefDate, DefStr, DefObj, DefVar`

➤ `GoTo, GoSub, Return`

➤ `Option Base 0, Option Base 1`

➤ `VarPtr, ObjPtr, StrPtr`

➤ `Lset`

General Recommendations

Following is a list of my general recommendations. They aren't silver bullets, but they can ease the upgrade of your application and are generally good programming practices.

➤ **Use early binding.** You are more likely to run into problems if you declare a variable of type `Object` and assign an instance of a class to it at runtime. Instead, declare the variable using the actual type of the object.

➤ **Use explicit conversions.** If you need to use late binding, make sure you use explicit conversions. It makes the intention of the code easier to understand and will make your upgrade go more smoothly.

➤ **Use the Date data type to store dates.** This might seem obvious, but Visual Basic 6.0 allowed you to use the Double data type to store and manipulate dates.

➤ **Don't use default properties.** VB.NET does not support default properties the way Visual Basic 6.0 did. Make sure to use the name of the property you are referencing.

➤ **Use zero-bound arrays.** In Visual Basic 6.0, you could use any whole number for the lower bound of an array. In VB.NET, the lower bound number must be zero.

➤ **Use constants instead of specific values.** If a constant is available, use it instead of its value. The value of some constants has changed in VB.NET, but the names are the same.

➤ **Use True and False.** Do not use −1 and 0 for True and False.

➤ **Avoid fixed-size arrays in user-defined types.** Only use uninitialized arrays in structures. VB.NET cannot automatically initialize a fixed-size array in a structure.

➤ **Avoid fixed-length strings in user-defined types.** Use strings instead of fixed-length strings in structures. VB.NET cannot automatically initialize a fixed-length string in a structure.

➤ **Update data types for Win32 API calls.** The size of some data types has changed from Visual Basic 6.0 to VB.NET. You need to ensure that you use data types that match the size of the parameters of Win32 API calls.

Visual Basic 6.0 Compatibility Library

Conversion of some parts of an application isn't possible because of architectual or syntactical differences. In these cases, functions in the Visual Basic 6.0 Compatibility Library are used so that your application can run in VB.NET without extensive modification. The functions in the Compatibility Library mimic the behavior of those in Visual Basic 6.0, but they are compliant with the common language specification.

◆◆◆

CAUTION The functions in the Visual Basic 6.0 Compatibility Library are meant for use only during upgrades. Although you could use the library in a new application, there is no guarantee that these functions will be around in the next version of Visual Basic.

◆◆◆

The Upgrade Wizard

When you open a Visual Basic 6.0 project in VB.NET, the Upgrade Wizard automatically runs. The wizard steps you through the process of creating a new VB.NET project from your Visual Basic 6.0 project.

After the upgrade, you will need to make changes to your application so that it runs. You might also want to make changes to take advantage of some of the new features available in VB.NET. To help with the changes, VB.NET adds an upgrade report to the new project. The upgrade report itemizes problems that the wizard encountered and adds comments in your code to indicate statements that need to be changed.

 TIP The comments are displayed to tasks in the new Task List tool window. You can double-click on a task to navigate to the code that needs to be updated.

For detailed instructions on using the Upgrade Wizard, you should see the "Upgrading a Project with the Upgrade Wizard" topic in VB.NET help.

Changes to the Visual Basic Language

VB.NET introduces quite a few changes to the core Visual Basic language. Some of these are modifications of the way Visual Basic has worked for years. Others are brand new additions to the language.

What's New in the Visual Basic Language

VB.NET offers many new and improved language features that make it a robust, powerful, object-oriented programming language.

➤ **Inheritance.** Inheritance allows you to define classes that serve as the basis for derived classes. Derived classes inherit and can extend the base class. Because the forms you design are really classes, you can use inheritance to define new forms based on existing ones.

➤ **Exception handling.** Structured exception handling combines a modern control structure (`Try...Catch...Finally`) with exceptions, protected blocks of code, and filters. Structured exception handling makes it easy for you to create and maintain programs with comprehensive error handlers.

➤ **Overloading.** Overloading allows you to define properties, methods, or procedures that have the same name but use different data types. Overloaded procedures allow you to provide many implementations to handle different kinds of data, while giving the appearance of a single procedure.

➤ **Overriding.** Overriding allows derived objects to override properties and methods that are inherited from parent objects. Overridden members have the same arguments as the members that are inherited from the base class, but they have different implementations.

➤ **Constructors and destructors.** Constructors control the initialization of new instances of a class. Destroy frees system resources when a class leaves scope or is set to `Nothing`.

➤ **Data types.** VB.NET introduces three new data types: `Char`, `Short`, and `Decimal`.

➤ **Interfaces.** Interfaces describe the properties and methods of classes, but they do not provide implementations.

➤ **Delegates.** Delegates are sometimes described as type-safe, object-oriented function pointers. You can use delegates to specify an event handler method that runs when an event occurs. You can also use delegates with multithreaded applications.

➤ **Shared members.** Shared members are properties and procedures that all instances of a class share.

➤ **References.** References let you use objects that are defined in other assemblies.

➤ **Namespaces.** Namespaces prevent naming conflicts by organizing classes, interfaces, and methods into hierarchies.

➤ **Assemblies.** Assemblies replace and extend the capabilities of type libraries. They describe all the required files for a particular component or application.

➤ **Attributes.** Attributes enable you to provide additional information about program elements.

➤ **Multithreading.** VB.NET allows you to write applications that can perform multiple tasks independently. By causing complicated tasks to run on threads that are separate from your user interface, multithreading makes your applications more responsive.

Array Changes

Arrays in VB.NET changed from previous versions; therefore, arrays are treated the same in all languages that support the .NET Framework.

➤ **Bounds.** The lower bound of every array dimension is 0.

➤ **Dimensions.** The number of dimensions of an array is fixed when it is declared.

➤ **ReDim.** You cannot use ReDim as a declaration.

Data Type Changes

VB.NET changes the size of some of the standard data types. These changes could cause subtle differences in your program's operation. Make sure you are using the data type that is most appropriate for your data. Table A.1 summarizes the data type changes in VB.NET.

TABLE A.1 DATA TYPE CHANGES		
Size	**Visual Basic 6.0 Type**	**VB.NET Type**
16 bits	Integer	Short
32 bits	Long	Integer
64 bits	(none)	Long

Declaration Changes

VB.NET includes some changes to how and where you declare variables. Some of these changes clarify syntax from Visual Basic 6.0, whereas others are because of unsupported or changed functionality in the language.

➤ **Multiple variable declaration.** In VB.NET, you can declare multiple variables of the same type in a single statement without repeating the type keyword. In Visual Basic 6.0, any variable that was lacking an explicit type keyword defaulted to Variant.

➤ **Fixed length strings.** You cannot declare a string to have a fixed length.

➤ **Type statement.** The Type statement is not supported in VB.NET. You should use the Structure statement instead.

➤ **Block cope.** In VB.NET, a variable that is declared inside a block is available only with that block. In Visual Basic 6.0, variables that were declared within a block were still accessible outside the block.

File Changes

In Visual Basic 6.0, you accessed files using functions such as Open, Input, Output, and Append. In VB.NET, all file handling is accomplished through the System.IO namespace. The System.IO namespace duplicates and expands the functionality of the functions that are available in Visual Basic 6.0.

Object and Component Changes

VB.NET is now a full-fledged object-oriented language. With this new status comes some changes to how objects and components are handled. These changes help support the features that characterize an object-oriented language.

➤ **Object creation.** VB.NET has no implicit object creation. This means that you can no longer declare an object variable As New and count on Visual Basic to create the object for you the first time you reference the variable. You must now explicitly create an object and assign it to the variable.

➤ **Parameterized constructors.** Classes can have constructors that can accept arguments. In Visual Basic 6.0, there was no means to pass an argument when an object was created.

➤ **Binary compatibility.** Instead of the Binary Compatibility option used in Visual Basic 6.0, VB.NET uses attributes to accomplish binary compatibility. Attributes give you direct control over what information is placed in your compiled component.

➤ **Default members.** In Visual Basic 6.0, you could specify any method or data member as the default member for a class. In VB.NET, only a property that takes one or more arguments can be the default member.

➤ **Indeterminate lifetime.** In Visual Basic 6.0, when the last reference to an object instance is released, the object is terminated immediately. In VB.NET, an object's destructor is not necessarily called as soon as the last reference is released. The garbage collector runs in the background and releases objects when it determines that they are no longer used.

Procedure Changes

Like changes to other areas of Visual Basic, some changes to declaring and using procedures are cosmetic, whereas others could affect the behavior of your application. The way these changes can affect your application's behavior can be subtle, so pay close attention to VB.NET's procedure syntax.

➤ **Default passing mechanism.** In Visual Basic 6.0, procedure arguments defaulted to being passed ByRef. This meant that the calling program could see changes made to the parameter of a procedure. In VB.NET, parameters default to ByVal. ByVal parameters cannot be changed.

➤ **Parentheses.** In VB.NET, parentheses are required for any procedure call with a non-empty argument list.

➤ **Return statement.** In VB.NET, you use the Return statement to pass a return value from a function back to the calling procedure.

➤ **Optional arguments.** VB.NET requires that every optional argument have a default value.

Property Changes

VB.NET introduced a new syntax for declaring properties. The procedures for getting and setting the property's values are now included inside the Property statement. The new syntax is simpler and allows VB.NET to get rid of the `Property Get`, `Property Let`, and `Property Set` statements. Here is an example of the new syntax:

```
Private MonthNum As Integer = 1
Property Month( ) As Integer
    Get
        Return MonthNum
    End Get
    Set(ByVal NewMonth As Integer)
        If NewMonth < 1 Or NewMonth > 12 Then
            ' Error processing for invalid value.
        Else
            MonthNum = NewMonth
        End If
    End Set
End Property
```

As you can see, the `Get` and `Set` procedures are nested inside the `Property` statement. A `Property` statement without a `Set` procedure is read only. A `Property` statement without a `Get` procedure is write only.

NOTE Property arguments might not be `ByRef`. If a property procedure includes a `ByRef` argument and changes its value, unexpected behavior might result. Make sure all property arguments are `ByVal`.

Control Flow Changes

VB.NET has removed some control flow legacy keywords from the Visual Basic language. Most of the removed keywords do not encourage good programming structure. If you follow modern programming practices, you shouldn't be impacted much by these changes.

➤ **GoSub.** Not supported in VB.NET.

➤ **On...GoSub.** Not supported in VB.NET.

➤ **On...GoTo.** Not supported in VB.NET.

➤ **While...Wend.** `Wend` keyword changed to `End`.

➤ **On Error/Error/Resume.** Still supported for unstructured error handling. The preferred method is to use the `Try...Catch...Finally` statement for structured error handling.

Tips for Experienced Visual Basic Developers

This section provides a few quick tips for those of you who have worked with Visual Basic for some time. These tips have more to do with how you work than with the Visual Basic language. The tips should help you get into a new routine with VB.NET.

Project Changes

Projects in VB.NET appear similar to Visual Basic 6.0 projects; however, there are some underlying differences. Projects in Visual Basic 6.0 took a reference-based approach. The project file contained references to items by specifying their path in the project file. The files for the project were loaded from the path that the project file pointed to.

VB.NET takes a different approach. VB.NET projects use a folder-based model. The project folder hierarchy contains all project items. When you add a file to a project, a copy of the file is placed in the Project folder. That copy of the file is used when the project is loaded.

The Remove command in Visual Basic 6.0 simply removed a file from the project. In VB.NET, the Delete command replaces the Remove command. Delete removes a file from a project as well as deletes the file.

TIP   To remove a file from a project in VB.NET, use the Exclude From Project command.

VB.NET introduces the concept of a solution. Solutions are like project groups in Visual Basic 6.0, but they can include projects that were created in any combination of languages that Visual Studio .NET supports.

Project types have also changed in VB.NET. Some project types have changed names, whereas others are no longer available. Table A.2 shows the project changes in VB.NET.

TABLE A.2 PROJECT TYPE CHANGES	
Visual Basic 6.0	**VB.NET**
Standard EXE	Windows Application.
ActiveX DLL	Class Library.
ActiveX EXE	Class Library.
ActiveX Control	Windows Control Library.
ActiveX Document	No equivalent.
DHTML Application	No equivalent. Use ASP.NET Web Application instead.
IIS Application (Web Class)	No equivalent. Use ASP.NET Web Application instead.

Debugging Changes

I have some bad news. Edit and Continue is gone from VB.NET. That means no more changing your code while your application is running and having the changes take immediate effect. In VB.NET, any changes you make in break mode while your application is running require your project to be rebuilt before the changes take effect.

In Visual Basic 6.0, syntax errors in your code would display an error message dialog box during debugging. VB.NET displays most syntax errors in the Task List window at design time.

 **CAUTION** VB.NET uses different keyboard shortcuts for debugging commands. Before you start pounding away on the function keys, make sure you know which command each key represents.

Setup and Deployment Changes

The Package and Deployment Wizard was used in Visual Basic 6.0 to create Setup programs to distribute your application. In VB.NET, you use Deployment projects to create Windows Installers to manage installation of your application.

Windows API Changes

You will probably find little need to make direct Windows API calls. Instead, you can use the classes found in the .NET Framework to produce the same functionality.

Run Time Changes

In Visual Basic 6.0, a client computer had to have the Visual Basic runtime (Msvbvm60.dll) installed for the application to run. Usually the Setup package would install this file if necessary. In VB.NET, applications need the .NET Framework Common Language Runtime (CLR). The CLR files are automatically included in installers built using Visual Studio deployment projects.

Summary

That sounds like a lot of changes to Visual Basic, doesn't it? Well, it is. VB.NET is not just a minor update to the Visual Basic language. VB.NET is more of a revolution than an evolution. The new features in VB.NET allow you to more easily create robust, maintainable applications. More importantly, VB.NET allows you to produce solutions to business problems in a more timely manner than ever before.

Visual Basic .NET Quick Reference Guide

➤ Variables

➤ Data types

➤ Control flow

➤ Operators

➤ Exceptions

➤ Procedures

➤ Scope

➤ Classes

➤ File access

➤ Web controls

➤ Web services

This Appendix is your quick reference to the VB.NET language. Use it as a guide while you are learning the syntax of the VB.NET language.

Variable Declaration

Syntax

```
[ <Attributes> ] [{ Public | Protected | Friend | Protected Friend |
Private | Static }] [ Shared ] [ Shadows ] [ ReadOnly ]
Dim [ WithEvents ] name [ (boundlist) ] [ As [ New ] type ]
   [ = initexpr ]
```

Example

```
Dim m As Integer       'Declare m as an integer
Dim n As Integer = 3   'Declare n as an integer and set it to 3
```

Data Types

TABLE B.1 VISUAL BASIC .NET DATA TYPES			
VB.NET Type	**Type**	**Size**	**Range**
Boolean	Value	2 bytes	True or False
Byte	Value	1 byte	0–255
Char	Value	2 bytes	0–65,535
Date	Value	8 bytes	January 1, 0001–December 31, 9999
Decimal	Value	16 bytes	$10^{-28}-10^{28}$ *
Double	Value	8 bytes	$10^{-324}-10^{308}$ *
Integer	Value	4 bytes	−2,147,483,648–2,147,483,647
Long	Value	8 bytes	$-10^{20}-10^{20}$ *
Object	Reference	4 bytes	Any type
Short	Value	2 bytes	−32,768–32,767
Single	Value	4 bytes	$10^{-45}-10^{38}$ *
String	Reference	Varies	0–2 billion Unicode characters *
*Approximate range			

Data Type Conversion

TABLE B.2 TYPE CONVERSION FUNCTIONS	
Function Name	**Return Type**
CBool(expression)	Boolean
CByte(expression)	Byte
CChar(expression)	Char
CDate(expression)	Date
CDbl(expression)	Double
CDec(expression)	Decimal
CInt(expression)	Integer
CLng(expression)	Long
CObj(expression)	Object
CShort(expression)	Short
CSng(expression)	Single
CStr(expression)	String

Array Declaration and Access

Syntax

```
[ <Attributes> ] [{ Public | Protected | Friend | Protected Friend |
Private | Static }] [ Shared ] [ Shadows ] [ ReadOnly ]
Dim [ WithEvents ] name [ (boundlist) ] [ As [ New ] type ]
    [ = initexpr ]
```

Example

```
Dim MyArray(10) As Integer
Dim i As Integer
For i = 0 To 10
    MyArray(i) = i + 100
Next i
```

Enumerations

Syntax

```
EnumDeclaration ::=
[ <Attributes> ] [ EnumModifier+ ] Enum Identifier
[ As IntegralTypeName ]
    EnumMemberDeclaration+
    End Enum
EnumModifier ::= AccessModifier | Shadows
```

Example

```
Public Enum DayOfWeek
    Sunday = 1
    Monday = 2
    Tuesday = 3
    Wednesday = 4
    Thursday = 5
    Friday = 6
    Saturday = 7
End Enum
```

Structures

Syntax

```
StructDeclaration ::=
[ <Attributes> ] [ StructModifier+ ] Structure Identifier
    [ TypeImplementsClause+ ]
    [ StructMemberDeclaration+ ]
    End Structure
StructureModifier ::= AccessModifier | Shadows
```

Example

```
Structure ContactInfo
    Public FirstName As String
    Public LastName As String
    Public Age As Integer

    Public Function FullName() As String
        Return (FirstName & " " & LastName)
    End Function
End Structure
```

Collections

Example

```
Dim Numbers As New Collection()
Dim i, Total As Integer

'Add the numbers 1 - 5 to the collection
For i = 1 To 5
    Numbers.Add(i, "Item" & CStr(i))
Next

'Add up the values of all items in the collection
For i = 1 To Numbers.Count
    Total = Total + Numbers.Item(i)
Next
```

Control Flow

If...Then...Else

Syntax

```
IfStatement ::= BlockIfStatement | LineIfThenStatement
BlockIfStatement ::=
    If BooleanExpression [ Then ]
    [ Block ]
    [ ElseIfStatement+ ]
```

```
    [ ElseStatement ]
    End If
ElseIfStatement ::=
    ElseIf BooleanExpression [ Then ]
    [ Block ]
ElseStatement ::=
    Else
    [ Block ]
LineIfThenStatement ::= If BooleanExpression Then Statements ]
[ Else Statements ]
BooleanExpression ::= Expression
```

Example

```
If Num = 5 Then Console.WriteLine("Your number was 5")
If Num > 5 Then
    Console.WriteLine("Your number was > 5")
Else
    Console.WriteLine("Your number was <= 5")
End If
```

Select Case

Syntax

```
Select [ Case ] testexpression
    [ Case expressionlist
        [ statements ] ]
    [ Case Else
        [ elsestatements ] ]
End Select
```

Example

```
Select Case Num
    Case 1, 3, 5, 7, 9
        Console.WriteLine("You entered an odd number")
    Case 2, 4, 6, 8, 10
        Console.WriteLine("You entered an even number")
End Select
```

While

Syntax

```
WhileStatement ::=
    While BooleanExpression
    [ Block ]
    End While
```

Example

```
While Num < 1 Or Num > 10
    'Prompt the user to enter a number
    Console.WriteLine("Enter a number from 1 - 10: ")
    'Read the number and store it in an integer variable
    Num = CInt(Console.ReadLine())
    'Display the number the user entered
    Console.WriteLine("You entered: " & CStr(Num))
End While
```

Do While

Syntax

```
DoLoopStatement ::=
    Do [ WhileOrUntil BooleanExpression ]
    [ Block ]
    Loop [ WhileOrUntil BooleanExpression ]
WhileOrUntil ::= While | Until
```

Example

```
Do While Num < 1 Or Num > 10
    'Prompt the user to enter a number
    Console.WriteLine("Enter a number from 1 - 10: ")
    'Read the number and store it in an integer variable
    Num = CInt(Console.ReadLine())
    'Display the number the user entered
    Console.WriteLine("You entered: " & CStr(Num))
Loop
```

For...Next

Syntax

```
For counter = start To end [ Step step ]
    [ Block ]
Next [ counter ]
```

Example

```
For c = 1 To Num
    Console.WriteLine("This message is in a For loop")
Next
```

Operators

TABLE B.3	ARITHMETIC OPERATORS	
Operator	**Meaning**	**Example**
^	Raises a number to a power	x = 2 ^ 2 'Returns 4
*	Multiplies two numbers	x = 3 * 4 'Returns 12
/	Divides two numbers	x = 10 / 4 'Returns 2.5
\	Divides two numbers	x = 11 / 4 'Returns 2
Mod	Calculate the remainder	x = 11 / 4 'Returns 3
+	Adds two numbers	x = 4 + 3 'Returns 7
-	Subtracts two numbers	x = 4 − 3 'Returns 1

TABLE B.4 NUMERIC COMPARISON OPERATORS	
Operator	**Meaning**
=	Equality
<>	Inequality
<	Less than
>	Greater than
<=	Less than or equal to
>=	Greater than or equal to

TABLE B.5 LOGICAL OPERATORS	
Operator	**Returns**
And	True if both expressions are true
Or	True if either expression is true
Xor	True if one expression is true and one is false
Not	Opposite of expression

Exceptions

Try...Catch...Finally

Syntax

```
Try
    [ tryStatements ]
```

```
[ Catch [ exception [ As type ] ] [ When expression ]
    [ catchStatements ] ]
[ Exit Try ]
...
[ Finally
    finallyStatements ] ]
End Try
```

Example

```
Try
    'Some code that might fail
Catch 'Optional filter
    'Code to handle an exception
[More Catch blocks]
Finally
    'Code that always executes
End Try
```

Procedures

TABLE B.6 PROCEDURE TYPES

Type	Description
Sub	Performs actions but does not return a value to the calling code. (All event-handling procedures are Subs.)
Function	Performs actions and returns a value to the calling code.
Property	Returns or assigns values to properties on objects or modules.

Subs

Syntax

```
[ <Attributes> ] [{ Overloads | Overrides | Overridable |
NotOverridable | MustOverride | Shadows | Shared }]
[{ Public | Protected | Friend | Protected Friend | Private }]
Sub name [ (arglist) ] [ Implements interface.definedname ]
    [ statements ]
    [ Exit Sub ]
    [ statements ]
End Sub
```

Example

```
Sub GetNumbers(ByRef Input1 As Integer, ByRef Input2 As Integer)
    'Prompt the user to enter numbers
    Console.WriteLine("Enter your first number:")
    'Read the first number and store it in an integer variable
    Input1 = CInt(Console.ReadLine())

    Console.WriteLine("Enter your second number:")
    'Read the second number and store it in an integer variable
    Input2 = CInt(Console.ReadLine())
End Sub
```

Functions

Syntax

```
[ <Attributes> ] [{ Overloads | Overrides | Overridable |
NotOverridable | MustOverride | Shadows | Shared }]
[{ Public | Protected | Friend | Protected Friend | Private }]
Function name [ (arglist) ] [ As type ]
[ Implements interface.definedname ]
    [ statements ]
    [ Exit Function ]
    [ statements ]
End Function
```

Example

```
Function DoDivide(ByVal Num1 As Integer, _
                  ByVal Num2 As Integer) As Decimal
    Dim Result As Decimal

    Try
        Result = Num1 / Num2
        'Display the result
        Console.WriteLine("The result of " & CStr(Num1) & _
            "/" & CStr(Num2) & " is " & CStr(Result))
    Catch e As Exception When Num2 = 0
        'Display an error message
        Console.WriteLine("Denomenator cannot be 0!")
        Console.WriteLine(e.Message)
    Catch e As OverflowException
        'Display an error message
        Console.WriteLine("Overflow exception caught!")
        Console.WriteLine(e.Message)
    Finally
        'Display an error message
        Console.WriteLine("Look ma, I didn't crash.")
    End Try

    Return (Result)
End Function
```

Properties

Syntax

```
[ Default ] [{ Public | Protected | Friend | Protected Friend |
Private }]
Property propertyname [ (argumentlist) ] As datatype
    Get
        [ statements ]
        Return expression
    End Get
    Set [ ( ByVal newvalue As datatype ) ]
        [ statements ]
```

```
        lvalue = newvalue
    End Set
End Property
```

Example

```
Private MonthNum As Integer = 1
Property Month( ) As Integer
    Get
        Return MonthNum
    End Get
    Set(ByVal NewMonth As Integer)
        If NewMonth < 1 Or NewMonth > 12 Then
            ' Error processing for invalid value.
        Else
            MonthNum = NewMonth
        End If
    End Set
End Property
```

Scope

Scope	Description
TABLE B.7 ELEMENT SCOPE	
Scope	**Description**
Block	The element is only available within the code block in which it is declared.
Procedure	The element is only available within the procedure in which it is declared.
Module	The element is available to all code within the module, class, or structure in which it is declared.
Namespace	The element is available to all code in the namespace.

Classes

Syntax

```
[ <Attributes> ] [{ Public | Protected | Friend |
Protected Friend | Private }] [ Shadows ]
[ MustInherit | NotInheritable ]
Class name
    [ Inherits classname ]
    [Implements interfacenames ]
    [ statements ]
End Class
```

Example

```
Public Class Automobile
    Public NumDoors As Integer
    Protected Color As String
    Private GallonsOfGas As Integer
    Public Sub StartEngine()
        'Put code here to make the car use gas
    End Sub
    Public Sub StopEngine()
        'Put code here to make the car stop using gas
    End Sub
    ReadOnly Property OutOfGas() As Boolean
        Get
            Return (GallonsOfGas = 0) 'Returns whether the car
                                      'is out of gas
        End Get
    End Property
End Class
```

File Access

TABLE B.8 FILE ACCESS CLASSES	
Class	**Description**
BinaryReader	Reads primitive data types as binary values
BinaryWriter	Writes primitive types in binary to a stream and supports writing strings
File	Provides static methods for the creation, copying, deletion, moving, and opening of files
FileInfo	Provides instance methods for the creation, copying, deletion, moving, and opening of files
FileStream	Exposes a stream around a file, supporting both synchronous and asynchronous read and write operations
TextReader	Represents a reader that can read a sequential series of characters
TextWriter	Represents a writer that can write a sequential series of characters
StreamReader	Implements a TextReader that reads characters from a byte stream
StreamWriter	Implements a TextWriter for writing characters to a stream

Web Controls

TABLE B.9 WEB SERVER CONTROLS	
Control	**Description**
Label	Displays text in a set location
TextBox	Input control for inputting text
Button	A push button control
LinkButton	A button with an embedded hyperlink
ImageButton	An image that responds to mouse clicks
HyperLink	A link to another Web page
DropDownList	Single-selection drop-down list
ListBox	Single- or multiple-selection list box
DataGrid	Displays a table of data from a data source
DataList	Displays a template-defined data-bound list
Repeater	A data-bound list based on a template
CheckBox	Allows selection of a True or False state
CheckBoxList	Multi-selection check box group
RadioButtonList	Single-selection radio button group
RadioButton	Single-selection radio button
Image	Displays an image
Panel	Used as a container for other controls
PlaceHolder	Used as a placeholder for dynamically added server controls

TABLE B.9 WEB SERVER CONTROLS (CONTINUED)

Control	Description
Calendar	Displays a single month of a year
AdRotator	Displays ad banners randomly from a fixed set
Table	Displays an HTML table
XML	Displays an XML document
Literal	Used to reserve a location on the page to display text
CrystalReportViewer	Displays a Crystal report

TABLE B.10 VALIDATION CONTROLS

Control	Description
RequiredFieldValidator	Signifies that the input control is a required field
CompareValidator	Compares the input value to another input value or constant
RangeValidator	Ensures that the input falls within a specified range of values
RegularExpressionValidator	Ensures that the input matches the pattern of a regular expression
CustomValidator	Performs user-defined validation rules against the input control

TABLE B.11 HTML SERVER CONTROLS

Control	Description
Label	Displays text in a set location
Button	A generic push button control
Reset Button	A button that resets the form's controls to their initial values
Submit Button	A button that submits the form
Text Field	A single-line text input control
Text Area	A multi-line text input control
File Field	A file upload control with a text box and a Browse button
Password Field	Same as a Text Field control, but the input text is not displayed
CheckBox	A check box control
Radio Button	A radio button control
Hidden	Used to transmit state information back and forth to the server
Table	Used to format content into rows and columns
Flow Layout Panel	A panel that supports the flow layout model
Grid Layout Panel	A panel that supports the grid layout model
Image	Displays an image
ListBox	Used for list boxes or drop-down lists
DropDown	Used for list boxes or drop-down lists
Horizontal Rule	Draws a horizontal rule (line)

Web Services

To make a procedure in your application available as a Web service, you simply include the WebMethod attribute to the procedure. The procedure must be declared as Public and include WebMethod for the procedure to be exposed as a Web service. Following is an example of a procedure that is exposed as a Web service:

```
<WebMethod()> Public Function Add(ByVal a As Integer, _
                                  ByVal b As Integer) As Integer
    Return (a + b)
End Function
```

Summary

This Appendix only hits the highlights of the VB.NET language. Although this information should help you get up to speed quickly with VB.NET, sometimes you will need more detailed information. The Help system that is available in VB.NET should be your next stop. There, you can find detailed information about every aspect of VB.NET and Visual Studio .NET.

INDEX

P